Culture & Cognition

*This book is dedicated to the memory of
Thomas Schweizer, whom I appreciated not only
as a colleague, but also as the warm human being he was.*

Culture & Cognition

Implications for Theory and Method

Norbert Ross
Vanderbilt University

SAGE Publications
International Educational and Professional Publisher
Thousand Oaks ■ London ■ New Delhi

For information:

Sage Publications, Inc.
2455 Teller Road
Thousand Oaks, California 91320
E-mail: order@sagepub.com

Sage Publications Ltd.
6 Bonhill Street
London EC2A 4PU
United Kingdom

Sage Publications India Pvt. Ltd.
B-42, Panchsheel Enclave
Post Box 4109
New Delhi 110 017 India

Printed in the United States of America

Library of Congress Cataloging-in-Publication Data

Ross, Norbert.
Culture and cognition : implications for theory and method / by Norbert Ross.
    p. cm.
Includes bibliographical references and index.
ISBN 0-7619-2906-1 — ISBN 0-7619-2907-X (paper)
    1. Cognition and culture. I. Title.
BF311.R6542 2004
306.4′2—dc21

                            2003011981

This book is printed on acid-free paper.

03   04   05   06   07   10   9   8   7   6   5   4   3   2   1

Acquisitions Editor:	Jim Brace-Thompson
Editorial Assistant:	Karen Ehrmann
Production Editor:	Julia Parnell
Copy Editor:	Kristin Bergstad
Typesetter:	C&M Digitals (P) Ltd.
Indexer:	Michael Ferreira
Cover Designer:	Janet Foulger

Contents

Introduction

This book will have many opponents. Experimental psychologists will accuse me of introducing flaws into essential aspects of experimental design and supporting an approach that lacks the necessary rigor to provide meaningful results. By the same token, many psychologists will question the need and virtue of studying nonstandard populations (non-undergraduate students).

Trained as an anthropologist, I tended to think that by defending their positions psychologists tried to maintain the status quo of their research, a highly time-efficient (and comfortable) research setting, where student subjects are forced to participate in studies, often run by their student colleagues.

By now I have come to think of an additional reason for this choice. Many cognitive psychologists still do not regard culture and social processes as of any interest for an understanding of processes in high-level cognition. While I have no sympathy with researchers who try only to maintain their research settings intact, I hope that this book will be read by more inquisitive minds in cognitive psychology and maybe even interest them in the topic.

Obviously, the approach proposed in this book also differs significantly from the more traditional anthropological approach of studying people from different cultures in their normal day-to-day context. While anthropologists will agree with my quest to abandon the study of undergraduate students, many will reject the idea of introducing formal experimental methods and statistical models into the field. Again, I hope their opposition does not prevent them from engaging with my arguments. I hope they will agree with me about the dire need to develop methodologies that allow us a better understanding, combined with more detailed theories about human culture, human thought, and human behavior.

In a sense, then, this book attempts to chart some middle ground between the two fields of inquiry, trying to unite the different perspectives of two academic disciplines that should never have been separated in the first place.

—*Norbert Ross*

Acknowledgments

This book is the fruit of many peoples' ideas and influences in the course of my academic development. The manuscript was written while I was a postdoctoral researcher and later an assistant research professor at Northwestern University. Here I learned many of the skills and problems of cognitive psychology and had plenty of time to discuss my ideas with colleagues, both graduate students and faculty. Most of the ideas presented in this book are, therefore, not to be seen as a reflection of my individual achievement. Instead they represent a mirror of my intellectual development within a very encouraging academic environment.

I tried to give credit to this fact by citing as much as possible of the work that was developed within a team effort to understand folk biology and both the cultural aspects of cognition and the cognitive aspects of culture. Still, it is hard to account for the many nights of discussion and hours of advice that I shared in the Petén (Guatemala) or central Wisconsin with Douglas Medin and Scott Atran. Especially, Douglas Medin helped the shaping of many of my thoughts, although I know that he will not agree with everything said in this book. I also want to thank Professor Ulrich Köhler for steering me toward this topic. I know he probably expected a very different book, but once more he took on the task of guiding me on my detours, making sure that I didn't lose track on the way.

Finally, I want to thank my family. As on previous occasions, they allowed me the extravagance of writing a book, using time that should have been theirs.

1

Culture and Cognition

Ethnography of the Mind—
A Cognitive Approach to Culture

In recent years, several books and articles have targeted the field of culture and cognition.[1] Parallel with this, researchers have paid increased attention over the past three decades to the combination of anthropology and psychology. New journals like *Culture & Psychology* (first volume in 1995) and *Culture and Cognition* (first volume in 2001) and the development of specialized programs at major research universities are the progeny of this increasing interest (e.g., the Culture and Cognition Program at the University of Michigan and the Culture, Language and Cognition Program at Northwestern University). Both the programs and the journals target an interdisciplinary audience and address a major necessity in the field: combining the study of culture with an understanding of relevant cognitive processes, and the challenge of studying high-level cognition as embedded in a specific cultural context.

Fruitful as they are, these interdisciplinary collaborations between anthropologists and psychologists are the exception rather than the rule, and few individuals truly master both fields. Some examples of successful cross-discipline collaborations are the research projects conducted by Wassmann and Dasen (1993); the research project carried out by Cole and colleagues (Cole, 1996); recent work by Bloch, Solomon, and Carey (2001); and the long-term collaboration among the members of our research team, including Douglas Medin and Scott Atran.[2] On the rare occasions when both disciplines are equally engaged in developing methods and theory rather than applying psychological methods in "exotic settings," results often challenge previous theories and provide promising insights for both academic disciplines. Unfortunately, these kinds of research projects are rather exceptional and are rarely taken seriously by the respective mainstream fields.

Still, the findings speak for themselves and are gaining an increasing readership. For example, recent research in folk biology shows the existence of universal principles in cognition (see Atran, 1998; Berlin, 1992; López, Atran, Coley, Medin, & Smith, 1997) like the taxonomical sorting of animals and plants. Subsequent research addressed (a) the character of these universalities, but was also able to (b) establish clear cultural differences that go beyond the commonalities (see Medin, Ross, Atran, Burnett, & Blok, 2002; Ross & Medin, 2003; Ross, Medin, Coley, & Atran, 2003). It is important to realize that these accounts go beyond the efforts of previous research in that *culture* and *cultural differences* are not assumed a priori, but are systematically explored with the help of formal methods. Also, cultural differences once identified are not regarded as the endpoint of the research, but as the starting point for the more important questions that target the origin and character of these differences. I will turn to this topic in later chapters.

The field of culture and cognition is far from being widely recognized and still lacks meaningful integration of the different approaches. The aim is not to streamline efforts with respect to research questions, but to extend our research questions beyond the usual topics that have already been addressed in the different fields. To do this, we need to develop a coherent body of methodological and theoretical underpinnings.

The lack of cross-disciplinary integration is obvious in numerous articles and books that intend to give an overview of the field, but fall short because they don't consider the strength of the other discipline (see Medin & Atran, 1999, for an exception). Anthropological discussions usually lack conceptual and methodological clarity, preventing the field from developing a body of knowledge that can be discussed, challenged, or confirmed and that ultimately leads to an increase in knowledge over time. On the other hand, research in psychology all too often lacks a theoretical understanding of (and interest in) cultural processes and their effects on high-level cognition. As a consequence, research in anthropology generally lacks sufficient clarity and specificity to inform our understanding of cognitive processes and is, therefore, often ignored by psychologists. In contrast, most cognitive research in psychology either ignores culture as an important factor that should be considered, or treats culture as just another independent variable.

Ignoring culture often leads to universal claims for findings that are based on psychology's standard population—U.S. undergraduate students—that cannot be extended to different populations. When culture is treated as an independent variable, results are at best misleading. In both cases, the results are hardly of interest to mainstream anthropology and of only limited use for cognitive research. Obviously, this lack of interaction results in mutual ignorance of the different strengths of the two disciplines and results in a weakening of both fields. The different strengths of the two disciplines are on different levels within the realms of (a) theory and research interests, (b) methodology, and (c) pragmatic research concerns.

Looking at theory and research interests, the two fields couldn't be more diverse at first sight. Anthropology's main interest is to understand (though admittedly not always) phenomena such as human culture and social processes. It is, therefore, most often concerned with (nonuniversal) shared aspects of human thought and action. Psychology, on the other hand, is based on an individualistic ontology (see Bruner, 1996) and focuses more on individual processes as universal mechanisms of the human brain and mind. On closer observation, it seems clear that neither agenda can be fulfilled without the other. Nonuniversal aspects can hardly be understood unless they are investigated against the background of universals. Similarly, universals cannot be understood if we keep focusing on only the psychological standard population within highly artificial contexts (the laboratory). Unless we broaden our subject pool, we cannot really identify universals in human cognition. Similarly, we have to focus on real-world issues, understanding possible impacts of cultural processes on high-level cognition. To study these processes, we first have to develop meaningful concepts of culture and methodologies that can be applied in different contexts. It is here that anthropology and the recent accomplishments and discussions in the field can be instructive.

In recent years, anthropology has faced two major questions that have largely gone unanswered. First, *How do we deal with within-group variability?* And second, *How do we collect, analyze, interpret, and present our data in ways that strip our work of the authoritative statements found in earlier ethnographies?* (see *Current Anthropology*, Vol. 40, for a special issue on "Culture"; see also Greenfield, 2000). Both concerns are about the problem of an individual's performance in an anthropologist's account and point to the larger question of what the processes are that lead to the shared aspects called culture.

Obviously, exploring shared aspects is inseparable from the question of how to make sense of the aspects *not shared* by members of a group identified as a culture. A variety of answers have been proposed ranging from rejecting the concept of culture (again, see the discussion in *Current Anthropology*, Vol. 40) to a proposal to call every agreement between individuals *culture* (*Current Anthropology*, Vol. 40; see also Brumann, 1999; Strauss & Quinn, 1997, p. 7).

Both accounts are unsatisfactory on several grounds. By now it should be accepted that culture is not a physical entity to which humans conform, much less conform completely. There is no book of cultural knowledge that individuals have to memorize to become functioning members of *their culture*. If this were the case, not just the processes of cultural change, but patterned within-group disagreement as well would be hard to understand. I doubt that any anthropologist has ever suggested the existence of such a physical entity, but the way anthropologists have long written about culture suggests that they should have put some more thought into the concept they applied. As a result, many traditional ethnographic monographs *essentialize culture* in their description by not only ignoring within-group differences, but also misleading the reader with respect to existing individual cognitions. The data are often presented as if they existed in every individual's mind, when they might in fact be artificial constructs unjustifiably aggregated across several individuals. This is not to say that these accounts are necessarily wrong, but that they treat culture as *mindless*, something existing independently of individual actors and their cognitions. Examples are plentiful, and I don't want to single out individual anthropologists. It was this problem—among others—that opened the door for the *postmodern crisis* in anthropology, which, unfortunately, often led researchers to avoid regarding culture as a meaningful study topic. It is just as wrong to ignore patterns of agreement that exist among clearly identifiable groups of individuals. One suggested way out of this dilemma was to define *any* agreement between individuals as *culture*. This approach also misses the point and puts us in danger of ignoring the different processes that lead to different kinds of agreements (e.g., similar outside stimuli, cognitive universals, etc.). Rather than joining one of these (admittedly) extreme positions, it seems wise to look at processes within and across social groups—often self-identified as cultures—that might lead to patterns of agreement (or disagreement).

Cognitive psychologists approaching the topic of human thought from the opposite direction, with the individual as the center of attention and the elicitation of universal patterns as the main goal of research, soon ran into different kinds of problems. Ignoring social processes altogether, at least for a long time, allowed for the advancement of large-scale theories of human thinking and behavior and the development of rigid methodologies. Once cultural processes were detected as potentially important factors in human cognition, these theories and some of the methodologies started to fall apart (see Cole, 1996; Medin et al., 2002; and Ross, Medin, Coley, & Atran, 2003, for examples).

If culture influences individual processes of thought and reasoning, then the study of student subjects tells us only part—and a very small part, indeed—of the whole story (see Fish, 2000; Medin & Atran, 1999; Medin et al., 2002, for elaborations on this argument). This problem and its source are most obvious in (a) the informants usually used in psychological studies—college students, and (b) the laboratory context in which many of these studies take place. First, in the case of cross-cultural studies using undergraduate students, it is often not clear *whether* and in *what aspects* the study populations differ from one another and whether these differences extend to larger sections of the populations they stand for (think about differences in age, economic position, etc.). It is, therefore, often not clear how to interpret the results of such studies. Second, undergraduate students, given their age and background, are usually not very knowledgeable about the domains under study, and, hence, their reasoning processes might be very different from relative experts in their culture (see Medin et al., 2002). As a result, many of the so-called cultural differences might better be explained as differences in expertise (see López et al., 1997, for an example).

Similarly, if our reasoning processes are embedded in a web of naïve theories, models, and value frameworks (see Chapters 2, 3, and 6), then our studies have to account for this by incorporating these contexts instead of isolating the study targets by using artificial stimuli in the laboratory setting. Artificial stimuli might allow better control of many of the factors researchers are interested in, but this very control might be stripping the experiments of any meaning the topic might have for informants (see Medin & Atran, 1999). Laboratory tasks are a far cry from simulating real-life decisions and/or exploring real-life cognitive processes.

Recent trends indicate an increasing interest in "culture" as a topic of psychological inquiry (see, e.g., Choy & Nisbett, 2000; Hatano & Inagaki 1994; Markus & Kitayama, 1991; Masuda & Nisbett, 2001). Most of these studies are designed and conducted in an atheoretical manner, however. Rather than pursuing clear theories and hypotheses, they often attribute experimental findings to vague *grand theories of cultural differences*. This prevents both clear results and convincing ethnographic descriptions (see Chapter 2 for examples).

All of these differences aside, a comparison of the strengths and weaknesses of the two fields—anthropology and psychology—is instructive. In a sense, they reflect the different epistemological and methodological approaches of fields that should never have been separated in the first place.

Early on, anthropology focused on the study of cultural systems, often questioning the need for and possibility of comparative methods. This is precisely the strength of cognitive psychology. Anthropological descriptions often treat cultural knowledge like a "free-floating entity" within a culture; something that is freely available to both the natives and the anthropologists. Ignoring individual differences often produced authoritative and essentializing descriptions of culture and cultural patterns.

The lack of clear methods not only results in problems of how best to represent the data, but also has broad implications for testing and replicating previous findings. As a consequence, scientific controversies often remain unresolved (see Chapter 3 for an elaboration of this point; see also Greenfield, 2000).

Anthropology's holistic view, on the other hand, emphasized the interconnectedness of ideas, models, and native theories, a concept that is largely ignored in the cognitive sciences. An example is the line of research that looks at the cultural differences between Asians and U.S. Americans. Most of the studies are useful illustrations of some of these problems. What is most striking, however, is how researchers in the field virtually ignore each other's findings, explaining their data with radically different theories as if their individual data were completely isolated from other research (see Chapters 2 and 3). To make matters worse, in most of these studies little effort is made to root the research in a wider theory of culture and cultural processes. Rather, it seems that culture is regarded as personal attributes of individuals, similar to gender and age. In these approaches, methodological rigor and the need to explain individual factors often control away important features of culture, such as the interrelatedness of features. In a sense, this rigor often led to methodologies that are not only inapplicable across cultures and contexts, but also often resulted in studies void of any contact with real-life situations. Medin and Atran (1999) pointedly called this the *rigor mortis* of (many) cognitive studies (p. 7).

This brings us finally to the third difference between the two fields, their respective pragmatic concerns and research topics. Again, taking the "cultural perspective," anthropologists are much more concerned with "cultural processes" than with processes on the individual level, which is the focus of cognitive psychology. This results in differences in both theory and methodology. Observing cultural processes on larger scales might not tell us much about the individuals involved, the actual carriers of these processes. This prevents us from truly understanding the processes under study, their dynamics, causes, and potential consequences. For example, in my own work among the Lacandon Maya of Chiapas (Ross, 2001, 2002a, 2002b), I can show how severe changes in the livelihood of these lowland Maya people introduced striking changes in environmental cognition and decision making on the individual level. Yet these changes make much more sense when we analyze the data in light of recent findings on the interaction of expertise and culture (see López et al., 1997; Medin et al., 2002). Different activities lead to different knowledge structures due to the development of expertise. This is not to suggest a unidirectional causal connection between activities and expertise; this link is probably much more complex and combined with values, emotions, and the like. The changes encountered among the Lacandones affected the group in a well-structured way, though with a different effect on younger adults than on older adults (Ross 2001, 2002a, 2002b).

In this particular study among the Lacandon Maya, a theory of the interaction between knowledge structure and expertise was helpful in understanding the underlying processes. In fact, without such a theory the general research question would never have emerged. A solid knowledge of the historical and cultural setting was necessary to (a) envision the study subject—intergenerational change—and (b) to create an experimental design that would address the relevant questions. This is the anthropologist's strength. Being immersed in (or rather exposed to) a certain locality not only provides the researcher with a lot of situational knowledge (the questions that are important and that make sense), but also allows the anthropologist to establish a good rapport with the people, usually while developing the necessary language skills. Aside from this, situational knowledge also provides ideas and testable theories about causal relations and processes.

This is a setting almost opposite to psychology's data collection. Psychology often relies on unmotivated student subjects, whose performance is at best doubtful. Further, in most instances the researcher knows next to nothing about the informants (see Fish, 2000). Not knowing our informants comes with the price of not being able to locate their responses on a level finer than the obvious: gender and the like. These more obvious differences are often targeted as study objects in psychological studies. However, due to our lack of more specific knowledge about our informants the findings often fall short of explaining the issues at hand; for example, why women respond differently to a task than men do. With student subjects, for example, even simple things like their particular fields of interest and expertise are usually not known to the researcher. In light of these examples, a research design based on the study of undergraduate students seems to be largely counterproductive for the endeavor of understanding human cognition (and culture) in context.

It is probably fair to say that the problems of the two disciplines originate in a similarly underspecified notion of culture, and I argue in this book that culture has to be seen as a distribution of shared individual cognitions and representations (see Garro, 2000; Strauss & Quinn, 1997). In this view, our final task is to understand the social factors, bundles of which we often call culture, that cause certain patterns of agreement and disagreement. Obviously, this distribution is partly driven by human universals, but also by direct and indirect exchanges between individuals and by a constantly stimulating social and physical environment.

It is not my intention to promote the already abandoned harmonious and overly stable concept of culture. Both physical and the social environments are in constant change, and even the interpretations to which these stimuli lend themselves are not exactly the same from one person to the next. These interpretations are often the cause of social struggle as described, for example, by Bourdieu (1991). However, even social/political movements that promote change are sometimes forced to adopt the ideas of the very same structures they try to escape.

Again, these processes are much more complicated than outlined here. One of the complicating factors is that culture is not only a research topic for the social sciences, but also a concept that has its own life in the everyday situations of human beings. This adds yet another dimension to cultural studies, for we often have to distinguish between conscious and unconscious processes of meaning formation. *Inventions of traditions* (see Hobsbawm & Ranger, 1983) can be seen as extreme expressions of conscious processes, while unconscious heuristics, knowledge structures, or habits of the mind (Medin, Ross, Atran, Cox, & Coley, 2003) are examples of unconscious processes.

Still, it would be wrong to define culture based solely on a distribution of shared representations. Both material objects and social constructs like institutions have to be taken into account: First, they constitute the materialization of representations and ideas (Johansen, 1992); second, they provide a rather stable environment and the basis for some general agreement based on similar stimuli (see Strauss & Quinn, 1997). Still, as Garro (2000) shows, behind any general agreement there is always sufficient space for disagreement as well.

In this view, culture is an emerging phenomenon evolving out of shared cognitions that themselves arise out of individual interactions with both the social and the physical environments. The natural and physical environments include both institutions and physical objects (natural as well as artificial). This view shares some features with Tylor's (1871) original definition of culture. It differs in that it does not depend on either (a) absolute agreement or (b) agreement across different domains. Therefore, it shifts our focus toward studying social processes and their results—shared cognitions—rather than culture per se.

Of course, this account implies that shared cognitions can be based on different processes, the study of which should be at the heart of our endeavors in both anthropology and psychology. Such a perspective allows us to account for both patterned agreement and disagreement among our informants. Obviously, these accounts should initially be limited to specific domains until we have evidence and a theory that is able to explain cross-domain agreement. I will turn to this discussion later. In this enterprise, exploring the content and the origins of these agreement patterns will be a fruitful and important area of study. In a sense, this kind of approach might help us to explore and understand the "fading quality" of culture. The "fading quality" refers to the fact that the more finely graded our analyses are, the more salient become the within-group differences. It is in part due to this observation that many anthropologists argue for abandoning the concept of culture. Nonetheless, it might prove to be one of the most productive areas of study. We might start looking for something like a "basic" or "preferred level" of cultural agreement, one where agreement between members of given social groups emerges. Of course, much more research is needed to address these topics.

Looking at the development of the two fields over the past decade, one cannot avoid noting a certain irony: Just when anthropology is struggling with the notion of culture, psychologists seem to embrace the concept with increasing frequency.

Nevertheless, it often seems as if psychologists are reinventing the wheel, rather than building on the foundation provided by some of anthropology's work. This is best illustrated by the fact that it is still worth a book chapter to discuss the inappropriateness of Western-standardized intelligence tests across different cultures (see Cole, 1996). Furthermore, psychological studies often either ignore historical accounts and processes altogether, or pay them only superficial attention. The same is true with respect to the interdependency of *features* and *themes* across individuals (see Chapter 2 for some examples).

It doesn't look much better on the other side of this academic divide. Few studies in anthropology are based on a clear methodology, and even fewer studies even take findings in psychology into account. Similarly, studies that explore patterns of agreement and disagreement are rather rare in the field. Even less frequent are instances of clear theories (and theory testing) that deal with the origin of the encountered and described patterns. Rare, too, is the researcher who struggles to integrate formal methods into the research to enhance its precision and the possibility of replication of the data. All these factors combine to discourage a productive discussion of findings, methods applied, and theoretical implications on a larger scale.

The lack of clear methods and theory-guided research is responsible for the meager accumulation of general knowledge in the field; something that becomes apparent when browsing through textbooks of the past several decades. The changes encountered are often only changes in terminology, not real advances in our knowledge of human culture, human thought, and human behavior.

This is not to say that anthropologists haven't gathered important information. However, most of these data are of little relevance for our understanding of human behavior and human cognition. At best (and often unintentionally), these data serve to reject previous theories. Anthropologists have also developed important tools and methods. Yet statistical models like the cultural consensus model (Romney, Weller, & Batchelder, 1986; see also Chapter 5) have not made their way into mainstream anthropology, and it is only recently that the cultural consensus model has gained importance (again, most of this does not take place in mainstream anthropology).

What, then, is left of cognitive anthropology? In general, cognitive anthropologists moved toward a theory based on different *schemata* to explain both different modes of thought and different ways of doing things (D'Andrade, 1995; Garro, 2000; Shore, 1996). In this view, schemata are organized frameworks of objects and relationships that are not yet filled in with concrete detail (D'Andrade, 1995, p. 124; see discussion in Chapter 6). These schemata can also be conceptualized as cultural scripts, often representing predictable social and public artifacts (Shore, 1996, pp. 43-44). Maybe the best known of these scripts is the restaurant script, which allows individuals to predict certain behaviors in a restaurant (ordering, paying the bill, leaving a tip, etc.).

Although schemata were first conceptualized in psychology (see Shore, 1996, p. 44), they soon captured anthropology's imagination, where they blossomed. As I will elaborate in Chapter 6, however, schema theory probably introduces as many problems as it resolves. While schemata are convenient metaphors to think with (for researchers), they are not specific enough to build clear theories and research designs around them. Again, a look across the border to other disciplines might be helpful. In cognitive psychology, researchers seem to be more concerned with the exploration of naïve theories (Hatano & Inagaki, 1994), mental models (Gentner & Stevens, 1983), and cultural models. By "cultural models," I refer to the shared version of individual (idiosyncratic), but not universal models (see Kempton, Boster, & Heartley, 1995, p. 11).

In a sense, the notion of *naïve theory* extends the concept of schemata because it explores the existence of a coherent body of knowledge that involves causal understanding (Hatano & Inagaki, 1994, p. 172). Naïve theories provide us with explanatory frameworks to make sense of our environment, helping us to make inferences about it and to incorporate novel knowledge and situations (Carey, 1985; Medin, Lynch, & Solomon, 2000; Murphy & Medin, 1985). These framework theories differ across domains of experience. A framework theory for understanding and predicting the behavior of physical objects necessarily differs from one that allows us to predict the behavior of sentient beings. Obviously, these theories can occur in different levels of abstractness. Some naïve theories are embedded within others, and some even connect different domains of cultural knowledge. Religion, for example, provides a very strong framework theory, often modeling and guiding more elaborated theories of sentient beings (see Ross, 2002b, for an example; see Chapter 6 for further discussion).

In a sense, the different focuses (on theories and schemata, respectively) reveal one previously mentioned difference between anthropology and psychology: the different methodological approaches applied in the two disciplines. Schemata are normally observed and implied from qualitative interviews (see Garro, 2000; Strauss & Quinn, 1997). It is hard, however, to find clear and convincing evidence for their existence and their psychological validity, or for whether schemata have meaning in the daily lives of real humans. Mental models and naïve theories are very different; once elicited, these theories can be compared with each other and tested against a set of predictions and observations. This means we are able to evaluate, refute, and reformulate the hypotheses, enhancing the understanding of our study topics.

Obviously, this kind of approach has to be embedded in a clear theoretical framework and equipped with sound methodologies. If successful, it has the potential to contribute to significant advances in the field. Not surprisingly, an increasing number of anthropologists are looking to this approach (and the field of psychology in general) to establish a new methodology in anthropology (see Antweiler, 1993, Cole, 1996, Greenfield, 2000, and Wassmann, 1995, for some examples).[3]

Unfortunately, this incorporation of new methods often comes at the expense of traditional anthropological strengths: the locating of data within a wider context and the incorporation of research questions of broader interest. As a consequence, little of the recent work in cognitive anthropology seems to trigger interest within the field of anthropology generally, and rarely do cognitive anthropologists actually succeed in demonstrating the importance of these methods to their fellow researchers and students. Unfortunately, due to a lack of methodological and theoretical rigor, cognitive anthropology does not play an important role in the cognitive sciences, either.

In general, one gets the impression that two equally problematic approaches arose in cognitive anthropology: One is somewhat of a copy of cross-cultural psychology with a strong emphasis on methodological issues; the other is somewhat in between traditional cognitive anthropology and psychological studies, but without the methodological rigor. Neither field connects to anthropology at large, because they both address topics that are only of marginal interest to the field. Compared to general anthropology, these studies now often include a high rate of using student subjects. Unfortunately, little is done to address (and include) important criticisms that anthropologists introduce into the respective research designs (see Antweiler, 1993, Schweizer, 1996a, 1996b, and Wassmann, 1995, for some exceptions). Sometimes, not even the very basic problems already identified in the field of cross-cultural research are addressed (see Cole, 1996).

Obviously, this is not to say that anthropologists should stay away from formal methods. The opposite is true. Switching to a psychology of "the other" is definitely not going to help the case, however. As mentioned earlier, psychology has its own share of problems, often complementary to the ones anthropology is currently experiencing (see Chapters 3 and 6 for an elaboration on this topic). To be sure, important advances have been made in both anthropology and psychology, but when it comes to the areas of culture and cognition, they are still the exception rather than the rule.

When psychology and anthropology discovered cognition as a meaningful and important field of inquiry, they did so from different perspectives and with different interests. Psychology, based on its individualistic ontology, recovered from behaviorism to study mental processes in a manner that separated these processes completely from the outside world, including human activities (Bruner, 1996). Culture, if it was considered at all, was something that people conformed to, even though it was not at all clear *what* they conformed to, *why*, and *how*. These limitations have their origin in the underlying assumption that processes of the mind should be rather stable and that a good science should strive to detect universals within thought processes, reasoning, and the like (see Medin & Atran, 1999, p. 2). Hence, many psychologists argue that the search for universals is the only worthwhile scientific endeavor.

In general, there is nothing wrong with an approach that tries to understand universals in human cognition and behavior. However, discovering the nature of these universals is difficult, because often it is not entirely clear at which level of abstraction to search for them (see Greenfield, 1997, p. 334). In fact, it seems that we cannot fully understand one without the other: cultural differences without an understanding of similarities (and maybe universals), or universals without an understanding of cultural differences and peculiarities. This might best be illustrated with an example: In the domain of folk biology, López et al. (1997) compared native Itza' Maya of the Petén (Guatemala) and Michigan students regarding their taxonomical knowledge of mammals and their category-based reasoning strategies. At first glance some clear universals seem to appear, because both groups sort the respective mammals close to what a scientific taxonomy would look like (see also Atran, 1998). Members of both groups also show some similarities with respect to their reasoning strategies (e.g., they use their taxonomical knowledge to reason about the species involved). Yet when it comes to category-based reasoning strategies, the researchers describe clear differences between the two groups, with the Michigan students relying significantly more on the taxonomical classification than their Mayan counterparts. The latter often use their ecological knowledge when reasoning about mammals. But what do these results actually tell us? Should we classify these differences as cultural and the respective similarities as universal? Further studies with U.S. tree and bird experts (Bailenson, Shum, Atran, Medin, & Coley, 2002; Medin et al., 1997) indicate that the reasoning strategies of these experts are similar to the ones found among the Itza' Maya of Guatemala, but different from the ones observed among U.S. undergraduates. These findings suggest that reasoning strategies are a function of (or at least influenced by) levels and kinds of expertise. This raises the question of whether certain cultural differences might be best conceived as differences in activities and goals that produce different kinds and levels of expertise. Related to this is the question of whether the similarities found across experts from different cultural backgrounds are best thought of as a universal feature in themselves. Differences in attention, activities, and goals definitely are an important part of cultural realities. The Itza' Maya of Guatemala depend on the rain forest in which they work to make a living. Obviously, their work is guided by a lot of knowledge and hands-on experience. This is not true of Michigan undergraduates, however, who probably know barely 10% of the plants in their immediate surroundings. These experiential differences might tell us only half the story, though. For example, in a recent study, we were able to show that Native American and Majority Culture (nonprofessional) fish experts in central Wisconsin share a common knowledge base, but still follow different "habits of the mind," or cultural models, that guide and channel their knowledge (Medin et al., 2003; Ross & Medin, 2003; see Medin et al., 2002, for an overview of the role of culture and expertise in categorization and reasoning).

These studies reveal, among other things, that culture provides us with (a) certain framework theories that guide our thinking and attention, and (b) certain knowledge structures that make particular kinds of information more salient than others. These features seem to interact with specific value systems and goals. Framework theories can be either unspecified principles (e.g., for many Menominee all natural things are in balance) or more specific theories, such as elaborated in religious systems. Older Lacandon Maya, for example, cannot conceive of animals causing any harm to plants, because they do only what they were created for by *hächäk'yum*, the Lacandon creator god (see Ross, 2001, 2002a, 2002b). Obviously, these framework theories can have an important impact on human values, goals, and behavior.

Some of these theories can go very deep, while others can be comparatively shallow and might even stand in competition with other models and theories. For example, some culturally shaped heuristics might surface only in instances when individuals recall or activate certain modes of thinking. This line of research has recently become the focus of attention of a series of studies (see Hong, Morris, Chui, & Martínez, 2000). Simple priming (e.g., showing a U.S. or a Chinese flag to Chinese Americans) triggered strikingly different modes of thinking that were previously thought of as rather stable cultural features. The study indicates that certain cultural differences might appear and disappear under different circumstances of priming. In fact, it might even suggest that culture itself might have to be regarded as a priming force, the details of which are yet to be explored.

While migration has become a major focus in anthropology, research on the effects of binationalism and biculturalism has drawn little attention from anthropologists. This is despite the fact that it seems to be of utmost importance in all kinds of cross-cultural encounters, identity formation, and the roles of ethnic communities in urban agglomerations.

It is not clear yet how stable these effects are and to my knowledge no replication of this study has been conducted. Also, nothing is known with respect to these effects across different populations, or with subjects who are not bilingual, and so on. Still, this line of research adds an important aspect to the above-outlined framework for studying culture. As indicated, we might conceive of social contexts (in both their material and social aspects) as a constant priming force that continuously evokes certain cultural styles, thereby maintaining them across time and individuals.

Obviously, these approaches emphasize the situational aspect of cultural identity and the volatile status of some of the cultural differences encountered. It is not yet entirely clear, however, exactly what these results mean for cultural studies as a field of inquiry. With respect to the approach taken by framework theorists, however, this line of research offers exciting new questions and areas of study; for example, anthropologists increasingly studied phenomena of cultural change and processes of acculturation over the past century. How deep do these processes actually go? And how exactly do they work? Do individuals actually hold different competing models at the same time (similar to bilingual individuals' processing the two languages in parallel)?

Of course, it is unlikely that these processes are the same across different domains, kinds of models, and situations. Still, the question remains as to how individuals actually formulate coherent models out of competing information (outside stimuli). What kinds of models coexist with each other and under what circumstances?

I won't offer an answer to these intriguing questions. However, it seems that these questions are ready to be asked by both anthropologists and psychologists and, if these questions are addressed properly, the results should advance both fields, even when viewed from the different ontological viewpoints. They should enhance both our understanding of individuals' thinking and of cultural processes in general. So far, I have identified four major dangers in the course of studying culture: (1) Addressing culture as a serious study issue is not to be confounded with pretending that everyone in a culture thinks or acts the same way; (2) the kind of research needed to integrate anthropology and psychology has to be grounded in clear methodology, allowing for comparison across groups and tasks. These methods have to be sensitive to the individual cultural context, and we have to verify that they produce comparable data across cultures (see Cole, 1996); (3) cultural comparison that is not embedded in a deep knowledge of the cultures dealt with and that is not tied to a clear theoretical framework leaves us with little to understand in terms of the underlying processes and causal phenomena; (4) if we do not understand the questions of *why* different cultures vary on certain aspects, we run the risk of essentializing culture and engaging in a circular argument. Again, one way to avoid this is to view our research findings from a perspective that focuses on the relevant processes, trying to capture the origin of the differences encountered. Points 3 and 4, in particular, should make one thing clear: Finding cultural differences in cross-cultural studies should constitute the starting point and not the endpoint of our research endeavor.

As outlined above, danger 1 seems more likely to be a problem for anthropologists (see Brumann, 1999, & comments), who are much more prone to exploring intra-cultural differences than to conducting cultural comparisons. For psychologists, the opposite seems to be the case. Many psychological accounts lack sufficient sensitivity to understand or even explore within-group differences fully (see Fish, 2000).

Danger 2 also seems to be a more serious issue for the field of anthropology than for psychology. After a short peak in the 1960s, mainly in the form of cognitive anthropology, insistence on clear and replicable methodologies is almost nonexistent in today's cultural anthropology. It is only recently, and with exceptions, that some anthropologists are searching for clear methods in order to create comparable and, often, more precise data that are less prone to personal judgments (see, e.g., Antweiler, 1993; Bernard, 1995; Wassmann, 1995).

It should be clear by now that rigid methods are by no means a "fix" for all problems. In fact, if lacking the necessary sensitivity and theoretical background, these applications might well create as many or more problems as they set out to solve. In the best scenarios, we might be confronted "only" with nonresponding informants who might simply refuse to participate in our tasks (see Antweiler, 1993, and Wassmann, 1995, for examples). In the worst situations, we might not even know what our data actually mean (recall the discussion above on priming effects) and whether our data are comparable across cultures (see Cole, 1996, for the latter problem).

This ties into dangers 3 and 4, the need for research that combines sound ethnographic knowledge with clear theoretical frameworks in order to avoid essentializing culture. Again, to resolve these issues it is not enough to conduct a psychology of the other by simply applying psychological experiments in the field. Nor should one simply extend psychological theories to an anthropological setting. This mistake seems to underlie Hartmut Lang's (1998) attempt to describe culture as the outcome of the human urge or need to conform. To be sure, conformity is an important aspect of processes of enculturation. Yet as a theoretical approach, Lang's concept accomplishes little toward explaining who the people that do conform are, and to what they actually conform. He also leaves out the even more complicated question of different "modes of thought" or "habits of the mind" that cannot simply be picked up and conformed to. His attempt is nevertheless noteworthy for it at least tries to connect a larger theory of culture with a theory of the mind and behavior (see also Linger, 1994). For another attempt to bring aspects of discourse analysis together with a cognitive theory of meaning and culture, see Chapter 3.

Unfortunately, for a long time anthropology was so preoccupied with the phenomenon of culture that it tended to ignore the individual level of analysis as well as individual differences. In part, it was the uneasiness with this situation, the ignoring of individual differences, and the resulting oversimplifications of cultural descriptions that led many anthropologists to ignore any theoretical reference with respect to culture, or to give up on the concept altogether.

The result is a largely atheoretical anthropology.

This seems to be a strange judgment on anthropology. Yet clear data on human thinking, behavior, and culture are sorely missing in the field (I will return to these issues in Chapters 3 and 6).

This led us to an ironical situation: Nowadays, an increasing number of psychologists explore culture as a thought- (and action-) shaping factor, while anthropologists no longer think of culture as a worthwhile study topic (see Brumann, 1999; Shore, 1996; Strauss & Quinn, 1997). However, there is the danger that in the process of approaching each other, little achievements will be carried over from one field to the other and that researchers will end up reinventing the wheel all over again.

This book is about culture and cognition and ways of combining the two unfortunately separate fields of inquiry into one meaningful research agenda. To be clear, most cognitive research in the past 15 years took place outside the field of anthropology; it is only recently that psychology started to formulate culture as a potential factor in its inquiries. This had and continues to have serious implications for both academic endeavors, as each field seems to lack important inputs from the other. The intention of this book is to bridge this gap. Several books and articles have been published representing somewhat similar aims,[4] but most of them are either short and sketchy (as Medin & Atran, 1999) or are rather superficial in their approach to both methodology and theory. Garro (2000), for example, elaborates on a theory of culture that allows a more finely graded understanding of processes and differences within cultures. Yet her approach falls short of both methodological clarity and theoretical rigor. Similar issues can be observed in the works of Shore (1996) and Strauss and Quinn (1997). Again, theoretical issues are rather undeveloped, and methodology is almost ignored.

In a sense, then, this book tries to establish both a guideline for methodology (data gathering and analysis) and a foundation for a theoretical framework to guide cultural and cross-cultural research.

Chapter 2 focuses on some basic theoretical problems and the question of how to frame cultural and cross-cultural studies. This chapter is based on a literature and research review, and presents some of the major obstacles to sound cognitive studies of culture and cultural studies of cognition. This discussion leads to Chapter 3, in which I develop a preliminary cognitive theory of culture.

Chapter 4 is intended to pick up some of the issues discussed and to describe some methodological concerns with respect to data gathering. Examples of methods are presented that have been applied successfully in the field. The intention of this chapter is not to give a complete handbook of methods, but rather to elaborate on some basic methods that can be used by the individual researcher to design and adapt more specific methods for the individual researcher's purpose. Obviously, our methods of data gathering will determine the kind of data we collect and, hence, the kinds of arguments we can or cannot make. While designing or adapting certain methods, one should have a basic idea of what the possible procedures for analyzing the data are. As these procedures vary from task to task and might include several different ways of processing the data, I decided not to include a chapter on data analysis in the strict sense of the term, but instead refer the reader to easily accessible statistic handbooks. Instead, Chapter 5 looks at one specific aspect of data analysis: the exploration of the patterns of agreement/disagreement between informants (both across and within cultures). This issue is often neglected in both anthropology and psychology. In both fields, researchers often look only at average (or extreme) responses. However, any sound cultural study depends on the understanding of how cultural knowledge is distributed. Exploring the distribution of cultural knowledge can tell us a lot about the processes involved in its production, maintenance, transmission, and so on. It seems to me that these questions should be at the heart of any cultural theory.

Chapter 6 summarizes the aims of the book, trying once more to show the necessity of a cultural theory of the mind as well as a cognitive theory of culture, and, hence, the fact that neither psychology nor anthropology (with their original ontological viewpoints) can stand by itself.

I try to illustrate my arguments as much as possible with both good and bad research examples. Because the intention of this book is to establish both a theoretical basis as well as some methodological guidelines, I will refer to specific articles in the hopes of increasing an awareness of how a sound approach with respect to both methodology and theory can bear some very important fruit. This kind of approach should help us enhance our understanding of the intricate and complex relationship between culture and cognition.

Notes

1. See, for example, D'Andrade (1995), Wassmann (1995), Cole (1996), Shore (1996), Strauss & Quinn (1997), Medin & Atran (1999), and Medin et al. (2002).

2. See Atran et al. (1999), Atran et al. (2002), Medin et al. (2002); Ross, Medin, Coley, & Atran (2003), and Medin et al. (2003).

3. Many more could be named, such as Schweizer (1996a, 1996b) on social network theory; Bernard's (1995) methods book; and Kimball Romney, who is probably the most outspoken anthropologist addressing this need.

4. See Medin & Atran (1999), Shore (1996), Strauss & Quinn (1997), and Wassmann (1995).

2

Cultural Studies and
Comparative Design

In the introductory chapter, I discussed the importance of combining different theoretical approaches and methodologies to gain a better understanding of culture. This is particularly important in the field of cross-cultural comparisons. Here it is not only important to identify and document differences, but also to explain these differences as a result of social processes, including interactions with specific physical environments. In order to explore the quality and content of difference, a clear theoretical framework is needed, which was briefly discussed in Chapter 1. The framework has to address culture as a process rather than as a label for a distribution in both time and space of knowledge, habits, and the like. The next two chapters will deal explicitly with the elaboration of such a theoretical framework from a cognitive perspective. Several books and articles deal with similar issues, but very few of them actually develop theoretical guidelines for cultural studies in cognition or cognitive studies of culture.

The Logic of Cultural Studies

It is often argued that being able to predict certain patterns, findings, or outcomes is the true challenge for any scientific enterprise. Citing Le Vine's (1984) recounting of how he experienced his fieldwork data as replicating and reconfirming previous studies in the area, D'Andrade (1990) makes the point that anthropology is indeed able to make accurate predictions about certain features of cultural knowledge and models (p. 66). He goes on to suggest, however, that pure prediction might not always be a good measure of scientific success for the following reasons:

(a) Although behavior might be culturally constrained, these constraints almost always allow for individual deviation; (b) cultural change makes it important to understand the forces that drive and influence these changes; and (c) much behavior is not (or sometimes not yet) conventionalized and, therefore, couldn't possibly be explained (D'Andrade, 1990, p. 67). I completely agree. Yet D'Andrade might have ignored the most important problem for cultural studies: In a sense, we study culture because we are interested in aspects shared across a group of individuals identified as a culture. Still, what have we really learned if we find that members of culture X make black pottery? To what extent is it an important prediction that the members of one village of a given culture X are likely to have black pottery because members of another village of this culture make it?

To be sure, these predictions are necessary as a first step, creating the basis for further studies to help us delineate and identify certain differences and similarities. Predictions of this kind, however, should not be the end product of our research. If they are, we stop short of gaining a deeper understanding of culture as a process and as an abstract entity that exists only through the individuals that carry and perform it. Identifying social processes behind the shared aspects has two important consequences: Once we are able to link patterns of agreement with specific social processes, we are in a much better position to understand and maybe even predict the outcomes of certain changes that affect cultural groups. Focusing on agreement patterns also forces us to look at individuals and their performance rather than describe synthetic group models. This approach focuses more on individuals than previous attempts in anthropology. Still, it is a far cry from trying to explain idiosyncratic differences. Rather, it focuses on agreement pattern based on individual's cognitions.

If our efforts focus only on predicting certain observations across groups, based on similar previous observations, we are merely mapping the distribution of items across space. This approach might have merit, but it also carries the risk of circular reasoning: We define a culture by a set of features only to become intrigued by the repeated discovery of these features in that culture. This line of thought is not at all intended to discard the ethnographic approach or use of observations described by Le Vine's (1984) recounting of his fieldwork (p. 71). On the contrary, these recurrent observations are important if we want to establish a meaningful research design. We have to be careful, however, not to overestimate their value in our scientific endeavor. What do these observations tell us about culture as an abstract concept?

In the pottery example, we learn that the members of a certain culture X at a certain time have a preference for black pottery. Obviously, this adds some knowledge about this particular culture. However, it does not tell us much about the impact of culture on our thinking and behavior, about the reasons for the distribution of pottery preferences, or about the emergence of these particular traits and, hence, the emergence of culture and cultural differences. An approach of counting and comparing existing traits also has a hard time explaining cultural change and related processes. If the existence of certain traits defines a culture, then, by definition, once these traits are gone the culture is gone. This, however, goes back to defining cultures as static and unchangeable. Furthermore, it is not at all clear whether some traits are more important than others to our subjects (or if all should receive equal attention from the researcher), and how to deal with interrelated traits that either condition or directly cause one another (see discussion in *Current Anthropology*, 1999, Vol. 43). I will return to this discussion in the next chapter. At this point, it is sufficient to say that some of these discussions led to the rejection of early models of evolutionism in anthropology.

Though this might seem to be rather trivial, it contains one of the major challenges for cultural studies and cultural comparisons: How do we account for differences within and between recognized groups of individuals? What do they mean, what do they stand for, and how do they emerge?

This leads to a further point of criticism. If we constrain ourselves to describing observations, the result, at least implicitly, is always a comparison: "Culture X has a preference for black pottery" includes, at least implicitly, a comparison to some assumed standard. Traditionally, the comparative base is the anthropologist's and the reader's culture. Exotic descriptions and the production of otherness are possible (and dangerous) consequences of this kind of approach (Friedman, 1994, p. 207). Note that this is very different from an explicit comparative approach that looks at two or more groups and discusses the differences found.

Two solutions are possible: Either narrow down or expand the research questions.

First, we have to distinguish between (a) the study of culture specifically shared by a group of people (the culture of . . .), and (b) culture as a more abstract principle that reflects the distribution of patterns of agreement in individuals' thinking and acting.

One is illustrated by the pottery example: Members of culture X share a preference for black pottery. In the other view, however, culture is seen as a community of thoughts and practices to the extent that there is a corresponding and often causally connected distribution of mental representations and public behaviors across a given population. It's the second view that is of particular interest here. From this standpoint, cultures are no longer rule systems, codes, worldviews, independent variables, or definable sets of any kind. From this perspective, cultures do not have lawlike essences or clearly definable boundaries, and they do not exist independently of the individuals who constitute them. We often find different populations reliably associated with different distributions of cognitions and the related behaviors, however. Those are patterns we can identify across or within different populations. Such patterns have a history, a present, and a future connecting them through time and space. Still, our research methods provide us only with snapshots of time that often make it hard to understand the underlying processes by which cognition and culture are both shaped and shape one another.

This perspective allows for two strategies of cultural studies. First, it isn't enough to describe commonalities among the people of a culture: We have to document these commonalities explicitly within the light of deviances (and vice versa). Exploring the agreement and disagreement between informants helps us understand the underlying dynamics within a given domain in a given culture. It is here that the methods described in Chapters 4 and 5 should help create a better understanding.

Let me elaborate a little more on these issues with the help of some examples. In cultural psychology, it is often assumed that members of Asian cultures hold a more holistic and interdependent view of the self than the more independently oriented Westerners (see Markus & Kitayama, 1991).[1] Yet, other findings suggest that in so-called Western culture, women are more interdependent than men. This finding might pose some challenges for classifying a culture as independent or interdependent to begin with, but it might also offer opportunities to gain a better understanding of the problem. For example, within-group differences might provide us with a theory of the underlying causes of cross-cultural differences. Once we understand the resulting (non-random) pattern of informant-agreement, we are in a position to formulate hypotheses, to venture into different realms, and to predict and explain possible outcomes of these features of human life. Note that the power of prediction indicates success; however, these predictions are on a different level from the ones put forward by D'Andrade. This is because they describe connections across and between different domains (e.g., cognition and action) within a culture, focusing on the explanation of specific causal connections.

This kind of approach renders the holistic endeavor of analyzing different domains as interrelated (not necessarily harmonically integrated) within anthropology more productive. When we can connect features, like independence and interdependence, to specific causes and can predict the behavior that will follow, we have gone a long way toward understanding cultures and the roles of individuals therein. Predictions like this—not the kind mentioned by D'Andrade—make cultural studies a scientific endeavor and expand its meaning and realm of theoretical implications. To draw an analogy, predicting that an apple falls down if dropped (knowing that a pear does) might not seem too surprising. This, however, was the level of prediction invoked by Le Vine when he observed how the data he collected replicated prior data in neighboring communities. This is very different from formulating a theory of gravity and predicting instances that go beyond observation (e.g., an apple wouldn't fall if dropped on the moon). While the former is a sign of more or less good observation skills, the latter represents a much deeper understanding of the processes involved (e.g., the laws of gravity).

Returning to the pottery example, this means we could derive explanations for why a certain group prefers black pottery, rather than predicting (after the observation) that they like it. Obviously, in this example it would be necessary to establish (a) that other types of pottery are known and (b) their manufacture is possible by the group under study. For example, if soil conditions and technical know-how allow for only certain types of pottery, there is no need for further exploration into why other techniques do not exist. In this sense, our cognitive/cultural research does not have precedence over more material approaches, but does have to be in constant interaction with them.

Any anthropologist with field experience will realize immediately that this view is carried with a great deal of optimism about what's possible. Still, going beyond mere observations and actually making, and confirming or rejecting, predictions derived from our data is what makes cultural studies a scientific field. Obviously, if we want our predictions to cross the barriers of different domains, we need fine-tuned methodologies that allow for formal comparison of the individual results. In Chapter 4, I present an example of combining different theories, and their respective methods, as diverse as social network analysis and the cultural consensus model (the cultural consensus model is described in detail in Chapter 5). Most of these theories are related to the quest of analyzing and explaining within-group differences. This strategy was successfully applied in several studies. For early examples see articles by Garro (1986), who looked at differences in expertise in medical knowledge, and by Boster (1986a), who explored the impact of kinship on the transmission of names for local manioc species.

My own research among the Lacandon Maya (Ross, 2001, 2002a, 2002b) continues this tradition of exploring the distribution of mental models of the environment across expertise and generation, and relating these distributions to possible causes and resulting behavior. It is important to note that none of these studies assume that the content of cultural knowledge is distributed equally among the members of a given population.

Therefore, the content description of the explored models is not the only result of the research. Equally important are the further explorations of *who*, among the informants, shares *what type* of knowledge and/or behavior. This kind of research not only tolerates the idea that different kinds of knowledge exist within a community, but takes it as the center of attention. This focus allows further explorations into the causes that lead to both patterns of agreement and of disagreement.

This strategy enables us to collect data on similar issues across different domains and to formulate a theory of their relations. This includes an exploration of the development, transmission, and change of knowledge and of cultural patterns in general, as well as the emergence of patterns of informant agreement and disagreement.

Once we develop a precise understanding of the agreement pattern, we are able not only to understand its emergence, but also its relation to actual patterns of behavior.

A note of caution is needed here. Most of these studies are correlational: We might be able to establish a relation between two domains, but not have a clear understanding of the specific causal connections. For example, we might find a strong correlation between the mental models of individuals and their behavior within a given domain. This happened in a cross-cultural study I conducted with colleagues in the Petén, Guatemala (Atran et al., 1999). The models that individual native Itza' Maya held about species interaction in the rain forest allowed the researcher to predict their actual behavior (e.g., which trees they protected, etc.). However, correlation must not be confused with causation. In this particular study, it is not at all clear what the causal chains are that lead to this specific correlation. Do Itza' Maya protect certain trees because of their mental models, or do they form their mental models about these trees because of their action? Asked more generally, does cognition cause our behavior or does behavior shape our ways of thinking? In general, the two measures might be (a) cause and consequence, (b) interdependent (both informing each other), or (3) both might be caused by a third, yet unknown, factor. Obviously, further studies, comparative sets of data, and deep ethnographic knowledge are essential for exploring and explaining these correlations. Analytical methods are an important step, but unless they are embedded in an extensive knowledge of the study's context, including historical and sociocultural settings, they could make things worse!

Developmental studies are but one example. The main goal of most of them is to follow the developmental pattern of children across ages and thereby understand the formation of knowledge and its distribution. The vast majority of developmental studies, however, are based on white, middle-class, urban children in the United States. This limited distribution of our subjects does not match the rather extensive ambitions of most researchers: to detect and describe universal patterns. This mismatch of broad ambition and a subject pool of limited diversity comes with the erroneous basic assumption that the underlying adult models (toward which children supposedly develop) correspond to scientific knowledge and, therefore, do not need to be tested. In fact, the two come together as it is the latter assumption that lures researchers into paying little attention to the diversity of their subject pool.

Both assumptions violate, or rather illustrate, the lack of ethnographic knowledge. Anthropological writings are full of descriptions of cultural differences with respect to reasoning and causal models. Therefore, urban, middle-class, U.S. children represent a very restricted sample of informants, as do college students, the standard population of psychological studies. Therefore, the data gained from these studies are hardly suitable for describing universal patterns in the development of high-level cognition (see Coley, 2000; Ross et al., 2003). Our studies continuously show that even within the United States, adult members of a culture not only hold views different from each other's, but also different from the often implicit scientific standard.

And this occurs even with respect to supposedly obvious phenomena. Kempton (1987), for example, conducted a study looking at adult beliefs about the functioning of thermostats. One of the findings of this study was that many adults believe thermostats work like car accelerators (the higher you put the temperature, the faster the room warms up). With the help of additional data, Willet Kempton could, furthermore, show that this model informs people's behavior in heating their homes; for example, when entering a cold room they turn the thermostat high in order to speed up the heating process. This, however, is contrary to the actual functioning of thermostats; it might result in wasting energy, but it doesn't heat the house faster or make the individual feel comfortable more quickly. Obviously, then, we cannot assume that adult models equal scientific knowledge.

Furthermore, if adults always converged toward the scientific model, then cultural differences other than differences in expertise (e.g., knowledge) should not exist. Yet studies in folk biology show differences in expertise as well as cultural differences in how individuals perceive their environment (species and their role in nature; Atran et al,, 1999; Medin, Ross, Atran, Burnett, & Blok, 2002; Medin, Ross, Atran, Cox, & Coley, 2003; López, Atran, Coley, Medin, & Smith, 1997). For example, in a cross-cultural study with nonprofessional fish experts, we found Menominee Native Americans and Majority Culture fish experts of central Wisconsin to differ on an array of measures (Medin et al., 2002; Medin et al., 2003). Not only do members of the two groups attach different values to the different fish species, they differ both in the ways they sort these species taxonomically and in their perception of the interactions of the several fish species. These differences cannot be explained as differences in expertise (e.g., knowledge of the underlying science model). These findings have important implications on at least two levels for developmental studies: First, to understand how children within a given culture develop knowledge (in a given domain), we have to understand the potential end product of their learning—the adult model (which is at the same time an important input for the learning child!). However, we should not expect the kids to become complete reproductions or "copies" of their parents—otherwise cultural change would be hard to understand. Second, not only should we expect to find within-group differences (gender, etc.), the development of which we should be able to trace, but also differences between generations as new influences impact upon each subsequent generation of children (e.g., new knowledge being introduced, and learning environments being significantly altered).

Again, my own work among the Lacandon Maya shows some indirect evidence for this kind of cultural change. Based on a synchronic research design, the study shows how individuals of two generations adjusted in different ways to a changing sociopolitical environment. Second-generation adults, who were either born in the community or came as young children, developed interests and goals strikingly different from those of their parents. While the parents still maintained (as much as possible) their dispersed settlements close to their agricultural fields and in the forest, the younger Lacandon adults decided to settle close to each other, away from the forest and their agricultural plots. This shift in household pattern can be seen as a physical expression of changing values with respect to social life and the forest. As a result, these differences are paralleled by differences in folk-biological knowledge and the respective values of the members of the two groups (Ross, 2001, 2002a, 2002b).

While studies with adults are instructive for understanding results of developmental studies, the latter can also inform our understanding of differences encountered among adults. If we do not understand the emergence of cultural knowledge, we fail to appreciate the quality and underlying causes of differences we encounter among adult models. Ignoring these interrelations leads to mistakes in interpreting our research data, something that has happened and continues to happen in cognitive research. A good example is Susan Carey's (1985, 1995, 1999) seminal work on the development of folk-biological thought. Based on a sample of white, urban, middle-class children, Carey's study seemed to show that children develop their models of biology via a folk psychology. In this theory, children start out by identifying human beings as the prototypical animal. In a truly ingenious task, Carey was able to demonstrate that the children in her sample showed a clear bias toward humans when reasoning about animals. The task (see Chapter 4, "Property Projection Task") involved teaching children that a certain element, the *base* (e.g., human, bee, etc.) has an unknown property, a *splin*. In a series of questions, Carey asked the children to judge whether other elements, the *targets* (both animals and nonliving items), might share the property of the base. For example, the researcher would show the children (individually) a picture of a dog and tell them: "We just learned that all dogs have a *splin*. We don't know exactly what a *splin* is or what it looks like, but we know that all dogs have it." After this instruction, the child was shown another card and asked: "Now here is a bug, do you think bugs have *splins* just as dogs do?" The idea behind this task is to understand the underlying concepts children hold about items (here animals, plants, and non-animate things; Carey, 1985, 1995, 1999). For example, if children have a notion of biological affinity, then this knowledge might guide their inductive reasoning. If this is the case, children should be more likely to project a property from dogs (base) to wolves (targets) than to birds (targets), because dogs are more similar to wolves than to birds (see Ross, Medin, Coley, & Atran, 2003).

Carey's data support her theory that young children in her sample hold an anthropocentric view of biology. First, she finds that humans provide a stronger base for projection than any other element. Children were more likely to project from humans as a base than from any other element. Second, the data show clear asymmetries. For example, children were more likely to project a *splin* from humans to an animal than from the same animal to humans. Finally, Carey found clear violations of similarities, as children were more likely to project from humans to an insect than from a bee to an insect. These data, together with further evidence, seem to suggest that children under 10 have an anthropocentric view of biology. Thus, Carey (1985) argues, children must go through a conceptual change (the title of her book) to achieve adult knowledge (e.g., a scientific understanding of biology, where humans are just another mammal). For a long time, this was assumed to be the general developmental path children used to acquire folk-biological knowledge.

Interestingly, few researchers realized the apparent contradiction between Carey's claim that children see humans as a privileged animal, and the findings that most human cultures draw a sharp distinction between human beings and other animals. Johnson, Mervis, and Boster (1992) found just that (see also Anglin, 1970). In their study (based on a triad similarity comparison; see Chapter 4, "Triad Comparison"), children and adults showed converging patterns of similarity relationships among mammals. Adults, however, considered humans more like other mammals than children did. Indeed, when presented with human-nonhuman triads, children almost never paired a human with another animal. These data suggest quite the opposite of Carey's theory, namely that children see humans as much more distinctive and peripheral mammals than adults do.

These evident contradictions, as well as preliminary results from Yukatec Maya children (Atran, Medin, Lynch, Vapnarsky, & Ucan, 2001), gave rise to a series of studies in which we specifically tested Carey's findings in a cross-cultural setting. We compared rural Native American children (Menominee of north-central Wisconsin) with their rural Majority Culture peers and Majority Culture children from an urban setting. Our urban sample was made up of Boston children, the area of Carey's study (Ross et al., 2003). Contrary to Carey's universal claims, our findings show that her results are not applicable even to other populations in the United States. Carey's children, as our Boston sample, had little or no knowledge about animals and plants. As a result, humans provided the only base from which these children could reason about animals. Rather than representing a universal developmental trait, it is a lack of knowledge that forces these children to go through a developmental shift and achieve a broader conception of biology and living things. Rural U.S. children, in contrast, start out differently because they are involved in outdoor activities from an early age. This environment provides them with specific knowledge about living things: animals, plants, and human beings. While more data are needed for a complete understanding of these differences, within-group differences among Yukatec children (Atran et al., 2001) and Japanese children (Inagaki, 1990) present further evidence for the impact of base knowledge in children's reasoning. In the study of Yukatec children, Atran et al. (2001) detected gender differences that were paralleled by differences in the upbringing of girls and boys. In this particular case, boys were more likely to make inferences about wild pigs, which they encounter when visiting the forest with their fathers, than were girls, who usually stay at home with their mothers. These differences were not found for dogs, animals that are equally salient for boys and girls of this community. Similarly, and possibly more striking, Inagaki (1990) found differences in how Japanese children reason about frogs based on whether or not goldfish were raised at home. Children who had goldfish at home used this specific knowledge to make inferences about frogs.

As a consequence, the data for our urban sample might be best explained as resulting from their lack of experience due to their minimal exposure to nature. As urbanization (and the resulting lack of exposure to the natural environment) itself is only a relatively recent phenomenon, it is both important and possible to examine the history of the changes that affect individuals' cognitions. My work among the Lacandones identifies some of those changes. Forced to live in fixed settlements and being directly connected to the government and other communities (government agencies and roads), offered the second-generation Lacandones new opportunities and at the same time took others away (exposure to the forest). This move into fixed villages and the resulting relative separation from the forest have taken place over the past 30 years, which allows us to study their effect on this particular group. However, changes in the natural and/or social environment, as well as the resulting devolution of folk-biological knowledge, are not unique to either urban children in the United States or to the Lacandones. In fact, similar instances of the loss of folk-biological knowledge have been documented for several indigenous groups, such as the Piaroa of Venezuela (Zent, 2001) and the males of the Tzotzil Maya community of Zinacantán, Chiapas, Mexico (Ross in press; Ross & Medin, 2003).

The kinds of studies discussed so far allow only for tracing ongoing or rather recent changes. In comparison, Wolff, Medin, and Pankratz (1999) chose another approach. Taking advantage of the online version of the *Oxford English Dictionary (OED)*, which allows one to search for (and count) dictionary entries back to the 16th century, they investigated the frequency of tree terms (including different levels of specificity, e.g., oak vs. red oak). In their analysis, the researchers report a decline in listed tree terms on all levels of specificity. The way the *OED* is organized, this seems to reflect (at least in part) the actual language use at various times. It is important to note that the researchers report a similar decline in other folk-biological categories, but not in the naming of artifacts. Therefore, the data indicate a devolution of folk-biological knowledge from the 16th to the 20th century. The data allow for further qualifications: Knowledge about trees evolved during the 16th and 19th centuries (increase in specificity), but it declined sharply during the 20th century (Wolff et al., 1999, p. 199). Obviously, the human brain is not a container filled (or not) with knowledge bites with a lack of knowledge implying an empty space. The issue of loss of knowledge should instead be viewed from the perspective of specificity, saliency, the organization of knowledge, and the absence/presence of specific theories. Also, as the issue is loss of knowledge within a specific domain (here folk biology), the measure does not imply anything related to intelligence or the like. Rather, it looks at cultural processes that put certain types of knowledge at the center of individuals' attention. For 21st-century U.S. citizens in urban areas, this implies that folk species are not very salient. Similarly, for average 21st-century Zinacantán men, tree species in their local environment are less salient than for their women. This can be explained by the fact that their natural environment is not only depleted of big forests, but also that land scarcity and increasing employment opportunities outside the agricultural sector severed the man–nature link within this community (Ross, in press; Ross & Medin, 2003).

Many more studies of different domains and topics could be cited, but the main point should be clear: Cultural research in cognition and cognitive research in culture need to address within-culture processes as well as cross-cultural phenomena. This is important not only for understanding the processes of cause and effect, but also for avoiding authoritative descriptions of static conditions (see Zent, 2001, p. 190, for a similar point about traditional environmental knowledge). This means that we focus on the making and remaking of cultural knowledge (as these emerge through individuals' cognitions), centering our attention on specific domains and their interrelations.

This approach includes exploring interactions between cultural models and mental models, how the former affect the latter and vice versa (see Hollan, 2000, p. 543), and how both are constrained and shaped by cognitive universals and the social and physical environment. Again a note of caution is necessary. While the holistic view in anthropology has led to important understandings in the field (see Brumann, 1999), it is important to realize that not all cultural knowledge is necessarily interconnected. Therefore, the predictive models discussed above might work only within domains. This is yet another reason why in-depth ethnographic knowledge is absolutely imperative. Although by now we have a good understanding of processes affecting patterns of knowledge and knowledge distribution within a single domain (e.g., folk biology), little empirical data exist with respect to the workings or even the existence of broader foundational schema that cross domains. For example, Menominee Native Americans often state the general idea that "all things are in balance." It is conceivable that such general schema (held by many Native American groups) affect how individuals reason in different domains. This kind of cross mapping of different schema or models between domains (see Shore, 1996, p. 117) needs empirical support.

Taken together, the preceding paragraphs outline a new research agenda for cultural anthropologists. Instead of writing more "no-name ethnographies" (a term borrowed from Barrett, 1996, p. 179), anthropologists should focus on two basic areas: (a) First, they should develop concrete descriptions of both the content of different knowledge domains and the distribution of that knowledge among the members of a study population. A critical feature for a sound understanding of the processes involved is that these knowledge structures are developed over time (including changes across adults and the development of this knowledge among children). (b) Then, on a broader level, we have to focus on the more general processes of formation, transformation, and transmission of knowledge in general and within specific domains. This requires detailed research based on formal models. As already mentioned, however, these methods cannot stand alone, but have to be informed by in-depth knowledge of both the population and the domains studied. The strategy of an "anthropology of predictive models"—where empirical models are the foundation for sound cultural descriptions—allows us to compare data not only across tasks but also across different methods and theories. This strategy takes the holistic approach of anthropology seriously by explicitly building its research agenda around the interrelatedness of models and domains. This interrelatedness should be explored and tested rather than assumed. This includes exploring the existence of underlying framework theories, or foundational schema as Shore prefers to call them (1996).

Cultural studies as a scientific field (not to be confused with the academic discipline of cultural studies) are long-term endeavors. Precise and often microscopic knowledge is needed to understand the issues under investigation and to find the correct interpretation of the data. Unfortunately, in the field of cross-cultural studies precise knowledge is often ignored altogether or abandoned.

Cross-Cultural Studies and Comparative Design

It should be clear by now that only a detailed theoretical framework allows formal methods to show their full strength through the prediction and the exploration of patterns in culture and cognition.

For example, applying two or three formal experiments (like those described in Chapter 4) in the field might look like a quick and easy task. However, the results of this approach might be frustrating at best or misguiding at worst. As discussed in Chapter 4, the tasks to be used have to be chosen and adapted to each specific field setting and to the question under investigation. The best-designed study is worthless if informants don't understand the task, or if any of their rules or norms prevent them from responding to some of the questions. This happened in Röttger-Rössler's (1989) study when informants refused to compare and rate individuals of their community according to prestige and status. In other studies, informants have declined to answer questions that did not make sense to them. Problems like this can usually be avoided with pilot studies that test the methodology and the specific questions. These are, therefore, minor issues compared to the conceptual problems discussed in this chapter.

Cross-cultural research is essential for exploring how individuals and groups of individuals organize their knowledge, how this knowledge is culturally shaped (Cole, 1996; Medin & Atran, 1999), and how it is related to other aspects, such as behavior.

Cross-cultural research and the interpretation of its results involve significant conceptual challenges. Ignoring the challenges results in a weakened theoretical position and a poor reputation for the field generally—among anthropologists as well as psychologists, who are used to experimental research. Examples of basic errors are easy to find. One of the most often-studied "cultural differences" is the difference in cognitive styles between "Asian" and "Western" thinking. This line of research even got *New York Times* coverage. The general assumption is that Asians show a more dialectical and holistic cognitive style compared to a more analytical, "Western," way of thinking. At first glance, this might seem like a worthwhile topic to explore. However, the general design already has some conceptual problems. First, given the broad focus (Asia vs. the West), most approaches usually fail to account for cultural processes. To make matters worse, many scholars would be hard pressed to say which cultures/nations belong to either of the categories and why. As an effect of this rather unspecific approach, culture is treated as an independent variable that can easily be controlled by assigning individuals of separate groups (Asians vs. Americans) to the tasks.

For example, in a study on hindsight bias, Choy and Nisbett (2000) concluded that Asians are more prone to showing hindsight bias than Americans. Hindsight bias occurs when a person reports little surprise at a given outcome of an event, even if the person's predictions (without knowing the outcome) were contrary to the actual outcome (see Fischhoff, 1975). I don't like to single out individual studies, but this one serves to address several symptomatic problems in cross-cultural studies in general and those comparing Asians and Westerners in particular. As in most of these kinds of studies, the authors base their hypothesis on different philosophical roots for Asian and Western thought. In this particular study, the authors reason that Asians, because of their holistic approach, should be much less surprised by any outcome of an event, even if they would not have predicted this outcome (Choy & Nisbett, 2000, p. 891). No further information or rationale for this hypothesis is provided that would allow us to assess the connection of philosophical traits and cognitive styles to the particular tasks and the interpretation of the study. The problem is aggravated by the remarkable absence of hindsight bias for the American informants in this study. After all, hindsight bias was first established and continuously documented for U.S. American informants (Fischhoff, 1975)! This reveals at least two important problems: The theory, predictions, and interpretations are not specific enough to relate to the actual data (why does a holistic worldview lead to hindsight bias?). Therefore, the hypothesis can neither be confirmed nor rejected. This problem is magnified by the fact that the study does not connect its findings to previous studies (and theories) that document clear hindsight bias among U.S. Americans. Finally, the underlying concept of culture is confused with a concept of civilizations. In principle, there is nothing wrong with comparing different civilizations, as long as (a) these civilizations are clearly defined, and (b) the predictions are clearly related to empirical findings among the different populations making up the relevant civilizations. If we look at the usual "subject pool" (the psychologists' informants or research participants) for these kinds of studies, it is obvious that this is not the case. For example, in the cited study U.S. American and Korean undergraduate students were used to represent "Westerners" and "Asians." Using student participants is controversial because they are not at all representative of their larger society (see Medin & Atran, 1999). In this case, however, things are worse because findings from student participants from a single country are extended to whole civilizations. In addition, no thought was given to the question of whether college students in Korea are comparable to college students in the United States. Lacking specific knowledge about Korean colleges, one might well suspect that certain selective mechanisms could be at work that bias the Korean student sample in ways different from the sample of U.S. college students. These mechanisms might include differences in income, socioeconomic position, and maybe specific education, or things as simple as gender biases. For example, psychology majors in the United States are mainly female. If, for example, the majority of the Korean students were male, then the question would arise of whether the data reflect gender effects rather than cultural differences. Obviously, one could (and should) report the gender composition of study samples; even then our knowledge of *who* the informants are would still be very limited. As mentioned above, problems like this are not at all unique to this particular study; unfortunately, they seem to be the norm rather than the exception in cross-cultural psychology.

To these conceptual problems must be added the issue of the stimuli used in the study, and particularly the problem of differential familiarity with the stimuli used. In the cited study, the researchers used (among other scenarios) a scenario involving a seminary student. It is doubtful that Korean students in Korea are very experienced with the concept of a seminary student. It is not clear whether this created a problem for the study, but it definitely didn't help strengthen the researchers' argument.

Besides the under-specification of our informants and our hypotheses, we can also find the opposite mistake in cultural studies. In another study, on expectations of high-school students of different ethnic backgrounds (here, culture), the researchers were overzealous in controlling as many factors as possible (Yager & Rotheram-Borus, 2000). Comparing Hispanic, African American, and Caucasian students, the authors made sure that all students came from families with similar incomes. However, this is a rather unusual feature for the particular study groups. It led to several undetected biases of the sample toward relatively wealthy Hispanics and African Americans versus relatively poor white families compared to the average income for each ethnic group. If social position plays a role in social expectations and behaviors, the authors might have "controlled away" important aspects of the living worlds of the members of these different ethnic groups, and the results of the study are, at best, artifacts of their selection methods. Unfortunately, we can't tell from the presented data.

In a sense, both of these approaches see culture as just another independent variable that can easily be separated from other aspects of human society like income and environmental input (both social and physical). This is not to say that we can't study the impact of social position, environmental input, and the like separately, just that a much more sophisticated approach has to be taken than the ones used in these studies.

This discussion of the two studies should combine to make one clear take-home message: Comparing two (or more) groups on a set of tasks might lead to statistically significant results, but statistical significance must not be confused with intellectually meaningful results. Unless guided by clear and informed theory and embedded in a series of testable hypotheses, the results might not be interpretable beyond saying that members of Group A are different from members of Group B on a given task. Any two given populations probably differ in a myriad of potentially relevant aspects. Therefore, the question concerning the meaning of these results remains unanswered (see Medin et al., 2002, for a discussion of some of these issues).

Some leverage can be gained by exploring the development and emergence of cultural knowledge and the existing patterns of informant agreement within each of the groups compared. Once we have identified these structures and their underlying causes, we are in a much better position to investigate existing cultural differences in a meaningful way. This also prevents us from comparing "apples" to "pears" and interpreting the results in inappropriate ways (see Cole, 1996).

Further examples from research comparing Asians with Americans help clarify this point. Markus and Kitayama (1991) review studies describing differences in concepts of the self. They propose an *interdependent view* of the self where an individual defines him- or herself based on other individuals and specific situations, and the corresponding *independent view* as the most fundamental schemata of an individual's self system (p. 230). Although the interdependent view is generally ascribed to Asian cultures, on a global scale it might be generally much more common than the independent view usually assigned to Americans and Europeans (p. 226). This has important albeit largely ignored implications for any interpretation of results. At a minimum, it should show that any large-scale explanation based on differences between Asian and Western philosophical thought could not account for these variations. Rather than trying to come up with complicated theories to fit the story, it might be better to look at the history of Western society to try to understand the emergence of this rather peculiar way of perceiving the self as completely independent. For this endeavor, reported within-group differences (Markus & Kitayama, 1991) might be much more fruitful for understanding some of the processes involved.

These general differences present further possible confusions as Markus and Kitayama reinterpret data presented earlier by Bloom (1984, cited in Markus & Kitayama, 1991). They state,

> It is our view that the differences in responses between the Americans and Chinese may be related to whether the respondent has an independent or interdependent construal of the self. . . . Respondents with interdependent selves might focus on the motivation of the person administering the questions and on their current relationship with this person. (Markus & Kitayama, 1991, p. 234)

In other words, Chinese informants might be responding more to what they think the researcher expects them to say, and, hence, introducing a response bias that drives clear cultural differences in the resulting data.[2] However, these differences (if the authors are right) represent only different concepts and levels of attention to the researchers' expectations. Other response biases can be thought of, and the problem should be clear: Although these biases might represent kinds of cultural differences, it is hard to separate them from the original research question and hypothesis. This brings us to yet another problem cross-cultural research has to deal with.

For example, Cole and colleagues (Cole, 1996) gathered cross-cultural data on memory, asking their informants to recall a previously presented list of items. For the Kpelle of Liberia the resulting recall lists were not only unstructured (compared to the lists elicited in the United States), but also remarkably short (p. 64). The researchers were sensitive to the problem, however. Rather than assume that the Kpelle have low and unstructured memory compared to U.S. Americans, they explored several other methods, resulting in large recall lists for these informants (Cole, 1996, p. 64). This demonstrates the importance of considering the format, context, and content of our studies, as well as the tools we apply. This has serious implications in cross-cultural studies. Two groups that consistently differ on certain measures (e.g., one having consistently lower ratings than the other) might be the result of (a) a general response bias among the members of one group, and (b) the task not being context-sensitive enough for cross-cultural application. This relates to a question raised by Markus and Kitayama (1991): How deep or pervasive are cultural differences, really? Are they primarily a reflection of differences in styles in expression, or do they also reflect differences in phenomenology accompanying behavior (p. 247)? As with the study by Cole and colleagues, one might ask to what extent our methods are easily translatable (see Cole, 1996, for the application of IQ tests across cultures) into other languages and cultures. For example, can we safely assume that "embarrassment" in Japanese means the same as in English (Markus & Kitayama, 1991, p. 248)? This might still be an answerable problem if we take it as an empirical question (Romney, Moore, & Rusch, 1997). The topic becomes more difficult, however, if we compare emotion systems of two different cultures that do not have a fully overlapping set of counterpart elements (see Kitayama & Markus, 1990, cited in Markus & Kitayama, 1991, p. 238).

By now, one point should be clear: One of the basic challenges in cross-cultural research is the problem of comparing the data directly across populations. Unless we are happy with rather empty cultural explanations, we have to take into account that any two populations will differ in many potentially relevant aspects. Rather than just assuming all these aspects as "the culture of a people," however, we should try to understand some of the dimensions on which the two populations differ.

Again, this might best be illustrated with an example. A study comparing Itza' Maya (Guatemala) and University of Michigan students (López et al., 1997) revealed clear differences in how the members of the two groups reason about mammals. Just as in the studies described above, members of the two groups differ on an infinite number of aspects, including age, language abilities, level of literacy, and levels of expertise with nature. Do we learn anything by labeling these differences "cultural?" Studies with tree experts in the United States (Medin, Lynch, Coley, & Atran, 1997) and with Itza' Maya and U.S. bird experts (Bailenson et al., 2002) show (a) that experts reason differently than novices and (b) that experts across cultures often share more with one another (with respect to their reasoning patterns) than they share with nonexpert members of their cultural group. These results are further confirmed by a cross-cultural study among Native American and Majority Culture freshwater fish experts in Wisconsin (Medin et al., 2002). Although these two populations differ in many ways with respect to their folk-ecological model, no differences were found with respect to levels of expertise and the ways they reason about freshwater fish (Medin & Ross, unpublished data; see Chapter 4, "Category-Based Reasoning"; see Medin et al., 2002, for an overview of these studies with respect to the role of culture and expertise).

At a minimum, these studies should caution us not to treat culture as just another independent variable and not to be too quick to draw conclusions. Unless we have a good understanding of the study topic within each of the populations under study, our interpretations of the data will be at best vague, and possibly simply wrong. (Note: In these cases, statistical significance is not a safeguard against erroneous interpretations!) As illustrated, research on within-group agreement wisely coupled with cross-cultural comparisons can provide us with important insights into high-level cognition and the role of cultural processes. Furthermore, the examples should show that rather than relying on only one measure, a series of independent tasks should be applied that allow us to confirm (or challenge) our findings across different methods.

Again, predictive models can give us some leverage (both for within-group and between-group results). In addition, different samples of each group or the comparison of more than one group can allow us to identify important aspects that might drive the differences we encounter. The latter method has been termed triangulation strategy (see Bailenson et al., 2002; Medin et al., 2002; Ross et al., 2003). The idea behind this strategy is to compare three groups with each other rather than only two groups. Ideally, the third group resembles one of the other groups in some aspects and the remaining group in others. Comparing the agreement patterns across groups should then help us to understand better certain dimensions involved in the distribution of shared cognitions and knowledge. Again, an example will be helpful in illustrating this approach. In a study on how children develop their folk-biological knowledge, we applied this strategy among three groups of children: Menominee Native Americans, rural Majority Culture children living adjacent to the Menominee reservation, and children growing up in Boston. Applying the triangulation strategy, we reasoned that when rural Native American kids and rural Majority Culture kids agree with each other, but do not agree with urban Majority Culture kids, a difference in expertise might be the best candidate for explaining this pattern. On the other hand, when Native Americans are the "odd group," differences in framework theories provided by the culture of the children might be the best explanation (Ross et al., 2003). Note that this approach is not a cure-all. However, it does help us to identify and further explore the differences encountered.

Once we have identified differences across groups, developmental studies that focus on both the development of cultural models and the differences in environmental inputs (social and natural environment) should allow us to pinpoint the differences encountered among the adults, including within-group differences (e.g., gender). This approach differs drastically from the cited comparative studies dealing with "Asian" and "Western" thinking. Rather than stopping at the point of encountered differences, the differences are taken as a starting point for further study to try to gain a better understanding of the role of culture, including how children are raised. Finally, this offers a new vision for developmental studies as well. Rather than taking the goal of children's learning for granted—adult knowledge as represented by scientific knowledge—these adult models have to be seen as targets of empirical research in themselves. Adult models rarely stand the test of scientific knowledge.

I think these examples suffice to illustrate that cross-cultural comparison is not without danger and is definitely not a research field that allows short-term research. Comparisons can be a reasonable strategy only if they are embedded in a clear theoretical rationale of expecting specific group difference to start with (e.g., Markus & Kitayama, 1991), or if they are used to guide further research exploring the causes of the encountered differences. Failing to find differences might not only be frustrating to the researcher (who could possibly be interested and publish the results), but also leads to the question of whether the methods used were powerful enough to detect differences.

To sum up this chapter, we have to be careful with our predictions and interpretations and be sensitive to an array of issues:

(a) Our studies have to be guided by specific theories; (b) these theories have to be based on detailed ethnographic knowledge; (c) it is only with solid knowledge of the topic under investigation and of the groups we are studying that we can develop clear hypotheses; (d) on the basis of these hypotheses we can identify the best samples of informants needed to address the hypotheses; and (e) identify and develop the appropriate tools for gathering and analyzing data.

In psychology, these points are all too often ignored in cross-cultural studies, and the results are, therefore, often sketchy, inconclusive, or simply wrong. On the other hand, rare is the anthropological research that embraces such a specific research strategy. It is important to note that this strategy does not make "participant observation"—one of the major paradigms of the field—obsolete. On the contrary, detailed knowledge of the study topic and context are of utmost importance. However, it is also important to realize that participant observation is all too often mistaken for a research method—which it is not.

It is clear that making predictions across and within cultures and eliciting differences in developmental processes creates some major challenges. However, there are pragmatic concerns and obstacles that are even more difficult to overcome. Data gathering across different populations is time-consuming and expensive unless we restrict ourselves to the rather atypical sample of college students, as in most psychological studies. Student participants, moreover, are often not only inattentive to the tasks, but also represent a rather peculiar sample for most of the world's cultures (including the United States).

Furthermore, working at this level of detail requires extensive knowledge about (a) the cultures and (b) the participants involved. Acquiring this knowledge in a cross-cultural design with three groups normally exceeds a single person's ability and facilities. Language abilities and long-established contacts are needed not only to get permission for some studies (e.g., with children), but also to design sensitive methods and arrive at meaningful conclusions about the results. This kind of research can usually be achieved only in a long-term collaborative effort that includes several principal researchers, ideally with different specialties, and a large staff of highly trained local research assistants.

One can easily see that such an endeavor is fraught with additional problems, including the mundane question of long-term funding. Yet once these barriers are overcome, the gains are substantial and the results intriguing when it comes to understanding human cognition in natural contexts or to comprehending the interrelatedness of culture and thought.

In this chapter, I often identified the way researchers conceptualize and construct culture as a major source of problems in their studies. Similarly, the methodological approach I propose depends largely on the a priori conception of who the relevant informants are for our studies. At several points, I described the need for a clear theory to guide our research. In order to come up with such a theory, however, we first have to establish the appropriate level for our studies. In a sense, this addresses a major question that anthropology has confronted over the past two decades: *What constitutes culture?* In the next chapter, I elaborate on the possibilities of a cognitive concept of culture. This discussion should clarify some of the strategies and approaches described so far.

Notes

1. Later, I address some problems inherent in most of the studies.

2. It is interesting to note how detached the studies comparing "Asian Culture" with "Western Culture" are from one another, as several of the different hypotheses brought forward by different authors seem to contradict each other. Again, this indicates the shallowness of many of the attempts to understand Asian and American thought.

3

Toward a Cognitive Theory of Culture

The Problem With Culture, Folk Beliefs, Scientific Concepts, and Their (Ab-)Use

In the first two chapters, I discussed cultural processes and cultural differences and how to study them. For example, if we are to study cultural differences it is clear that the initial definition of "who is in" and "who is out" is absolutely vital. This requires an a priori decision of what we mean by culture.

Similarly, if culture lies at the heart of the anthropological[1] endeavor (Hirschberg, 1988, p. 269; Knorr-Cetina, 1993, p. 167), every theory or paradigm applied in the field has to be evaluated for its contribution to the development and use of a scientific concept of culture. In other words, we must constantly examine the usefulness of any applied (although often hidden) concept of culture with respect to the improvement of our understanding of human thinking and behavior.

In this chapter, I outline a cognitive theory of culture. In a sense, this is needed to respond to ongoing discussions and criticisms over the past two decades in anthropology: *Does culture exist outside of folk-anthropological[2] beliefs (including the ones held by scientists)?* and *Does a concept of culture provide meaningful insights into the life, thinking, and behavior of human beings?*

Some decades ago, asking these questions would have been seen as nonsense or merely a rhetoric trick, especially if posed by an anthropologist. Things have changed, however, and today these are important questions that anthropologists and cognitive scientists who think about culture have to answer one way or another. These questions might be quite disturbing to both folk notions and scientific disciplines as people increasingly regard culture (often confounded with race; see Fish, 2000) as a concept basic to an understanding of human beings. At German universities, for example, this trend is accounted for by the changing labels of academic schools (*Fakultäten*) from *Geisteswissenschaften* ("humanities") to *Kulturwissenschaften* ("cultural sciences"; Brumann, 1999, p. 10). At the same time, "Cultural Studies" and "Ethnic Studies" are flourishing departments in many U.S. universities and bookstores.

Marked changes are also found in other academic fields. In psychology, for example, this trend can be seen in the number of handbooks in cross-cultural psychology (Berry, Portinga, Segall, & Dasen, 1992; Berry, Portinga, & Pandey, 1997), and the work by Cole (1996) and Shweder (1991), to mention just a small sample of publications in the field. Other fields, too, show an increasing focus on culture as a unit of analysis, as can be observed in literature studies (Said, 1979), political science (Huntington, 1993, 1996), and sociology, to mention only three examples.

Given these developments, it is remarkable that it is within anthropology, for centuries the stronghold of the study of culture, that these concepts are now questioned (Abu-Lughod, 1991, 1999, pp. 13-15; Appadurai, 1996; Wagner, 1981; see also Brightman, 1995).

Different theoretical stances led individuals to criticize different concepts of culture. Although not all of them are based on scientific grounds, they have to be taken seriously in our discussion on culture. Both Brumann (1999) and Brightman (1995) present the main arguments against culture as a meaningful concept, and it seems that three major criticisms have to be addressed if we are to defend the importance of a scientific concept of culture[3]:

The first of these criticisms is that culture often implies the notion of clearly marked and separate units, consisting of homogenous and synchronized groups. Consensus and agreement are emphasized, often ignoring significant within-group differences (Aunger, 1999, p. 93; Clifford, 1988, pp. 232, 235) in both the position of individuals in the meaning-making process and their levels of agreement. As a consequence, human beings are often ignored as intentional agents with different life histories, feelings, wishes, and even more obvious issues such as different levels of expertise in individual domains. In the words of Friedman (1994), this approach "flattens out the extremely varied ways in which the production of meaning occurs in the contested field of social existence" (p. 207; see Appadurai, 1996, p. 12, for a similar position; see Brumann, 1999, p. 2, and Brightman, 1995, for further references and elaboration on this point).

The second is that treating cultures as clearly marked and homogenous units leads one to underestimate differences and conflicts over the production of meaning. This, in turn, leads us to perceive meaning (and, therefore, culture) as a *given fact;* an almost essential part of culture; a personal attribute of the members of a culture. From this perspective, meaning and culture are studied as fixed units rather than ongoing processes that entail both a history and a present. These processes often include negotiations and conflicts (Clifford, 1988, pp. 232-235; Friedman, 1994, p. 207). This is not to say that all meaning production is necessarily based on conflict. Neither is the opposite necessarily the case. For example, Bourdieu's (1991) work on censorship and the imposition of form provides illustrative examples of how certain forms are maintained almost invisibly through the exercise of power within educational systems. Most people are not even aware of these processes—a fact that makes them even more powerful tools. Meanings (and, as an extension, culture) is always negotiated and created in processes that should be studied as part of the anthropological endeavor. On the other hand, this does not imply constant conflict over the creation of meaning. Nor does it assume that meaning is completely volatile and cannot be studied. It is notable that even authors who write explicitly against culture (Abu-Lughod, 1991) recognize the existence of "shared routines" and that "different groups of people share certain things, ways of thinking and doing" (Abu-Lughod, 1999, p. 14).

A third criticism is leveled against identifying "culture" or "cultures." *What is the unit of investigation and on what grounds does the researcher choose this unit?* As Friedman (1994) wisely warns us (p. 207), culture is often used as a black box or container for differences. Whenever these differences are attributed to demarcated populations, we have culture or cultures. In these instances, culture becomes an independent factor used to explain observed differences in a regression analysis. This point is closely related to the problem of "culture as a unit," as described above and illustrated in several examples in the preceding chapter. The resulting arguments are generally circular. Yet even if the shown differences appear intuitively convincing to us, the question remains: *What are the meaningful study populations; what elements are studied; and what might be the reasons for the observed differences?* Depending on the answers to these questions, we might be able to respond to Renato Rosaldo's (1999, pp. 27-28) query about the stability of these units (called culture) in time and space.

All three points speak to real problems that have to be addressed in any serious attempt to construct a meaningful theory and concept of culture.

In the social sciences, it is often difficult to separate folk concepts from scientific concepts. The latter are often built upon the former by using "commonsense concepts" and their validity explored with scientific methods. The origin of the anthropological concept of culture can probably be explained this way. In fact, most of the "cultures" studied by anthropologists are probably identified either by the in-group or some out-group as a culture—that is, different from others. Generally speaking, there is nothing wrong with this approach, and, in fact, this might be the only reasonable way to get started in cultural research. It is imperative, however, that we continue to reflect on our initial choice of the target group and continue to take into consideration this original decision when interpreting our data. We must not confuse folk beliefs (often our own) and intuitions with what is needed for a scientific theory of culture. Otherwise, we might simply reinstate the existing stereotypes and folk models encountered prior to our study, engaging in a rather circular endeavor.

This is not to say that folk beliefs about cultural differences are necessarily wrong. Ultimately, one cannot, and should not try to, explain away certain differences. For example, the Tzotzil Maya of Zinacantán are in many aspects different from members of the neighboring community of Chamula—if only in their different ways of dressing themselves. However, such descriptions often fall short on two accounts: First, they usually describe observed differences and fail to link these observations to potential causes. As discussed in the previous chapter, saying that members of culture A differ from members of culture B on X (e.g., dress) is not a scientific account of culture because it merely reiterates the differences that initially led to separating the individuals as members of different cultures in the first place. Second, such an attempt does not account for within-group differences (e.g., in dressing, or the role of the hamlets as described in Cancian, 1992, and Ross, 1994), or similarities between the groups compared to other groups (e.g., both speak Tzotzil, not Tzeltal).

Wimmer (1999, p. 20) rightfully mentions that while many anthropological descriptions readily acknowledge within-group differences, these differences are hardly accounted for and included in the respective theoretical frameworks.

Brumann seems to commit this mistake. His distinction between the "core meaning of the word culture"—with which most classic and modern anthropologists presumably agree—and "theories about cultures"—where these current and classic scholars differ (Brumann, 1999, p. 4) is logically impossible. It is inconceivable that a theory of culture (defining culture) does not affect the "core meaning" of the concept to be defined: culture. For Brumann, the presumed "core meaning of culture" is the fact that culture somehow involves a sharing of certain features. He hastens to add that this does not necessarily imply an even distribution of these features among the informants, an aspect that has to be dealt with within the theory about culture.

While his effort to rescue some of the classic anthropologists from being criticized beyond reason is laudable, Brumann himself fails to provide a theoretical framework for culture.

In the remainder of this chapter, I elaborate on these issues. To foreshadow some of the discussion, I argue that "culture" has two important roles in our studies. Folk notions of culture are a powerful social construct that influences how people behave toward one another (in-group/out-group definition, behavior, and communication). I will also argue, however, that elaborating on folk notions of culture is of little analytical value in that folk notions of culture are much too broad and nonspecific to provide us with a fine-grained understanding of specific cause and effect relationships, which should be at the heart of the anthropological sciences.

This might explain why so many anthropologists agree on the "core meaning of culture" (Brumann, 1999, p. 4). It seems that the same paradigm guided generations of researchers to identify the culture they set out to study—"common sense and intuition." It is only recently that anthropology started discussing the foundational concepts of our discipline and their implications. Unfortunately, these discussions often miss the point by focusing on the concept of culture on a level too abstract for empirical research.

Before I proceed with my own approach to a cognitive theory of culture, I want to discuss in more detail the criticisms mentioned above and some of their backgrounds.

The Authenticity Crisis of Cultural Concepts: Cultural Differences and Different Cultures

Most of the comments summarized in Points 1 and 2 come from researchers who look critically at the function and role of anthropology and the anthropologist/ethnographer (see, e.g., Abu-Lughod, 1999). For example, Derek Freeman's (1983) work on the role of Margaret Mead and her research in Samoa, although by no means unchallenged in itself (Schweizer, 1989; Shankman, 2000, p. 5; Shore, 1996), continued a debate opened in O. Lewis's (1951) restudy of Tepoztlan. This central Mexican village was originally described by R. Redfield (1930) as a harmonious unit of rural Mexican life. Lewis studied this by-now-famous village several years after Redfield, and his description gives the impression of a completely different community, which he confounds with culture. The community was split into factions and riddled with conflict. General theories of change don't seem to be able to accommodate the extent and quality of the differences revealed in the two studies. This presents an important shortcoming in traditional anthropological methods, as one of the major axioms of scientific research seems not to hold: the ability to replicate research findings.

Of course, the obvious problem of non-replication of findings immediately challenged the general validity and authenticity of anthropological research in general (Manners & Kaplan, 1968).[4]

Once the question arose, two possible alternatives appeared on the horizon: The one emerging from the more traditional, scientific anthropologists who asked for the development of clear concepts and methodologies (Romney, Weller, Batchelder, 1986, p. 313), but it did not question the basic underlying concepts of the fields, such as "culture," or the role of the researcher. The second alternative produced a strong reaction against the scientific approach and argued against any anthropological endeavor that entailed negative political ramifications. In this perspective, anthropology's political implications are scrutinized and the general problem of understanding *the other* is examined (see Fabian, 2000). Entities such as culture are questioned and often regarded as the invention of the ethnographer, who creates rather than describes them. In general, the interaction between researcher and participant, and the question of how scientific knowledge is created plays a big role in this approach. The various perspectives embraced in the second view are often labeled *postmodernism,* although they include very different theoretical positions.

To be sure, understanding across cultures should not simply be taken for granted, and debates on the history of anthropology should definitely warn us against a simple acceptance of just any description of a culture. This should be clear from the last chapter. The opposite would be just as wrong, however. Pretending that cross-cultural understanding is impossible makes any anthropological endeavor—and as such the understanding of the human condition—unfeasible. What seems to be needed is a clear approach that allows fellow researchers to examine one another's methods, theories, and interpretations of the data.

This seems to be more in line with the earlier perspective that asked for better methodologies. Obviously, I support such a goal. However, some critical aspects of this approach have to be introduced.

Kimball Romney is arguably one of the most outspoken (and admittedly extreme) defenders of the quantitative approach in anthropology. In Chapter 5, I will introduce the cultural consensus model developed by Romney et al. (1986, pp. 313-314) to address some of the problems discussed here. This model is a tool to better understand the level of agreement and disagreement between informants on a given domain (see Garro, 2000, for a good intuitive description of the model and its assumptions).

Several researchers have critiqued this model, mostly with respect to its underlying concept of culture. They frequently throw the baby out with the bathwater, however, by underestimating and ignoring the value of the statistical model as a research instrument, and at times erroneously confound bad theories or applications with bad models.

For example, Linda Garro describes the cultural consensus model as assuming that the *same responses* indicate the *same cultural reality*, and that discrepancies are treated as errors (Garro, 2000, p. 306). In her discussion, Garro compares the cultural consensus model with what she calls the cultural models theory, which is identical to schema theory (Garro, 2000, p. 284; see also D'Andrade, 1992). Garro also misses two essential points: First, cultural models and cultural schema should not be treated as being identical. Cultural models revolve around the concept of mental models and tacit (naïve) theories. Schemata, on the other hand, are organized frameworks of objects and relations that must be filled in with concrete detail (D'Andrade, 1995, p. 125; see Chapter 6). In such a framework all models are schemata, but not all schemata are models or theories. Second, in recent years an increasing number of researchers used the cultural consensus model not to verify a particular set of answers as culturally correct, but to explore (a) the existence of general consensus among a group of informants and (b) to investigate similarities and differences (submodels) among these informants. This approach has been successfully applied across cultures (Atran et al., 1999; Medin, Ross, Atran, Burnett, & Blok, 2002) as well as in the exploration of within-cultural differences (La Torre-Cuadros & Ross, 2003; Ross, 2001, 2002a). An approach of this kind is far from classifying deviations from the consensus as errors!

Garro's (2000, p. 306) critique illustrates yet another important point: A cultural consensus (e.g., high agreement) on a given set of questions does not necessarily imply there are no underlying differences. Even more important, the similarities described by a consensus can be based on different processes (see Medin et al., 2002). Finally, informant agreement as encountered by the researcher might depend only on the level of concreteness, and, hence, on the quality of our data-gathering tools. All these issues, however, do not weaken the cultural consensus model, as they are not part of the package. Still, Garro's critique is important because it reminds us that a statistical model is not a tool to identify "culture"; it is an important tool to detect and explore agreement (and disagreement) patterns. As such, the model has to be embedded in a clear theory for selecting the study participants and for drawing conclusions from the resulting data.

Patterns of agreement provide us with important insights into the structure and content of the data—*who* knows *what*. Obviously, answering these questions goes a long way toward understanding the underlying social processes. Still, how deep our understanding goes depends on the tasks applied and the analyses conducted. In this sense, cultural consensus theory provides an important *tool* for exploring exactly the kind of agreement/disagreement pattern that Garro puts forward in her somewhat erroneous dichotomy between consensus theory and cultural model theory.

As already indicated, Garro is right when she argues that consensus should not be used as a definition of culture, as was implicitly assumed in the original paper. It is here that some clarifications are needed. The cultural consensus model should be used as a tool to explore systematic agreement patterns and deviations therefrom. However, it should not be mistaken for a theory of culture or, even worse, a tool to establish and define culture. None of this is inherent to the statistical model itself! In a sense, Romney addresses this point in his response to Aunger (1999, p. 103) about separating methods that support or reject a theory from assumptions, hypotheses, and theories. This important distinction becomes more obvious if we look at two conditions of the cultural consensus model: Culture is (a) shared among relevant participants and (b) learned as part of our social heritage (Aunger, 1999, p. 104).

While the second condition should remind us of the less-than-perfect sharing across our informants, it is the first condition, and especially the restriction, that is of particular importance: When applying the cultural consensus model, it is necessary to distinguish between *relevant* and *non-relevant individuals,* a fact that has to be kept in mind when interpreting the data. For example, it is obvious that findings based on studies with male informants do not allow us to make statements about members of both genders, and so on. If we have to decide, a priori, *who* the relevant members are, then the model itself cannot represent a theory of culture.

To be clear, the cultural consensus model, which I use extensively in my own work, is an important tool for discovering differences and similarities within a domain among different individuals. As is the case with any statistical tool, its success depends on clearly identified informants, and the results can obviously never be better than the quality of data gathered in the first place. It is here that Garro's critique hits the target. Romney and colleagues (Romney, 1999; Romney et al., 1996) fall short of combining the acknowledgment of salient differences with a sound framework of culture that (a) treats deviations as more than mistakes and (b) includes these differences without returning to (again) intuitive decisions about relevant members. It is here that the statistical tools are no longer innocent (see Chapters 2, 4, and 5). All this caution is necessary. It is, however, not meant to dismiss the enormous achievement the cultural consensus model represents in the social science tool kit. As mentioned, I make extensive use of the model and the results help support or reject hypotheses about consensus on certain beliefs and knowledge for a set of items within a domain among a group of individuals. In this way, the model helps me explore levels and patterns of agreement among a set of informants (see Boster & Weller, 1990; Weller, 1984a). This is of particular importance for much of cognitive psychology, where trends in the data are often identified without further consideration of agreement levels. In the worst case, this leads the researchers to misinterpret their findings completely!

I have mentioned already several times that the model does not rescue us from the dilemma of deciding *who the relevant individuals are, and on the basis of what theory and concept of culture* we select them. Nor does it suggest *how to interpret intracultural differences or on which level of agreement to apply the label "cultural."*

Brumann (1999), for example, seems to suggest accepting the labels "culture" and "cultural" for all differences that make intuitive sense, creating cultures based on gender, region, profession, class, and age (p. 12). So inclusive an approach does not allow for a clear, scientific concept of any explanatory value. Taken to an extreme, this view leads us back to a point—even before R. Linton, who was aware as early as 1936 of the existence of intracultural differences—where all differences are cultural (age, gender, etc.). In this view, cultures are homogeneous by definition.

To illustrate his point, Brumann invokes the world described by Tim Ingold (1993), "in which people dwell as a continuous and unbounded landscape, endlessly varied in its features and contours, yet without seams or breaks" (p. 226). However, Brumann (1999) then hastens to add that we would still "need a vocabulary for describing its mountains, plains, rivers, oceans, and islands"—his cultures (p. 12). But here Brumann misses Ingold's original point: The question is *how* one would know to distinguish mountains and hills and oceans from one another and to determine whether they are indeed real (or just our artificial creations).

Even worse, at least some of the proposed cultures, such as gender and age (and more could be found), cross the units that Brumann (1999) would like to describe as mountains and plains. This could lead to considering an individual to be part of an infinite number of cultures (p. 12) at the same time. I doubt that many of the classic or modern anthropologists would agree with this concept of culture (as Brumann suggests) because it makes it impossible to define any group of people in a meaningful way as a culture to be studied.

Could anything possibly be gained[5] from such an inclusive view? Or is the general perspective already misguided? I would argue the latter, because this kind of perspective neglects different processes leading to similarities and variations, ignoring more subtle differences. It also seems to pay too much attention to "culture" as a specific phenomenon, almost like the independent variable it is taken for in much of cultural psychology.

Where, one might ask, is the quest to understand "recipients' engagement . . . and the resulting practices" (Brumann, 1999, p. 13) if we regard almost all similarities as (different) cultures. What about a Chamula woman's engagement with gender issues and her situation in her specific society? Do we expect her engagement and the resulting practices to be exactly the same as the ones expressed by a female lawyer on Wall Street, a Menominee woman in central Wisconsin, or a Hindu woman in India? If not, what are the sources of their differences and similarities?

Applying Brumann's framework, we not only lose the possibility of studying processes of transformation and change, but also those of maintenance and rebuilding. Furthermore, the researcher loses the chance to locate culture historically as a set of evolving models, ideas, and values (Cole, 1995; Greenfield, 1997, p. 328). Balanced against these disadvantages is only the gain of the (not new) insight that people can be grouped together on different levels with respect to their agreement on different domains, with the numbers of differences being a function of the number of measurements taken and tools applied.

Including the processes of transmission, tradition, invention, and so on, does not necessarily mean that a concept of culture has to be infinitely flexible and that the members of a culture do not have to agree at all with one another. People often agree on an underlying cultural model but provide different interpretations of it (Garro, 2000; Strauss & Quinn, 1997). Again, unless these differences are randomly distributed, they give us some good ideas of the processes at work. Still, routines in thinking and acting, learning across generations, environmental (social and physical) input conditions, and a general striving for conformity (Lang, 1998, p. 7) should guarantee some agreement among the members of a group that share a physical and temporal space, be it virtual, immediate, or through generations.

My research among the Lacandon Maya serves as a good example. Although significant differences were found in comparing the members of the two living adult generations with respect to their folk-ecological models, these differences have to be seen against a common cultural model shared by all informants (Ross, 2001, 2002a, 2002b). This should make us aware that only against the background of similarity can we identify and evaluate deviations (Schweizer, 1996a, p. 66)—plains and mountains.

To use Argyrou's (1999) words: "[Sameness] is the axiomatic proposition that demarcates the epistemological space within which it becomes possible to study Others" (p. 31).

Culture as Socially Transmitted Models

In this chapter, I describe the cultural part of knowledge, beliefs, and values as "emerging from the bottom"[6] to avoid the danger of viewing culture as "a coherent body that lives and dies" (Clifford, 1988, p. 235) or as a "physical substance" (Appadurai, 1996, p. 12) that becomes—once identified and demarcated—an essence of the people carrying it (Friedman, 1994, p. 207). "Emerging from the bottom" means that cultural ideas are no longer treated in an abstract manner, with culture becoming a mere "anthropological abstraction" (Borofsky, 1994, p. 245; Strauss, 1992). On the contrary, cultural ideas are viewed as residing, at least partially, in each individual and are analyzed as such. In this approach, it is just as important to explore the cultural ideas (and differences) as it is to understand the formation of these ideas. The "cultural" part of these ideas and values has to be derived from the multitude of values and ideas found in each individual of the group under study. Because cultural knowledge is seen as socially transmitted, its distribution among the members of any given group has to be at the heart of such a project. How this transmission of information takes place depends on the kind of knowledge, the carriers, and the particular context. Because we often do not know all of these variables, studying the distribution of knowledge and models is the right place to start. In general, it seems necessary to explore at least four basic processes of knowledge transmission:

1. Transmission of knowledge and concepts across generations, both from one generation to the next (see Ross, 2001) and over long periods of time (see, e.g., Greenfield, 1997; Köhler, 1977, 1989).

2. Transmission of knowledge across spatial boundaries (in- and out-migration; also the use of virtual spaces of communication, etc.).

3. Transmission of knowledge across social boundaries, with and without close social contacts (across social groups, etc.; Atran et al., 1999; Atran et al., 2002).

4. Transmission of knowledge within clearly delimited spatial and temporal units (development of children's folk-biological knowledge; Ross, Medin, Coley, & Atran, 2003).

In this context, I use *knowledge* as shorthand for ideas, knowledge, concepts, biases, and every mental process that is subject to social transmission. The task is to explore the processes that guide the transmission and the resulting distribution of knowledge. Rather than just assuming them to be harmonious and free of problems, we have to explore them precisely in the context of changing frameworks (e.g., globalization) and social conflicts. Within these contexts, the processes are almost always less than perfect from the viewpoint of information processing.

Acknowledging this at the outset, we have to define culture as a process rather than a static entity, without necessarily giving up the ideas of agreement and sharing. While the latter might sound like a "harmonious sharing and agreeing" among individuals, it only means that there has to be at least some common ground (in the ultimate scenario, any countermovement does need something to counter). This agreement does not necessarily mean acceptance, but can be coupled with different interpretations (Garro, 2000; Strauss & Quinn, 1997).

This is evident in the ways many countermovements are organized. For example, in the Tzeltal rebellion in the Chiapas highlands in 1712, the Maya rebels used what they knew of the colonial systems in their vision of the new state; this included names and hierarchies within their military (Dürr, 1998, p. 779; see also Viqueira, 1993).

This view opens the possibility of exploring the connection between social position and knowledge distribution in a variety of domains. The study by Ramaswami Mahalingam (1999) should be seen in this light. His research in South India looks at the development of mental models of reincarnation within the caste system. Confirming his hypothesis, low-caste members showed less conviction of inborn destiny than members of higher castes. These differences, however, are only understandable against the background of a common caste system and a generally shared idea of reincarnation.

Agreement and difference can be explored and explained with the help of more complex theories of processes. Mahalingam looked at the distribution of mental models as a dependent variable of the social position of children; other researchers are more concerned with the transmission and distribution of knowledge and concepts across generations (see Köhler, 1977, 1989; Ross, 2001) and across ethnic groups (Atran et al., 1999). Once we understand these processes and the resulting distribution of socially shared knowledge, we are in a better position to explore the development of knowledge in children (Ross et al., 2003) and the possible consequences for behavior (Atran et al., 1999; Ross 2001, 2002a, 2002b).

All these different lines of inquiry have it in common that none of them regard culture and knowledge as unproblematic units that are endlessly (and perfectly) shared and transmitted among a group of people. Although it is often not made explicit, these studies address the problem of less-than-perfect social transmission of knowledge. As a result, they implicitly regard culture as an emergent system that consists of individual cognitions (and individuals' cognitions) distributed according to the processes involved in their creation. While some of these processes might create agreement among the members of a group, other processes, such as individual inventions, might not. This characterizes one major research focus of cognitive anthropology, namely, how cultural knowledge is organized in the mind (D'Andrade, 1995, p. 248). Viewing knowledge, or at least large parts of it, as inherently social connects this approach inseparably to the cognitive sciences and social theory.

Toward a Cognitive Theory of Culture

All this leads me to propose the first part of a concept of culture that's based in cognitive theory:

> A. *Culture describes all the mental processes that are (or can be) subject to social transmission.*

Note that this definition does not focus on the sharedness of the processes and their results. By mental processes, I mean concepts, theories, individual ideas, and inventions. The reason for this broad approach is to keep open the possibility of including not only change, but also processes of social domination (exclusion from knowledge) in the formation of the shared part of culture. Furthermore, a definition that primarily focuses on the shared part of culture tends to exclude individual ideas and inventions that appear only in certain contexts and are not necessarily agreed upon right away. For example, consider the flower industry in Zinacantán (Ross, 1994). Originally stimulated by the construction of a road, flower production emerged slowly on a small scale within the *milpa,* the traditional cornfields. Gradually, an industry evolved that included regional sales and flower imports from Mexico City (Ross, 1994). Under other circumstances, this development might have taken a different road, or might not have occurred at all (e.g., if there hadn't been a market, workforce, and already well-established trade routes).

In a similar vein, we shouldn't forget that even Galileo did not develop his ideas in a vacuum. This is not to say that his ideas were ready to be picked up, as history can tell us, but at a minimum he needed the telescope, an essential tool for his observations.[7]

Obviously, we cannot ignore cognitive universals or the role of similar stimuli leading to similar concepts (see Atran, 1998; Berlin, 1992; Boster, 1987a). While universals are responsible for some general features of agreement (all humans need food), it is often the level of abstraction applied (not all humans eat the same foods) that makes it difficult to explore and understand their role (see Greenfield & Childs, 1978, for an example). Still, similar external stimuli can lead to both group differences and agreements.

For example, the concept of "corporate culture" is widely accepted, often implying a global culture of management. No doubt, many features of this "corporate culture" are due to the transmission of experience and ideas (e.g., via staff and information exchange). However, it is less clear what impact similar stimuli have, such as the impositions caused by the organization of international trade and production.

This is not to say that it is not important to study similar stimuli; quite the opposite, as we can see in the role of cattle for the Nuer in East Africa (Evans-Pritchard, 1940). In the context of the East African cattle complex (a term coined by Herskovits), the cattle are not merely one more element shared by the Nuer. The fact that the Nuer, in a given region and time, made their livelihood with cattle creates many more elements that they share with one another (as well as with other groups). One can easily think of special- ized knowledge about the ideal mixture of a herd (number of castrated bulls vs. cows; see Evans-Pritchard, 1940, p. 33), which, again, might be shared across groups. Cattle diseases and nutrition are other good candidates.

This is a very important point, and it should warn us not to define culture as if it consisted of items on a shopping list, as was somewhat implied by Brumann (1999, p. 4) in his endeavor to save the concept of culture. Brumann himself subscribes in his reply to the importance of this fact: the interrelations and interdependencies of different features (p. 23). This aspect was recognized early on in anthropology (Kluckhohn, 1949a, 1949b). However, to "see" these inter- relationships we first need to establish the proper unit of investigation so we don't end up with an array of unrelated (e.g., different levels) similarities among ever-changing groups of individuals (based on patterns of unrelated agreement).

Some of these problems I explore in a little more detail by means of an example.

Ecological Knowledge Among Menominee Native Americans and U.S. Majority Culture Fish Experts

In a series of studies, we explored the folk biology that members of two groups living in rural Wisconsin hold with respect to freshwater fish and forest species. In previous studies, culture and differences in expertise were often confounded (see, e.g., López, Atran, Coley, Medin, & Smith, 1997). We, therefore, chose to look only at male experts in both groups. To further streamline our research design, we chose to interview only Menominee (Algonquin-speaking Native Americans) living on the reservation (Medin et al. 2002). The idea was to identify individuals who had closer ties to their community than Menominee living in urban areas. Members of both groups were asked to identify the individuals they regarded as most expert within the relevant domains (hunting and fishing). The expertise of each individual was further controlled with the help of a species identification task.

At first glance, the design looks convincing. However, our ethnographic work quickly produced several questions about which factors we should control for in our study. For example, *should we control for differences in occupation?*

This seemed rather trivial at the beginning, but it quickly became clear that the majority of Menominee males worked or had worked at some time in their lives in the logging business. This was not true of the male members of the neighboring community from which we drew our Majority Culture sample. Given these facts, shouldn't we expect clear differences—if only because of different experience with the forest? If so, would we have to restrict our Menominee sample to nonloggers (or the Majority Culture sample to loggers)? The questions were not about logging, but logging certainly presents people with outdoor experiences that we might expect to have some impact on their ecological knowledge and models (see Kempton, Boster, & Heartley, 1995). This question brings us back to one of the conditions of the cultural consensus model (Romney et al., 1986); namely that only relevant individuals should participate in the study (Romney, 1999, p. 104). It should be clear from the example that the choice of informants (the relevant individuals) is as important as it is difficult. Who are relevant individuals for what kinds of arguments? Why do we choose one over the other? In this case, for example, focusing on loggers prevents the development of a concept of culture that *precisely* allows for these differences within and across groups, and in which factors such as occupation form an integral part of the study design itself. This is important not only for cultural studies, but even more so in a cross-cultural context. Outside the Menominee reservation, logging does not play such an important role. If we were to restrict the study sample one way or the other, we could ignore some of the marked differences between the two groups and would probably not understand its possible impact on cultural cognition.

To give an extreme example, it would be like comparing Itza' Maya and U.S. undergraduate students, restricting the Itza' Maya sample to only individuals who do not know the forest. Unfortunately, these problems are not at all uncommon in cultural studies, as is shown in the already cited study on high school students (Yager & Rotheram-Borus, 2000).

In our case, the decision not to control for occupation led immediately to the next question: To what extent is the difference between the two groups (elicited through experimental studies with sample groups) based on the difference in occupation? *Does the difference we find depend solely on a person's occupation? If so, what does this mean for the study of culture?* Still, within a definition of culture it seems we have to allow for the fact that different elements are not always clearly separable from one another, but are often even causally connected. This cautions us against (a) approaches that are based purely on the comparison of similar features, as marshaled by Brumann (1999, p. 7), and (b) approaches that compare different factors (e.g., profession and culture) in a regression table. While in the first case culture is seen as the sum of a (probably infinite) number of different elements (with all the problems discussed above), in the second case culture is seen as an abstract force that has to be separated from all identifiable factors, at which point it will vanish from our explanations altogether, or be given an almost mystical character—when we run out of "other factors" (see Medin et al., 2002). Our expert study is of particular importance here. So far, our data show that differences in knowledge are not due to differences in expertise. First, we find clear, cultural differences among both Menominee and Majority Culture fish experts and nonexperts in the two groups. This indicates that expertise in folk biology is not based only on "objective observation," but on observation through a cultural lens that guides our learning to attend to specific features. Second, differences found among experts seem to be the result of differences in knowledge organization and saliency rather than knowledge base. For example, the very same questions under time pressure resulted in cultural differences that could be explained by the categorization produced by each of the two groups. These differences, however, disappeared when informants were given more time to contemplate their response (Medin et al., 2002).

Nevertheless, other studies along this line indicate that the increase in certain kinds of knowledge allows experts to use reasoning strategies that are similar across cultures, but different from those of novices (see Bailenson, Shum, Atran, Medin, & Coley, 2002; López et al., 1997; Medin, Lynch, Coley, & Atran, 1997). These data suggest that culture and expertise interact with each other, although some universal phenomena seem to be involved (e.g., the fact that experts' reasoning strategies deviate from strictly category-based models).

This interrelationship between elements does not always allow us to separate causes clearly from effects. According to Keller and Keller (1996), cognitive processes can depend on previous behavior and practice, as in their example of the creative behavior of blacksmiths: A blacksmith develops ideas during the actual work process. These ideas are, in part, derived from the instruments surrounding him in his workshop (pp. 107, 118). The exact nature of the relationship between cognition and behavior is not yet clear. Still, by now a good body of literature exists that establishes a relationship between mental models and behavior (see Atran et al., 1999 and 2002, for three populations of the Petén in Guatemala; see Ross, 2001 and 2002a and b, for two adult generations of the Lacandon Maya). The question remains, however, of whether cognition guides behavior, or whether behavior guides our thinking. In their attempt to combine cognitive aspects with aspects of practice and behavior, Keller and Keller suggest a double connection with both sides influencing each other.

This, then, forces us to reject (as does Brumann, 1999, p. 21) a definition of culture that is restricted to cognition alone, as suggested by D'Andrade (1999, p. 16). D'Andrade's suggestion has two basic problems: (a) as in the older cognitive definitions of culture (see Goodenough, 1964, p. 36), shared ideas tend to become another set of elements and (almost) fixed entities in and of themselves, and (b) cognition should not be seen as independent of human behavior or outside stimuli.

This adds another ingredient to our definition of culture:

> B. *Culture describes all the mental processes that are (or can be) subject to social transmission, as well as other elements of human behavior, including material goods and all kinds of institutions, that help to establish and form our mental processes. These different elements (mental, behavioral, and material) can often be understood only as a set of interrelated features, one causing/forming the other, that are in constant relation with the social, historical, and natural environment.*

It is important not to exclude the material aspects of culture, the different kinds of institutions, and public artifacts. We should conceive of material objects not only as materialized culture (e.g., materialized expressions of individuals; see Johansen, 1992), but also as stimuli on which humans reflect and reinstate—though never completely—part of their culture. In a sense, material objects are projections of often conventionalized understandings of reality, set in time and space (Shore, 1996, p. 44).

This view corresponds with the idea of the *cultured mind*, which is best understood as an interaction between the nervous system and a large set of models, both internal and external, on which the mind feeds (Shore, 1996,

p. 7). It is this set of models, materialized or not and in different degrees of formalization, that provides a good part of a group's cultural background. These models include conceptions of humankind as much as they include a screwdriver or a letter opener, although, obviously, they might differ in a variety of important aspects, including how they translate back into our thinking.

In the study of Menominee and Majority Culture men, the goal was to compare members of two groups with different historical and social backgrounds. This is not shorthand for getting around the "cultural background" of each group. However, the history of each group and the social frameworks of their life-worlds are very different and led us to expect clear differences in their mental models of the environment. This expectation was supported, although it applies only to the groups represented by our subjects—male experts in each group. This is important to keep in mind, because it addresses the third problem identified at the beginning of this chapter: How do we select our unit of study? On what level do we locate "culture?" And how do we define and identify it?

So far, the results of our Wisconsin studies show that the two groups of experts from two different social groups differ significantly from each other with respect to their mental models of the particular domain of environmental models. However, members of the two groups do not differ in their base knowledge about the environment (Medin et al., 2002). Related studies conducted among different groups in Guatemala (Atran et al., 1999, 2002) replicate these findings. However, in this case the study populations differ markedly in their knowledge base.

My research among the Lacandon Maya (Ross, 2001) and studies among tree experts in the United States (Medin et al., 1997) also show intracultural differences with different levels and kinds of expertise. Culture and expertise interact on different levels and shape individuals' cognition, often forming a clear pattern of cultural models. Expertise also has a cultural aspect (e.g., what is an expert, how does a person become an expert), so these findings open new and intriguing questions for our study:

To what extent do experts of two groups agree more with each other than with novices (or nonexperts) of their own group? Of course, the same question has to be asked for the nonexperts, too: *To what extent do nonexperts across groups agree more strongly with one another than with the experts in their own groups?*

If framed in the context of a study of two different social groups, these questions can tell us a lot about the role of expertise in cognition and cultural knowledge.

Do experts in particular domains but from different groups agree more with one another because of their knowledge (observation), or do they acquire specific cultural knowledge that distances them from one another depending on their social group?

We have some indications that experts and nonexperts indeed share some cultural models that are independent of level of expertise. Still, much more work is needed to answer these questions completely. Obviously, the questions become pointless if we define experts (those who agree more with each other than with novices of their group) as a culture. This relates to my argument: If we allow an infinite number of cuts as "cultural," we might just as well abandon the concept of culture altogether because it loses any scientific significance (see also Cerroni-Long, 1999, pp. 15-16, on this point).

To avoid this, we have to elaborate our definition of culture a little further to include a historical, process-oriented view of ideas (across space and time), as suggested by Gingrich (1999, p. 18; see also Greenfield, 1997). To do this, however, we have to delimit the realm of the ideas under study. Although many researchers argue against a notion of culture as requiring physical proximity for its production and maintenance (see Brumann, 1999, p. 23), I still argue against Brumann on this point. While "seeing, hearing or reading of one another may suffice for mutual imitation" (Brumann, 1999, p. 23), the question is whether imitation is the sole or even the main basis of cultural production. And again, rather than assuming these forces, we should study their specific context, comparing them to other factors such as child-rearing, schooling systems, and other processes of information transmission based on immediate contact. Maybe the "common cluster of knowledge items people acquire by being exposed to global mass media, news and education, etc. form the basis of a global culture," as Brumann suggests (1999, p. 23). However, focusing on a global culture blinds us to a deeper understanding of the internal workings and reworkings of these forces on local levels. After all, is it not the recipients' engagement with these products we are supposed to study?

If we assume that these global forces exert equal effect around the world, we are definitely not in the position to study the "cultural hybridizations" Abu-Lughod (1999, p. 15) asked for. These hybridizations, previously known as syncretisms, are at the heart of the processes outlined above, and according to Abu-Lughod, must be studied within the configurations of power, education, and wealth. These configurations often represent peculiar qualities of places (Abu-Lughod, 1997, 1999) and should, therefore, be observed and studied within these limited units.

It is important to keep in mind that the focus on the hybridization or syncretisms is not a study of "pure or traditional" versus "degraded" cultural knowledge, although often framed this way. It is, rather, the study of knowledge transmission under less-than-perfect and ever-changing conditions. It is not only the study of knowledge transmission, but at the same time the study of knowledge and meaning production within specific conditions. If these processes are at the heart of our endeavor, then it is clear that we need an identifiable unit of study as a starting point: a group of people at a specific place.

By now it should be clear that I do not want to reintroduce the "isolated group" studies of the first half of the last century. But unless we know that certain types of subcultures do not include cultural specifics,[8] we shouldn't discard the possibility of explaining some of their features with respect to local conditions (Abu-Lughod's "particular qualities of places"), such as power relations and local patterns of thought and style. Only from this perspective are we able to compare the formation and content of subgroups across different cultures, highlighting their cultural specificity (Cerroni-Long, 1999, p. 16).

How do fish experts from different groups perceive their natural environment? How do women from different localities perceive their respective situations of being a woman? How do the mass media influence and change these perceptions?

These studies should also help us to better understand the commonalities between these subgroups across cultures:

What do certain experts or females have in common that they do not share with novices or men of their own groups? What do they share with novices or men of their own group that they do not share with experts or women of other groups?

I have discussed one piece of research that looks at some of these issues (Coley, et al., 1999). The authors agree that much more work is needed to understand fully the roles of culture and expertise in the shaping of thought and behavior (see also Medin et al., 2002).

For all these reasons, it is not plausible to construct cultures (not culture as an abstract concept) around topics and domains as Brumann (1999, p. 12) suggests. Rather, we should understand the unit of *a culture* around more or less "enduring aggregates of people, recognized as such by their members, within which all functions necessary for the continuation of communal life are performed by in-members" (Cerroni-Long, 1999, p. 16).

This description of the proper unit of *a culture* does not exclude global forces like the mass media, nor does it essentialize a culture as a thing. Neither does it pose the self-sufficiency of a group or something similar. However, it does reject the assumption that the mere existence of global forces (e.g., mass media) is sufficient to promote a global culture. Once we identify the unit of study, we are in a much better position to explore within-group agreement and disagreement (representing, among other things, inconsistencies and change), one of the major concerns voiced in the criticisms of a culture concept.

This puts us into the position of elaborating a little further on our definition of culture:

> C. *Culture describes all the mental processes that are (or can be) subject to social transmission, as well as other elements of human behavior (including material goods) that help to establish and form our mental processes. These different elements (mental, behavioral, and material) can often only be understood as a set of interrelated features, one causing and forming the other, and are in constant relation with the (social, historical, and natural) environment. The abstract concept of* **culture** *has to be distinguished from* **a culture,** *which is a unit of study that is constituted by a relatively enduring aggregate of people, recognized as such by their members, within which all functions necessary for the continuation of communal life are performed by in-members.*

It should be clear that not just any type of (shared) group behavior should be regarded as culture, and that members of a culture can entertain different points of view and models (see also Garro, 2000, for this point). Therefore, this (still preliminary) definition does not depend on consensus and agreement. The members of a group are the carriers of cultural ideas and culture. However, although it is important in our studies to account for disagreement as much as for agreement within a given group, we have to be careful not to tie our concept of culture too close to the concept of community (see Kuper, 1994). While we might study a particular community, we still have to look beyond the borders of both space and time to understand the particular traits and features we are studying. This relates closely to the ideas developed in the previous chapter: Cultural studies should never stop at describing differences (or similarities). Rather, we should try to understand these differences and similarities in a historical, social, and geographical context. As such, this approach addresses yet another criticism anthropology often faces. Our studies are inherently comparative, if only because the reader compares the presented data to his or her own culture. Making this comparison explicit prevents the creation of the "other" taking away the perspective of the Western middle class as being the gold standard.

However, we should not forget that communities and ethnic groups often constitute self-defined social groups of interacting individuals, limiting access and transmission of information within more or less bounded entities, for example, their community or ethnic group. Therefore, it is important to include the *maintenance of communal life* as an important aspect of our definition of culture. (Note that this is different from self-sufficiency, etc.). While this might be a tricky theoretical problem for the researcher, it often seems less of a problem for our informants. An individual can be an ally on different levels (ethnicity, gender, profession, etc.) with a variety of individuals. These categorizations often depend on the given context. Still, there seems to be something special about ethnic groups, race, and culture (the three are often not distinguished in folk-sociological terms) that seems to make it a natural category for most of the groups we are studying (see Hirschfeld, 1995, 1996, with respect to race; and Bloch, Solomon, & Carey, 2001, with respect to kinship). For example, many people (in different cultures) hold the belief that learning the language of the biological parents is somewhat facilitated by genetic means. In this sense, culture, ethnicity, and race might provide something like a "basic level category" (see Rosch, Mervis, Gray, Johnson, & Boyes-Braem, 1976), an intermediate level of categorization that people prefer to appeal to when reasoning about human beings. Evidence so far shows that human beings essentialize categories like race (see Hirschfeld, 1995, 1996) and use a concept of innate species potential (see Atran et al., 2001; Bloch et al., 2001) to reason about biological inheritance.

The essential nature of these categories, together with some basic observations (e.g., language differences), might explain why cultural differences seem to be assumed rather than questioned. It is not unusual for anthropologists to be asked by their informants if they are able to eat the same food they (the informants) eat. These differentiations often lead to group differences based on limiting access to information, for example, that certain knowledge and behaviors are shared only among in-group members. It is in these instances that "culture" actually *does* something to the individuals. Still, it is important to note that it is the model of culture and not an essential entity that guides individuals' behavior.

It is in part through these imposed restrictions that cultures are constituted, created, recreated, and maintained. This is a rather important point because it reminds us once more to study ongoing processes rather than fixed units of cultures. In our quest to understand agreement and disagreement patterns within and across social groups, we often encounter differences in expertise as explaining some of the pattern. However, rather than seeing experts as members of a separate culture, we should treat them as a cultural resource, as members of a social group who focus on certain aspects of life (see Coley, Medin, Proffitt, Lynch, & Atran, 1999). These subgroups emerge due to different interests, attention, and professions. However, they also constitute important assets within a community, as in the case of the curers in the Tarascan community studied by Garro (1986, 2000). In general, members of a group are well aware of who the specialists in certain domains are (see Atran et al., 1999; Ross, 2001, 2002a, 2002b). Treating them as a different culture is like studying the religion of a group, but excluding the religious experts.

If my analysis is right, what is needed for a successful scientific concept of culture is to shift away from the focus on culture as the aggregation of shared elements of content alone. This rather traditional view (see Brumann, 1999, p. 3, for examples) has to be replaced by a concept that connects shared and not-shared content elements with processes of formation and deformation and that allows for variations across and within space and time.

This shift is important in order to avoid using culture as a container for otherwise not explainable differences (see Friedman, 1994, p. 207). The latter is especially dangerous because it removes any explanatory power a concept of "culture" would have. It would then be essentially useless to the social sciences. To say that members of group A do such and such because they are members of group A is (a) rather circular and (b) doesn't help to reveal the relations between culture, thought, and behavior. The feared and often criticized essentialization of culture (Friedman, 1994) seems to be the consequence (Friedman, 1994; Medin et al., 2002). Observing and describing cultural traits should, therefore, not be the end product of an inquiry, but rather a starting point for understanding the processes by which these traits (as well as material objects) emerged, are reproduced, and are changed.

Recognizing the importance of the processes and the resulting differences and similarities involved should not distract us from the general goal of the social sciences: the abstraction of general rules from real-life scenarios and the identification of larger patterns. The ultimate goal is to summarize large amounts of data and to predict certain consequences and results (see Chapters 2 and 5 on these issues; see also Romney, 1999, p. 105). This view, of course, assumes that there are structures and patterns to be found. This seems to be a rather safe assumption, given that even the critics agree with this basic idea (Abu-Lughod, 1999, p. 14). Still, it has to be tested empirically case by case (see Chapters 2, 4, and 5).

The Sharing of Culture and the Exploration of Cultural Differences

It is interesting to note that one of the oldest and most frequently cited definitions of culture, by Sir Edward Tylor, does not pay much attention to shared features as a necessary condition of a concept of culture. Tylor

(1871) equates culture with civilization and defines it as that "complex whole which includes knowledge, belief, art, law, morals, custom, and any other capabilities and habits acquired by a man as a member of society" (p. 1). In this definition, only the last part—the acquired habits—indicates the more-than-random sharing of certain features within a group. This aspect seemed to have gained increasing importance within more recent definitions of culture. Marvin Harris (1975), for example, speaks of the "patterned, repetitive ways of thinking, feeling, and acting that are characteristic of the members of a particular society or segment of a society" (p. 144). For Keesing (1981), culture refers to the "patterns for behavior characteristic of a partic-ular social group" (p. 68; note Keesing's reference to a "social group" as the study unit).

Culture has to be based, at least in part, on shared aspects of whatever it is we are trying to understand. Ultimately, if there are no nonrandom dis-tributions of certain features, there is nothing to explain and understand.

Nevertheless, the (never-perfect) sharing of certain aspects and features as part of a cultural heritage (Romney, 1994, p. 269) almost automatically implies differences among different members of a group.

Then again, the exploration of shared traits often depends on the level of abstraction at which we operate and the number of items we observe (see Wimmer, 1999, p. 20, for a similar point). Identifying culture as a set of shared items (whether mental, behavioral, or material) runs the risk of miss-ing the point because our resulting constructs might reflect only the trials and elements we tested for.[9]

Obviously, this is closely related to a problem concerning research meth-ods and general research design that was discussed in Chapter 2. If we com-pare two cultures on individual features, we find a myriad of ways in which these two cultures differ. However, we always run the risk of not knowing which of the encountered differences are crucial (see Bailenson et al., 2002; Ross et al., 2003).

All this makes an attempt to create a cultural mapping of similarities and differences on our planet pointless if not impossible (see Hannerz, 1999, p. 19).

Public and Private Culture:
The Emergence of Shared Meaning

By now two things should be clear: (a) Culture does imply certain aspects of shared meaning, and (b) this sharing should not be expected to be com-plete or endlessly perpetuated. These points are important to keep in mind;

otherwise our definition of culture could not cover basic processes of change and transformation.

In a sense, culture does not exist outside the individual's head. This needs some elaboration. Naturally, we have in our daily lives many instances of "material culture" as well as social institutions surrounding us, including touch, smell, and taste, as Hannerz (1992, p. 4) rightfully reminds us.

However, these instances should be thought of as expressions of the internal meanings of an individual (or a group of individuals; Johansen, 1992) that make cultural sense only if they evoke meaning in us (Shore, 1996). This they can achieve only if we are equipped with the right instruments for their interpretation (Hannerz, 1992, p. 4). This can best be illustrated if we think of objects, such as fancy cars or rare shells, that serve as prestige objects in one culture but not in another.

Still, even if we have the right instruments for their interpretation, the process of meaning making from outside stimuli is not at all simple. Physical objects or rules might evoke but do not contain meaning (again, think of a car as a prestige object). Therefore, shared interpretations should be treated as something to be explored rather than assumed.

In a way, this is illustrated in the work of Keller and Keller (1996). The researchers show how meaning is created in the process of a blacksmith's work and how ideas not previously conceived emerge during the work process. These kinds of processes, which are often guided by expertise, are, in part, what stimulate changes in meaning formation—the root of cultural change.

However, although meaning formation has emergent properties, people do not pluck new forms out of the air, as Strauss and Quinn (1997, p. 25) remind us. Change and reinterpretation always build on previously learned models and schemas (Strauss & Quinn, 1997). The example of the Tzeltal rebellion might once again be instructive. Although, the Tzeltal Indians in 1712 clearly wanted to change and overcome the imposed colonial system, they still resorted to exactly this system for some of their ideas (see Dürr, 1991).

This is not to say that they weren't ingenious in their efforts. But it is obvious that many of their new efforts were painted in "old colors," such as the organization of the military, including the different ranks of the soldiers (Dürr, 1998, p. 779). This should not come as a surprise if culture includes something of Bourdieu's (1977, p. 72) habitus—shared systems of rather imprecise but durable principles and representations that are not due to obedience or rules.

For Bourdieu (1977), the foundation of this habitus starts at birth and improves through apprenticeship, often without rules but through direct familiarization with the surroundings (p. 88). These habita guide the processes of meaning formation and many aspects have to be taken into account, including intentions, motivations, and emotions (Strauss & Quinn, 1997, p. 47; see also Keller & Keller, 1996).

To say that these habita guide the processes of meaning making does not mean that they are deterministic for these processes. The final stage in the process of meaning creation is necessarily individual, allowing for the creation of new meaning and the challenge of old interpretations. And again, some of these individual (idiosyncratic) inventions become established new norms while others do not get picked up. Many more studies are needed, exploring the conditions under which certain ideas are picked up and others not, in order to understand cultural processes and processes of cultural change.

If we take all the above seriously, a concept of culture based solely on whatever kind and amount of shared experiences as proposed by both Strauss and Quinn (1997, p. 7) and Brumann (1999) seems to be rather weak and offer little reward. First, in applying such a concept we lose the possibility to explore the history and embeddedness of ideas (Greenfield, 1997) and we will fail to understand the emergence, change, and disappearance of Bourdieu's habita over time.

Second, such a view also ignores the differences among the factors involved in creating agreement, such as oral transmission or similar social and physical stimuli. As a consequence, we are led to ignore and misunderstand the basic differences in the various processes involved. This is an important point: If all kinds of sharing experiences lead to culture (Strauss & Quinn, 1997, p. 7), it is a logical consequence that the shared experience of listening to music has the same ontological status as does the sharing experience of growing up in a typical Kabyle household (Bourdieu, 1977, pp. 80-81). Obviously, we'd lose much with such an approach because it would prevent our study of embedded processes—the essence of Abu-Lughod's (1999, p. 15) hybridization of cultures—and in a sense the essence of anthropology.

At this point, it is important to recall the group concept outlined in the attempt at a concept of culture. This is not to argue that sharing experiences by listening to the same music does not have an impact. It might lead to certain patterns of agreement, as Strauss and Quinn (1997, p. 7) argue. However, we have to look at different dimensions of such processes in order to understand an individual's cognition as well as patterns of agreement within and across cultures. What is needed is a meticulous study of the processes involved in individual meaning making within the context of its surroundings, including the historical, social, and physical aspects. This kind of study allows us to assess the larger processes involved in the evolution, maintenance, and change of cultural aspects.

This is not to say that cultures are clearly bounded and demarcated (e.g., Strauss & Quinn, 1997, p. 7). In fact, recent studies on so-called biculturalism seem to indicate different and competing cultural frameworks existing even within individuals (see Hong, Morris, Chui, & Martinez, 2000). Hong et al. showed in their research that Chinese Americans could easily be primed into one of two cultural response patterns—one called "Chinese" and the other "American"—simply by showing them pictures of items, such as the respective national flags. This form of biculturalism might prove to be the most extreme form of unbounded culture. Still, much more research is necessary to explore the stability of these patterns (beyond college students) and their effects on a person's cognition. Research with bilinguals, furthermore, showed that languages are processed in parallel rather than serially. In a series of truly ingenious experiments, researchers at Northwestern University were able to show that individuals fluent in Russian and English would attend to both languages in parallel when asked to perform certain tasks. This was done with the help of eye-tracking devices that showed that individuals, when given certain sound inputs, would attend to both languages to search for the relevant items (personal communication, Viorica, April 2003). Obviously, this opens the question of bicultural individuals attending similarly to respective tasks.

This is an exciting field of research that looks not only at the content of cultural differences, but also at their characteristics. In the research with Menominee and Majority Culture fish experts (Medin et al., 2003), we find clear cultural differences that vanish when informants are given more time for their responses. Here it seems that certain ways to organize knowledge privilege certain saliency effects over others while not affecting (or being affected by) an individual's knowledge base. Again, research is needed that explores the stability of these effects (replication) and their further consequences for human cognition and behavior.

A final word on this matter. Most anthropologists would probably agree that culture is socially inherited through the shared experience of a social world that preexists the individual (Strauss & Quinn, 1997, p. 16). However, we should not forget that the social world itself is the product of human agents. The decision of who is allowed to share certain experiences (e.g., who is an in-group member) is not always with the individual, and access to relevant information is often limited from the inside out. This relates our study of culture back to the folk concepts of culture, race, and ethnicity (see Gil-White, 2001). But then, as long as we focus on the processes involved in the creation of shared patterns, we might not have to be too concerned.

In this chapter, I outlined a cognitive concept of culture. Obviously, many aspects of culture are not located exclusively in the heads of individuals. Still, the processes of incorporating aspects like outside stimuli have to be understood on an individual level. Many of these features are shared among groups of individuals and might, therefore, lead to shared aspects with respect to the individuals' interpretation—the construction of meaning. However, we shouldn't be surprised if we find considerable cross-cultural agreement in many domains; for example, members of different social groups might differ on certain aspects but not on others.

Culture has to be understood as the distribution of knowledge, ideas, and values, and its study should focus on the exploration of the distributive patterns and the processes involved in its creation.

The study of the processes and patterns of distribution requires strict methodologies of both data gathering and data analysis. In the next two chapters I will turn to this point, probably the weakest area in present-day anthropology.

As the field of culture and cognition is rather new, the development of methodologies is in flux. Therefore, the following chapters are not intended to represent a complete method guide, but rather an outline and a point of departure for further exploration and developments. Many of these methods have been applied successfully in other fields. To be successful, however, they have to be used with sensitivity in the field. Also, as should be clear from the previous discussion, they have to be embedded in a sound theory of culture. When brought together with ethnographic and historical knowledge, they will provide us with good insights into the relationship of culture, cognition, and behavior.

To sum up: If this discussion is correct and culture is indeed a "natural category" for human beings, then we have to base our scientific approximation of culture on these understandings. They lead to specific processes of information sharing and the creation of meaning that should be at the heart of our investigation.

Obviously, once we focus on these specific processes and their effects we are on a much more specific level than "culture," allowing us to arrive at an improved understanding of both cultural processes and cultural differences.

In this kind of approach, then, "culture" serves as an initial shorthand for moving toward the real study subject: the distribution of patterns of agreement and disagreement among groups of individuals.

I will now turn to specific methods of data gathering and analyses to approach such a study topic.

Notes

1. Throughout this book, I use anthropology in the sense of "cultural anthropology," although one can probably find similar problems within the fields of linguistics and archaeology.

2. By "folk-anthropological beliefs," I refer to understandings people outside the scientific community hold about human beings. Although I draw a distinction between scientific and folk understandings, I am aware that both inform one another (see Atran, 1990, for one example).

3. These criticisms come from different theoretical backgrounds. However, they point at similar problems and issues, and it seems justified to summarize them for the present purpose.

4. We ought not to forget that Redfield was at the time a leading figure in the field.

5. Other than paying attention to differences and similarities on an ever-changing basis.

6. See the idea of "Emergenz von unten - emergence from the bottom" with respect to social structure as used by Schweizer (1996a:106). With respect to a dialectical emergent view of culture, see Ross (1994, 1997) with respect to the concept of emergence in discourse analysis.

7. We also should not forget that not all individual ideas and innovations get picked up, and that probably most of them vanish before they become noted (Barnett, 1958).

8. This relates to the following chapter on methodologies. In a sense, similarities are often less conclusive than differences, as the former do not exclude the possibilities that our tools simply aren't good enough to capture existing differences.

9. Carpenters in different areas probably share more material goods (tools) with each other than they do with noncarpenters of their own group. See also Keller & Keller (1996) on basic knowledge of blacksmiths.

4

Research Methods

Data Gathering

As discussed in the preceding chapter on the history and development of cognitive anthropology (see D'Andrade, 1995), methodology has always played a crucial role in this field of anthropological inquiry. In at least one wing of the field, the emphasis placed on methodologies (especially the analysis of data) became almost more important than the empirical findings and their implications. Much time was dedicated to the development of elaborated techniques that were then applied to U.S. samples only, and often only to undergraduate students. Rarely do we find studies outside the United States, and even fewer are those that ask important theoretical and empirical questions (see Berlin & Kay, 1969, and Berlin, Breedlove, & Raven, 1973, for an exception).

This development had two effects. First, the strong focus on methodological questions and the relative lack of empirical findings gave this wing of anthropology little appeal in the general field. Furthermore, lacking appeal to a wider audience, the respective methodologies never really made their way into anthropology. Second, the strong focus on methodological questions elaborated on the basis of undergraduate students led to the fact that most of these methods were never assessed within different cultural settings, and their universal applicability was often only assumed rather than tested (see Antweiler, 1993, p. 165, to this point). As a result, formal methods were frequently avoided in anthropology, not so much because they were not suited for certain tasks, but because anthropologists were not comfortable with them. (I recall a conference comment made to Thomas Schweizer, an outspoken defender of formal methods in anthropology, that "these methods were the reasons why we [anthropologists] left the other social sciences.") Unfortunately, this split often led to the exclusion of formal methods in student training. (At times, anthropology students are asked to take a statistical course without an explanation of why this could be helpful.)

Early on, the spread of formal methods was further hampered by the lack of powerful devices for data analysis, which are provided today by accessible and fast personal computers. Lacking this resource, these early approaches could target only limited areas, semantic fields and their structures as discussed in Chapter 1. Obviously, such a limited approach affected the theoretical foundations of such core concepts as culture. Culture almost automatically was constructed as a system of (completely) shared knowledge and meaning. Semantic systems were constructed as if they were representative for each individual member of the society (e.g., Paarup-Laursen, 1989), and existing knowledge in a community was often represented by adding and aggregating knowledge bits collected from different individuals into a systematic description of a knowledge system (e.g., Berlin, Breedlove, & Raven, 1974).

Although these constructs might explain a good deal of the content of an abstract system (the cultural system), they do not tell us anything about how these systems are represented in the actual cognitions of individuals and who the carriers of these cognitions are. This is what should be at the heart of our endeavor. Questions like "*whose knowledge*" or "*whose meaning*" were the logical consequences (see Chapters 2 and 3 for further elaboration on this topic). This lack of specificity prevented us from gaining an understanding of the underlying processes of knowledge formation and deformation and led almost by definition to rather static descriptions of cultural knowledge, fixed in time. Culture appeared as a blueprint, or a magic box, shared by the individual members of the culture.

A good example of the failure to conceptualize these problems is in the work of Paarup-Laursen (1989). In his work on the meaning of illness among the Koma of Nigeria, the author never describes his methodologies and results in a detailed manner. As a consequence, it remains unclear whether the presented models are "general models" shared by all individuals of the community studied or if they were provided by only a subgroup of individuals who more or less agree with one another. In this particular case, it would have been informative to know who his informants were and who of them agreed with each other and on what topics. Such an approach would have helped avoid yet another problem. In the author's account, we are left on our own to decide whether the described structures are the cognitive order of illness according to the Koma of Nigeria or are the researcher's intuition based on informal interviews (Paarup-Laursen, 1989). In a sense, the reader is left to judge the credibility of the data on pure faith (see Greenfield, 2000, and Chapter 3 in this volume for an elaboration of the consequences of this kind of research strategy) or through the use of examples from other areas, which might or might not be applicable.

In the late 1980s, a new paradigm entered the field: the exploration of informant agreement and disagreement (see the special issue of *American Behavioral Scientist*, 1987). With this shift in perspective, the "sharing of culture" moved well into the center of empirical research of a group of anthropologists (Romney, Weller, & Batchelder, 1986). Ever since, semantic systems are no longer seen as absolutely shared; it is the sharing itself of knowledge, models, and values that became the focus of empirical research (rather than being simply assumed). With respect to the acquisition of knowledge and its distribution, Boster (1986a) and Garro (1986) produced some interesting starting points for research. Garro compared experts and nonexperts with respect to intracultural differences of models about disease in a Mexican village (Garro, 1986). Rather than targeting the content of these models, the main focus of Garro's research was the distribution of knowledge among the members of the community. She found that, essentially, curers and noncurers shared one common model, but that the curers shared more of it, hence, were more expert in the topic. James Boster went in a somewhat different direction, exploring differential agreement patterns among the Aguaruna of Peru with respect to the naming of manioc species. In this study, he was able to show that agreement between two individuals was a factor of their kin relationship. In other words, he could demonstrate that kinship relations provided one of the networks for the distribution of certain manioc names (Boster, 1986a).

Obviously, this kind of research renders certain field methods (e.g., rapid appraisal techniques and informal interviews) no longer suitable. Previously, groups of individuals could be interviewed together (depending on the topic). The new goal of comparing individual cognitions, however, creates the absolute necessity that each person be interviewed separately, making research both more costly and more time-consuming.

One of the criticisms brought against this kind of work is based on the lack of content analysis and description, as well as a certain lack of relevance. Focusing on theoretical models of knowledge distribution, based on quantitative methods, the relevant research often ignored to a certain extent the content of cultural knowledge. However, this shifted the focus away from what used to be the heart of anthropology: an engagement with content differences based on qualitative methods. This shift in focus away from content increased the split between the two approaches. The two approaches quickly became associated with their underlying methods; quantitative and qualitative research. Yet as important as this shift toward informant-agreement was, it does not mean that we should no longer examine the content of cultural knowledge. On the contrary, an in-depth content analysis of the models should still be at the heart of anthropological research. However, we might be forced to describe differing bodies of knowledge (as held by different individuals). In the end, the combination of both aspects will help us make better sense of our general findings and descriptions. Furthermore, as seen in the preceding two chapters, differences and similarities between groups of individuals are of great importance to theory building in anthropology. To reach this goal, we need sound methods for both data collection and analysis, which are the focus of this and the subsequent chapters.

There is a multitude of methods available for both data gathering and analysis, with a stronger focus on analysis than on data gathering (Antweiler, 1993, p. 259; Kokot, Lang, & Hinz, 1982, p. 343). In this chapter, I look at data-gathering methods and weave them into the larger context of anthropological fieldwork and its main paradigm, participant observation. The application of these particular methods cannot be separated from data analysis, which is the topic of the next chapter.

Presenting successful research methods should not blind us to local peculiarities and the need to carefully design and check the applied methods from case to case. To say that a certain method is universally applicable (Weller & Romney, 1988, p. 9) does not mean that it can be endlessly copied and mechanistically applied in all different contexts and to all possible questions.

Many methods in the field are amazing both in the creativity and sensibility (or lack thereof) shown by the researchers who designed them, and in the data they produce. However, many are so specific in their applicability that I will not include them here. The methods I present are chosen based on their general usefulness for developing further methods. I present only methods that were successfully applied in the field.

My aim is twofold. I intend to explain specific methods in detail. These methods are important in themselves, but furthermore serve the goal of setting up a general framework within which individual researchers can adapt and create their own methodologies, to fit specific research questions.

It is very important to keep in mind that the proposed methodologies do not represent a complete set of methods, nor should they be seen as blueprints for research. On the contrary: Mechanistic application of formal methods can lead to frustrating results, as in Röttger-Rössler (1989, pp. 77-81). In her work, informants refused to sort real individuals according to prestige. This shouldn't be too surprising, but might have been avoided or remedied post hoc by the use of a less direct research design.

Unfortunately, the typical reaction in anthropology, given such frustrations, is to abandon formal methods altogether. Consequently, the importance of formal methods for a better understanding of human cognition is usually underestimated. This lack of experience and interest has led to many misguided conceptions. For example, Antweiler (1993, p. 263) seems to confuse the simplicity of a task (which is, in fact, its strength!) with the complexity of the data produced and the possible knowledge derived. The latter depends mostly on the creativity with which we deploy and adapt these methods, not so much on the methods themselves. For example, free-listing tasks are often thought to be of limited use. In these tasks, people are asked to generate a list of items. Most researchers employ these techniques only to get at the elements of a domain to be studied. If applied correctly, however, they might tell us quite a bit about the organization of knowledge and related saliency effects across a group of informants (see Ross & Medin, 2003).

The Experimental Design

Before I start describing research methods, I want to draw attention to two important general considerations in all formal research dealing with human subjects: (a) the selection of our informants and (b) how we present our stimuli (questions, pictures, etc.) to them.

Selection of Informants and Sample Size

In the social sciences, a common assumption exists that large sample groups are always better, more reliable, than small ones. While this is correct in principle, it needs some qualification. The sample size depends on (a) the task at hand, (b) the population studied (existing levels of agreement and disagreement), (c) the format of the research, and (d) the level of confidence we want to achieve. One has to keep in mind that not all tasks are equally likely to detect differences or similarities, for this depends partly on the number of data points elicited in a study. The fewer the data points per individual and the lower the agreement, the more subjects we need to include in the study.

This has an important consequence. Cross-cultural differences elicited with a small set of individuals might be much more convincing because differences have to be much more salient to emerge within a small sample of informants. Any significant difference found with a small set of informants is bound to be (even more) significant, if we enlarge the sample size.

(Note that this is obviously true only if we keep the definition of the relevant participants constant.)

A second common assumption in the social sciences is that we need a random sample[1] to achieve trustworthy results. Again, this is correct in principle, and, again, there are qualifications. First, random sampling does not mean that we always take a random sample across the whole population. As Bernard (1995) rightfully advises us, it is normally much more important to get a good (representative) sample than to get a large sample (p. 80). *Representative* means that all individuals and subgroups needed in the study have the same chance of being included. Within small populations this is normally not difficult to achieve, although it definitely needs some forethought. Second, the issue of sampling becomes a little bit more difficult in cross-cultural studies (see Chapter 2). Here, we have to identify not only cross-cultural matches, but good samples within each group as well. As mentioned in Chapter 3, the selection of a sample is not at all theory-free—unless we can take a really large random sample, which is usually impossible with respect to both gathering data that are meaningful to anthropologists and analyzing the data later. For example, in a cross-cultural study in Guatemala, we consciously chose older Itza' Maya who spoke Itza' in order to compare them with members of immigrant groups that were matched in age. This biased our Itza' sample, which was not at all representative of the whole community. Still, this particular sample has two advantages: First, it provides us with the opportunity to study within-culture differences by allowing us to compare the data with similar data from younger Itza'. Second, with processes like loss of knowledge or "westernization," we are probably much more likely to find cross-cultural differences by looking at the older, presumably more traditional, section of the community (see Medin, Ross, Atran, Burnett, & Blok, 2002, for a discussion). An approach like this is justified because the task was not only to show differences, but also to tie them to activities and values. Obviously, in this case the data from older Itza' do not generalize to the whole community, and consequently we couldn't extend our findings to the community level (see Ross, 2001, for an example of intergenerational differences among Lacandon Maya).

To say that older Itza' Maya represent a more traditional view of Itza' culture might sound a little misleading. This is not meant to say that they represent the "real (isolated) Maya model" or that the older Itza' Maya model is more important than the ones held by their sons and daughters. It is merely to acknowledge the fact that cultural models change over time and that the possibilities of cross-cultural learning and common school systems might lead to less-pronounced cultural differences in certain areas and domains. Obviously, these decisions are necessary (a) in order to avoid masking within-group differences and (b) to establish who the relevant subjects are. However, they have to be justified on theoretical grounds and should not cause us to ignore the limits they present for the interpretation of data.

Finally, the question arises of how many informants are needed. This decision has become much easier with Romney et al.'s (1986) cultural consensus model. The cultural consensus model allows post hoc testing of whether a given number of informants is sufficient to claim that a consensus exists. The basic idea behind the model is that culturally more salient types of knowledge (cultural models) receive a wider distribution among a given population. Therefore, informants should agree more strongly with each other, which means that we need fewer informants to find a consensus. An example should illustrate this.

A researcher would probably need only a small sample of informants to understand the principles of the American Majority Culture system of kinship naming because informants probably share a great deal of the relevant knowledge. This might not be true for other domains (e.g., the workings of the economy or health issues), however, for which a larger sample size might be needed to find agreement among the informants (see Chapter 5 for a more detailed description). Less agreement means that the given problems (and their respective responses) are not as salient in a culture as others. For example, how to count from 1 to 10 is probably more widely distributed within a given adult population than knowing whether a particular car falls into the category of sports car. As should be clear from the previous discussions, we should not always expect consensus among our informants. Still, in order to make cross-group comparisons, consensus is necessary to make any claims about the "modal response" of the members of a group.

In this sense, the study of informant agreement provides important information about the domain and the respective elements we are interested in.

The outcome of a study depends partly on selecting the right informants. This can be a tricky issue in cross-cultural studies, as described in Chapters 2 and 3. It is not always obvious which groups are relevant for comparison, and, hence, from which part of the population to draw the sample. A good example of this problem is the study by Cancian (1972), who explored the relation between the social status of different groups of farmers within a culture and their willingness to introduce innovations. In this study, Cancian included in his sample only farmers who produced the same crop—corn farmers in Zinacantán, Chiapas—ignoring another group of men who had earlier given up corn farming to dedicate themselves to the production of flowers (see Ross, 1994, for a discussion of the development of the flower industry). By doing this, Cancian (without considering the implications for his study) might have excluded the most innovative group from his analysis—not a good choice, it seems, given the topic of his study.

In general, it is obvious that the more heterogeneous a population is with respect to a given belief system, the larger the sample must be to detect patterns of similarities or differences, as well as any overall agreement. Therefore, it is important to establish the relevant group of informants (Romney, 1999, pp. 104-105), or if unknown, to give every known subgroup of a population an equal chance to be represented within the sample. The latter obviously applies only if we want our conclusions to be valid for the population as a whole. In that case, we have to be careful how we select our samples to avoid a bias toward important dimensions of the study.

The difficulty of getting a large nonbiased sample can be illustrated with another example. In a study with Mexican migrants in Chicago, a basic survey was used to understand the composition of the target population, about which next to nothing was known at the time of the study (Ross & Sanchez, n.d.). Several samples of 100 individuals were taken at the regional Mexican consulate. This was done over a period of several months, and complemented by further samples in different communities and households. To our surprise, the different samples produced significantly different results. A sample taken at the consulate right before summer vacation showed a much higher average income than comparative samples at the same location later that year. The reason for this peculiar bias was rather simple, post hoc: Before the summer a high percentage of individuals visited the consulate to arrange their papers in order to travel home for summer vacations. On the whole, these people are much more affluent than the average Mexican in Chicago, who does not have the income (or papers) to make such trips.

Obviously, we do not always know which subgroups might make a difference for our study. The basic idea of the cultural consensus model (see Chapter 5 for more details) might help us resolve this issue. By turning the instrument into an exploratory tool, we can ask if a given set of informants shares a model about a certain domain and what personal attributes explain the patterns of agreement or disagreement detected. Once we identify the different groups (e.g., affluent vs. poor Mexicans in Chicago) we can explore the impact these dimensions have on the proposed study.

This method of detecting agreement pattern was applied in the study on intergenerational change among the Lacandon Maya of Chiapas (Ross, 2001, 2002a, 2002b). Starting with a random sample of individuals, the data (elicited in individual interviews) were compared across individuals to

(a) explore the extent to which all Lacandon informants agree with each other and (b) to investigate the emerging patterns of agreement, for example, which informants tended to agree with one another. The patterns of agreement showed clear differences between the members of the two adult generations, indicating an ongoing cultural change, a finding that could be confirmed with a series of different but related tasks. (Note: Although I expected to find these differences, the community was small enough to include all adult members of the community instead of taking a sample.)

Several other problems and solutions could be discussed with respect to sampling methods. However, as I am more concerned with specific methods of cognitive research, I refer the interested reader to Bernard's (1995, p. 71ff) excellent chapter on sampling methods for more information.

Presentation of Stimuli

Another issue of general importance is the presentation of stimuli. Most experimental studies present the informants with a set of stimuli to which they are expected to respond. These stimuli can include pictures, name cards, or entire questions. In this context, the anthropologist's questions must be seen as the stimuli provided to the informant to generate certain answers. Critical anthropology has often reflected on this fact by looking into power relations between anthropologists and their informants. While these are important issues, in this chapter I am more concerned with more formal stimuli, as used in cognitive research experiments. Whatever these stimuli are, one must always control for the fact that the order in which the stimuli are presented to the individuals can influence the responses. At least two possibilities have to be taken into account: First, the informants might get tired or bored—or more excited—toward the end of a task and, second, the order of stimuli might influence answers. Suppose you have a sample of 100 short questions in a task that takes about 40 minutes. At the beginning, the informant might be more attentive (maybe even too eager to be able to give good responses) than at the end of the task when boredom can set in. As a result, the informants might give much more thought and detail in their responses at the beginning of the task than at the end. A different bias might occur in the second case. Here the internal order of the stimuli might prime respondents to answer in specific ways to a given question. For example, after talking about bad air, air pollution, and the shortage of oil, to then ask an informant about the impact of automobiles on the environment might not be sensitive. Unfortunately, the biases introduced in our studies are not always as obvious as in these examples, and unless we specifically control for them we cannot rely on our results. Does the resulting pattern represent a meaningful result, which has to be explained, or is it just an artifact of the order in which the items were presented? To avoid these problems, we can either counterbalance the order of stimuli presentation or present the stimuli in a random order.

Ideally, we counterbalance by applying all possible combinations and orders. This allows us to explore the differences created by the order of presentation. As illustrated, the order of the questions is important not only in terms of what comes first, but also in terms of what goes together, even within a single session. Therefore, simply reversing the order of the questions for half of our informants might not be sufficient. In most situations, complete counterbalancing (all possible options) requires a high number of informants, something not usually available to anthropologists. In this case, we have to randomize the order to make sure that no pattern of presentation influences the results. Yet in this case, we also lose information on whether the order in which the stimuli were presented had any influence on the responses. Knowing this might seem trivial at first glance, but it can provide us with important information about the context dependency/stability of certain topics under investigation.

Scientific Methods and the
Role of Participant Observation

"The best (anthropological) training you can possibly have is a thorough drilling in the experimental methods of the psychological laboratory (Rivers to Bartlett)" (Bartlett, 1937, p. 416).

After reading Chapter 3, it should be clear that some of the problems anthropology has gone through, and to some extent is still going through, are based on decisions of how to design a research project: What constitutes scientific data, a hypothesis, a theory, and the like. These are among the reasons why cognitive anthropologists observe and borrow from other fields, like linguistics (see, e.g., Goodenough's (1956) development of the componential analysis) and psychology.

They often adapted and modified methods developed in other academic fields, such as George Spindler's (1955) application of the Rorschach test among the Menominee in central Wisconsin.

This is understandable, because research methods received (and still receive) relatively little attention in anthropological teaching. A clear understanding and agreement on these issues is required, however, if we want to advance anthropological knowledge by building on previous findings in the field. This is not at all to argue for giving up what might be anthropology's most important paradigm: participant observation based on long-term fieldwork. On the contrary, as I explained in Chapter 2, any sound experimental approach in cultural research has to be built around an in-depth knowledge of the research subject and formed with clear, theoretical expectations that can be tested. This is very important, as our research methods are not detached from theory: They never produce context-free data.

Yet, participant observation should not be regarded as a method in itself (though it often is in anthropological research proposals). Nevertheless, participant observation is more important than merely closing in on the people we want to study or seeing it as a starting point for conducting research, as suggested by Bernard (1995, p. 137). Participant observation constitutes an essential part in the process of developing the right methods to address a given question within a given situation. At least five issues are important:

One has to adjust the methods to the field situation. This is not always easy because language problems and particular field settings (such as one-room houses, lack of electricity, or informants' legal problems, e.g., if they are migrants) might prevent the application of otherwise suitable methods (Antweiler, 1993). There are many more reasons, as any anthropologist probably knows, and the number of anecdotes about failed field methods is probably just as high as the number of methods that actually turned out to be successful.

The second problem concerns both the design of reasonable questions and the establishment of the right research context. Artificial research settings might lead to wrong, or at least artificial, responses from informants. This fact is nicely illustrated in an anecdote reported by Diamond and Bishop (1999, p. 17). While collecting data about birds among the Foré in New Guinea, the lead author asked his longtime informants questions about mushrooms. These men, who were very knowledgeable about other aspects of the forest, denied even knowing different names for different species of mushrooms. On a later trip, the same informants showed a deep knowledge of mushrooms, including names of different species. When asked why they had refused to disclose this information before, the simple response was that they considered it a waste of time, as his ignorance with respect to mushrooms was rather obvious. It is rather interesting (for our purpose) to note that in an earlier publication the same author (J. Diamond) interprets a very similar situation as a meaningful data point. Here, he describes the fact that his Foré informants did not know any names for butterflies (Diamond, 1993, p. 261), arguing that this is due to the lack of utility value butterflies have in this society.

This point is also closely related to the ability to speak the local language. In 1962, R. Narrol observed that anthropologists who spoke the native language reported significantly more cases of witchcraft than those who did not (pp. 89-90). Narrol related this finding to the better rapport and, hence, the better understanding of local settings. In fact, any researcher who is able to speak the native language will readily agree that gossip on the street and indirect information are some of the richest sources in participant observation. In fact, gossip often provides us with the little edge that signals informants that the anthropologist is at least partially knowledgeable in the topic.

Participant observation might help to reduce the risk of reactivity: People often give rather peculiar responses if they feel observed or checked on. Long-term field research can help detect these inconsistencies, as formal results can be checked against day-to-day observations and informal talk or listening to other people talk. This can prove particularly important with politically sensitive topics like environmental behavior and indigenous groups, or topics like witchcraft.

For novel research, another important factor is to gain enough preliminary understanding of the study domain to be able to (a) formulate theories and hypotheses, which eventually can be tested; and (b) design meaningful and sensitive methods for the research question.

The preliminary understanding often provided by participant observation helps us with the interpretation of our findings, for it gives us an intuitive understanding of the domain in question. This was the case with work among the Lacandones (Ross, 2001, 2002a, 2002b). In this research, clear differences emerged in environmental cognition, decision making, and behavior among the members of the two adult generations of the community. In this particular case, it was important to understand both the history of the community and an individual's daily preoccupations and occupations with the environment. Taking into account a whole array of changes that had happened in the community, it became clear that the found discrepancies were not a simple difference in expertise that would eventually be overcome by the younger Lacandones adding to their knowledge. Rather, these differences seemed an expression of an ongoing cultural change from one generation to the next.

The whole research design, however, was based on earlier and intuitive understandings of these intergenerational differences, identified during informal research such as talking with informants, going out on forest walks, and working in the *milpa*—the agricultural field of the Lacandones. It is important that we don't treat this kind of intuitive knowledge (often the sole basis for anthropological accounts) as scientific results. On the contrary, we must always be open to the possibility that our intuitions might be wrong—which might be the case more often than we realize. In research conducted in Guatemala (Atran et al., 1999), we hypothesized that the migrant Maya group would be more likely to resemble the native Maya group than the migrant Mestizo group. This hypothesis was the result of informal interviews with several individuals of the three communities. However, our study proved our intuitions wrong. This changed many assumptions, theories, and subsequent research directions of our project.

Again, all these points are concerned with the so-called crisis in anthropology, because data not based on clear and transparent methods cannot be tested, replicated, or rejected. Yet being able to do so is one of the basic axioms of scientific research. Lacking the necessary validity, the results are subject to doubt and contradiction (both within and outside the discipline; see Greenfield, 2000, for a discussion of this issue and the "postmodern crisis in anthropology").

Research Design and Field Methods

In the above section, I mentioned that participant observation should not be considered a method in itself, but rather a necessary part of a larger research project that enables us to design and apply meaningful and sensitive methods to investigate problems. This is for at least three reasons: (a) In order to produce testable knowledge, we must establish a frame that allows other researchers (and ourselves) to check, replicate, and reject our findings. Although this is frequently a major problem in anthropological research, it can be even more pronounced because (b) we often might not be able to see our own biases and false intuitions unless we check them against a set of data. (c) Moreover, many research questions simply cannot be answered without a clear method, as in the case of informant agreement and the sharing of cultural features.

The basic paradigm used to test hypotheses and theories is an experiment. There are different kinds of experiments, or quasi-experiments, that can be of scientific use. Bernard (1995, p. 52) distinguishes four different kinds of experiments based on the degree of control researchers have over the design. While I wouldn't call all of the examples given by Bernard "experiments," I consider all of these approaches useful within anthropological research and cognitive research. Instead of following Bernard's classification, however, I prefer to distinguish among (a) laboratory experiments, (b) field experiments, and (c) observational studies. The latter can often be very similar in structure to an experiment and allow us to make similar inferences, yet we lack the necessary control over the design.

Laboratory experiments are very rarely used in anthropology, but can nevertheless provide us with important insights into real-life situations (Hirschfeld, 1996; Ostrom, 1998). It is their strength, however, that is also the problem: They are conducted under almost complete control in an artificial setting that never approaches real-life situations. Participants are normally well aware of the artificial situation of the experiment and the departure from real-life situations. This is a very important point for cognitive anthropology and the cognitive sciences in general (see above for the problem of reactivity).

Field experiments take place in the field context and normally engage people who are not used to this kind of work (contrary to undergraduates, who are used in most psychological studies). This can create significant problems, as was indicated in the case of the Foré of New Guinea who did not report their expertise in mushrooms. Clearly, both the context of the research and the participants' reactions are less predictable and, hence, create a setting that lacks some of the control the researcher has in laboratory experiments. These disadvantages are at the same time a big advantage. In laboratory experiments, we usually do not have access to people who are experts in a given domain or who have even the minimum of interest in the domain or the study; instead, the researcher depends on volunteers who might or might not be suitable informants. Also, the lack of meaningful context in a controlled/laboratory experiment encourages informants not to provide information, or to provide irrelevant and often even meaningless information. Again, the extreme cases are probably the thousands of psychology students who are required each year to participate in psychological studies (Medin & Atran, 1999). Most of the students are not at all interested in the research and, hence, some serious doubts arise concerning the effort they put into their responses. Accounts of students' boycotting the researcher's efforts with fake responses are numerous. Further problems are (a) the general lack of familiarity with certain domains and (b) the lack of information we have about our informants. The former imposes serious restrictions on the kinds of stimuli we can use, while the latter often hinders clear interpretation of group differences found among the informants.

In comparison, a practical problem for most of the field experiments is the selection of informants. Random assignments are often difficult, if not impossible, as is often the testing of a great number of individuals.

Another methodology is the use of *systematic observations* that might include interviews (as well as other sources). What distinguishes the latter data from the experimental setting is that we (a) have less control over the situation and (b) normally have no possibility to manipulate the settings. Hence, the logic is not that of building and testing a hypothesis with a set of experiments, but rather one of making inferences based on formal observations. We might frequently find situations where we can control, to some extent, several factors that might lead to a given situation. For example, in the study among the Lacandon-Maya of Chiapas, household locations of the members of the two living adult generations of the community were observed. In this case, older Lacandones tend to live in the surroundings, while the second-generation adults form the center of the community. Interviews and further observations allowed me to exclude factors like income, political connections, or availability of space as causal connections in the emerging pattern of household locations. One of the inferences drawn from this finding was that different values and preferences (closeness to forest and the agricultural field vs. being close to one's peers) led to the pattern. For the younger Lacandones, these changes represent a clear rupture with the more traditional models of "good livelihood" (Ross, 2001). This inference could be tested and confirmed with the use of experimental methods.

In a sense, observational data are often more convincing than many experimental data for they describe real behavior and its consequences rather than responses to hypothetical questions. Even so, the hypothetical questions allow us to test whether our ideas about existing models are correct or not.

Not all ideas, values, and models are expressed as clearly or are as easily observable as the data on preferred household location. Furthermore, the Ross (2001) study allows only a correlation analysis, which is not sensitive to small differences in the data or to causal connections. Nevertheless, observational data are often all we have and, as in this case, they usually provide a very good basis for experiments or further observations. It is here that participant observation has one of its most important roles: (a) finding the right units to study, and (b) making the necessary observations and successive inferences that allow us (c) to formulate hypotheses and theories, which we then can test in more formal experiments. This might sound somewhat circular and lacking the control we are supposed to have in scientific work. However, confirmation from different sources of data, as well as independent data from experiments, help us establish (or reject) our hypotheses (if the methods and data are indeed independent).[2]

All these points lead to a final observation. In cognitive research and the topic of culture and cognition in general, comparative studies play an important role (Coley, 2000; Ross, Medin, Coley, & Atran, 2003). However, one of the difficulties that has to be dealt with is designing studies that provide meaningful results.

Suppose, for example, a study that compares two cultural groups on one task. Two problems arise:

First, if the members of the two groups do not differ on this given task, how do we know whether the results are an outcome of real similarities (e.g., possible candidates for universals) or whether our methods were simply not powerful enough to detect existing differences? (Note: Not all methods are equally likely to detect differences!)

Second, if we indeed find differences, how do we assess the meaning and significance of these differences? As discussed in Chapter 2, there is probably an infinite number of ways to separate the members of any two social groups. Yet whether all possible distinctions are equally important for our research, especially if we take into account that there are probably also an infinite number of similarities that could be found between the same groups,[3] remains to be answered (see Medin et al., 2002 for further discussion).

Again, participant observation seems to offer some remedy for this dilemma, as it helps us a priori to formulate testable hypotheses.

Experimental Methods in the Field: Data Collection

After elaborating on general issues of research design as well as the role of participant observation, I turn now to actual research methods, focusing on experimental design and the process of data collection. The emphasis will be on research methods that have proven successful in cultural studies of cognition as well as cognitive studies of culture.

One of the critical points of successful cognitive research is the ability to speak with our informants in the language with which they are most familiar. This is made clear if we look at language as one of the forces (primers) for the creation and maintenance of cultural knowledge. Although the extreme form of this line of thinking, expressed in the linguistic relativity theory, (see Gumperz & Levinson, 1996) has found many critics, the general importance of language as a means of maintaining and transmitting cultural knowledge is basically unchallenged.

Consider an experiment that targets typicality ratings for animals and birds (see Rosch, 1975). To ask lowland Maya people for the *true* and best representative of a class of animals is likely to trigger certain species because this notion is already encoded in certain species' names, such as *hach kän*, the true snake, for the poisonous naviaca (*Bothropos asper*).[4] Running the same experiment in Spanish would ignore the fact that the language itself is a cultural means, and would, therefore, also ignore the natural context of human cognition.

However, the anthropologist's learning the language poses some interesting cognitive problems: *How do we know that the words we learn actually refer to the entities we ask about?*

This is not intended to question our general ability to understand different languages or cultures. However, human beings and their languages encode similar features and items in often quite different ways. Because bilingual individuals are frequently our greatest help in learning a local language, many of these differences might become obvious or not, depending on the analytical sensitivity of our local teachers. Consider another example: The lowland Maya word *ch'ich* usually translates into "bird" (see Atran, 1999, p. 123, for the Itza' Maya of Guatemala). All of my Lacandon informants told me *ch'ich*, when I asked them for the translation of the Spanish word *pajaro*, bird. But are these two categories really a perfect match, or do we just assume such a match because it approximates our understanding and helps establish the possibility of conversation? There is some indication that this is indeed the case for this example. As other Maya groups, Lacandon Maya classify the bat as *ch'ich*, although they readily acknowledge that the bat shares many features with mammals rather than with birds (Ross, 2001).[5] If this is correct, then we have to expand the category *ch'ich* from bird to "flying animal." How can we check this? One way, discussed below more in detail, would be to see how the same informants classify unfamiliar cases like flying dogs (or even invented species). Obviously, this is not a simple problem as both birds and the bat belong to the same category, *ch'ich*. This might be rather trivial for a description of the categories itself, but it becomes important when we look at larger theoretical issues and when our intention is to compare these categories across cultures.

To establish any locally perceived organization or structure of *emic* systems, we first have to explore and understand the components that constitute these systems. For this purpose, Goodenough and Lounsbury both proposed, independently of each other, the componential or feature analysis (D'Andrade, 1995, p. 21ff; see also Goodenough, 1956; Lounsbury 1956; Romney & D'Andrade, 1964). This analysis tries to identify the *distinctive features* of a term or an entity that distinguishes it from other similar terms or entities in the same domain. Kinship was one of the first domains to which componential analysis was applied (see Lounsbury, 1956; Romney & D'Andrade, 1964). I can illustrate the general idea behind componential analysis with a short example:

Table 4.1 describes a feature listing of the English terms "daughter" and "son."

The table shows that both "daughter" and "son" share a set of features, but have one distinctive feature: gender. If we change any of the other features,

Table 4.1   Feature Listing of the English Terms "Daughter" and "Son"

English Term	English Term
Daughter	Son
Consanguinal	Consanguinal
1 generation to EGO	1 generation to EGO
Direct	Direct
Descending	Descending
Female	Male

such as distance from EGO, we would produce different categories within the English kin system (moving up in distance would produce "brother" and "sister" instead of "son" and "daughter"). These systems are not the same across cultures, and a number of different kinship systems exist that have been identified and studied from very early on (see, e.g., Morgan, 1871). The Tzotzil Maya of the highland of Chiapas, for example, distinguish two terms for child: *'ol* and *nich'on*. Table 4.2 shows the relevant chart.

Again, both terms share a number of features. The distinctive feature in this case is not the gender of the child, but rather the gender of the parent (I hasten to add that there are terms for "girl" and "boy" in Tzotzil that can be used as "daughter" and "son" by means of a suffix indicating possession). During the early stage of my fieldwork among the Tzotzil Maya, I didn't recognize this distinction: My ways of learning the language were based on approximation, asking my bilingual informants how one would say such and such in Tzotzil. One of my main informants during these early stages of secondary language acquisition was the mother of the family I stayed with. Asking her about the different kinship terms, I learned to say *ho'on mu'yuk to k'ol*, a phrase that produced quite some laughter at the Sunday market (where I usually practiced my newly acquired knowledge), because it translates into "I [female] still don't have a child."

These examples should suffice to explain the basic principle of a componential or feature analysis. For further elaborations on the methodology, see the original articles by Goodenough, Lounsbury, Romney, and D'Andrade, and the short description in D'Andrade (1995, p. 21ff).

Componential analysis gives us a basic understanding of the structure and meaning of the systems under study—what the exact entities are that become encoded and how they differ from each other.

Although we conduct many of these calculations automatically (not all, as seen above) while learning a language for research purposes, we often have to be very strict about them. Therefore, one of the important questions to

Table 4.2   Feature Listing of the Tzotzil Terms "'Ol" and "Nich'on"

Tzotzil term	Tzotzil term
'Ol	Nich'on
Consanguinal	Consanguinal
1 generation to EGO	1 generation to EGO
Direct	Direct
Descending	Descending
Male or Female	Male or Female
Female-EGO	Male-EGO

start with is, *What are the relevant units and elements to be compared?* In this regard, Frake noted as early as 1962 that contrast sets are not unlimited. We most likely wouldn't contrast a hamburger, a sandwich, with a rainbow (to use Frake's example). Frake argued that *rainbow* does not constitute an uncontrived alternative in the set of hamburger and sandwich—another form of saying that it doesn't belong within the same *domain*, or area of conceptualization (D'Andrade, 1995, p. 34).

Weller and Romney (1988) define a domain as an organized set of words, concepts, or sentences, all on the same level of contrast, that jointly refer to a single conceptual sphere, within which the individual elements derive their meaning in a mutually interdependent system (p. 9). This can be illustrated with an earlier example: In English, "daughter" and "son" derive their specific meaning when compared with each other. This makes it clear that defining the domain is of crucial importance for any research. If the meaning of the elements studied, the words, concepts, or sentences described by Weller and Romney, emerge within an interdependent system, then it is obvious that the number and kinds of elements chosen influence the meaning we are bound to find for each of the elements.

Suppose one was to study differences among cars, but included only fast cars as elements in the domain. Applying the above-described feature analysis, one might not find that velocity is a distinctive feature, and, hence, the resulting structure (and meaning of each element) would be significantly different from a set that included trucks, vans, SUVs, and racing cars. This is not a problem if we know about the particular selection of elements (we could simply adjust by renaming the domain sports cars). But what if we do not know the content of the domain a priori?

Perhaps the most useful technique for identifying the elements of a domain is a *free-listing task* that specifically asks informants to name all the elements of X they can think of.

Free Listing, Saliency, and the Definition of Domains

Free-listing techniques tend to be used when we do not already know the elements and boundaries of a domain we would like to study (Antweiler, 1993, p. 260), which is probably the rule rather than the exception in anthropological research. The aim of a free-listing task is not necessarily to get an exhaustive list of elements, but to get a list of culturally relevant items on which most of the informants agree. Due to the method, these elements (or items) are usually in some relationship to one another, depending on the given question. Methods to elicit these lists differ and range from simply asking the informants to name all the elements of X, to sophisticated approaches like those applied by Berlin and Romney (1964). In this study, the researchers looked at numeral classifiers in the Tzeltal Maya language. Numeral classifiers are classifiers of nouns that are often used in enumerations and that indicate certain characteristics of the item described by the noun. To elicit a complete list of these classifiers (or at least as complete as possible), the researchers developed a computer-generated list of all possible consonant-vowel-consonant combinations, which is the form Tzeltal Maya classifiers usually have. (The list included a total of 4,410 combinations!) Using this list, informants where asked which of these combinations were actual classifiers (vs. nonsense combinations). This left the researchers with far more classifiers than any previous study had been able to generate. Still, their final list might be incomplete, and sometimes such a large number of elements is unreasonable to work with, depending on the actual research question.

Normally, we are not in a position to interview all relevant individuals, and even if we were, we could never be sure that they wouldn't forget one or more elements. However, with an increasing number of informants, the number of new elements added to an aggregated list becomes smaller. These new items tend to be more idiosyncratic (they are mentioned by only a few individuals), do not have the cultural saliency of other items that were mentioned by more individuals and earlier in the individual listings, and might not be shared by all the informants. In many cases it is, therefore, a reasonable strategy to choose the most frequently mentioned elements, those most culturally salient, which assures us that most of our informants are familiar with them. Obviously, it is essential to find a question that actually stimulates informants to think and respond productively as part of the research process (again, this can be achieved based on prior participant observation and pilot studies).

It should be clear that we have to keep these imposed limitations in mind when we think about the elements of the domains we study (which elements are selected and which are not). However, a free-listing task comes with further advantages. Because not all information is equally salient in a culture, this task provides us with not only a list of relevant elements, but also with important information about these elements. More salient, better-known, or more important items are usually higher up in the list: They are (a) mentioned earlier by the individual informants and (b) mentioned by more informants (Weller & Romney, 1988, pp. 10-11). Both indices of saliency are usually highly correlated with each other (see, e.g., Romney & D'Andrade, 1964, p. 155), and also seem to correlate with actual frequency in common speech (see Henley, 1969, for an example). I used free-listing techniques as an index of saliency in a study on folk-biological knowledge among the Tzotzil Maya of Zinacantán (Ross & Medin, 2003). Recent changes in the community led me to hypothesize that tree species should be more salient for women than men because the women engage these days in many more activities related to the forest than the men, who increasingly seek employment in sectors other than the traditional *milpa*-agriculture. Given that these changes are rather recent, and that individuals who are more involved in the "traditional culture" (participating in the rather expansive church rituals etc.) are also more likely to engage in agriculture, I also expected saliency differences among the men with respect to age and their participation in the traditional religious system of the community. A simple task, in which individuals where asked to generate tree species, confirmed these hypotheses. Women generated more species than men, and for the men we find a high correlation between both age and number of species generated and between participation in the religious system and number of generated species. While more studies are needed to confirm these data further, a simple task provided basic data to confirm a hypothesis on a rather complicated phenomenon. Obviously, we can't conclude from such a task that not generating an item equals not knowing the item. Still, not generating an item seems to be related to the saliency of this item for a given individual. From this perspective, it is often also worthwhile to take a closer look at the not-so-well-known items and their distribution among the informants.

Antweiler (1993, p. 260, footnote 11) mentions the fact that not all domains are suitable for this task and tells of an experience when free-listing tasks produced only a few items. At first glance, this might look like just a frustrating result for the researcher. From a cognitive perspective, however, this could be an interesting data point about the domain in general, as it might suggest that the domain is either very small or not coherent from an *emic* point of view. The latter is very important to keep in mind: The researcher's conception of a coherent domain might not coincide with the informants' conceptions! Obviously, as mentioned earlier, such interpretations apply only if we make sure that the responses (or their lack) are not a direct result of poorly chosen questions or an uncomfortable interview context.

In addition to looking at individual elements, free listing allows us to explore the occurrence of clusters of elements that appear together in the listings (compared across individuals). For example, are mammals clustered within the domain of animals—do their names occur in close order—and if so, do these clusters appear before or after other clusters (e.g., bird, etc.). In the United States, for example, we might expect birds to appear after mammals in a listing of animals, given the saliency of mammals in the U.S. concept of animals. If this is indeed the case, we might also expect the individuals to mention more mammals than birds.

Studies with children also show that free listing can provide us with a first idea about the content of certain categories. For example, when asked to name all the living things they know of, children in the United States usually mentioned human beings apart from animals, indicating that children indeed conceive of human beings as different from animals (Ross & Medin, 2000).

There are many ways to elicit these lists, depending on the domain explored. The main issue is to find the right kind of questions to elicit a fair number of elements that actually refer to the domain under inquiry. Approaches range from interviewing individuals alone to group interviews (note that in group interviews, the number of groups and not the number of individuals equals the number of informants), and from simply asking the names of all X to more complicated scenarios (see Weller & Romney, 1988, pp. 13-14). As discussed above, the number of informants necessary depends on the degree of their agreement with one another. Informant agreement can be tested with three indicators:

- The number of elements mentioned is more or less the same across the individual informants
- Once we have a significant number of informants, adding a new informant should not add many new elements
- The general order of elements should be similar across all informants

If these three conditions are met, we can assume that a clear structure of the domain exists and is known by the informants. As already described, the structure of the tabulated frequency list (percentage of individuals who mentioned an item) can tell us something about the domain. A normal distribution of the elements sorted by frequency (number of informants mentioning an element) should decrease gradually from top to bottom. A sharp drop-off after two or three items might suggest that the domain is small— containing just a few elements. This can also be an artifact of inadequate methods (with the informants not responding well) or an inadequate or incoherent domain (see Weller & Romney, 1988, p. 15). Because the task is not restricted, calculating agreement between informants (see Chapter 5) is often omitted for these kinds of data even though a statistical method to accomplish this has been available since 1932 (Driver & Kroeber, 1932). The Driver's-G, named for Harold Driver, calculates the agreement of two individuals as a measure of agreed-upon items and the absolute number of items mentioned by each individual (Driver, 1970; see also Barselou, 1989; Moore, Lizeth, & Rusch, 2001). The formula for calculating is

$$\text{Sqr of } (A/T1 * A/T2)$$

with Sqr = square root; A = number of items shared by the two informants and T1; and T2 being the absolute number of items mentioned by informants 1 and 2.

Let me illustrate some of these methods with an example from actual research. In a cross-cultural study, my colleagues and I explore how children in different cultures develop their folk-biological understandings. We interviewed approximately 100 children of different ages in each of three groups: the Menominee, a Native American group of central Wisconsin; rural Majority Culture children of central Wisconsin; and urban children from Boston and Evanston, Illinois. In the first task, we used a free-list format, asking each child individually first to name all the animals he or she could think of and, second, to name all the plants she or he could think of. Because of its simplicity, this task proved powerful in exploring cultural and experiential differences in the development of this kind of knowledge, as well as some of the underlying concepts the children applied (Ross & Medin, 2000).

Previous research comparing experts with novices indicated that experts tend to talk about living kinds with a higher level of specificity (e.g., cardinal vs. bird) than nonexperts do. Therefore, we expected to find a developmental pattern that would show increasing specificity with increasing age. However, only our rural Majority Culture sample fit this prediction. Menominee children applied the same specificity across all ages, while the urban group actually showed the opposite pattern: with an increase in age, the specificity of mentioned animals decreased. This result is striking, for it seems to suggest that for Boston city children specific animals are not at all salient, and saliency might even decrease with age. This already suggests a lack of knowledge among the city children, a finding that was further supported by other data (Ross et al., 2003).

Besides the level of specificity applied by the children, we also compared the kinds of animals (exotic vs. native to the area) mentioned by the children of each group. Menominee children mentioned more local species than nonnative species, and the Boston children named more exotic species. We found the same results for both plant and animal listings.

A third analysis showed rural Majority Culture children mentioned "bird" as a category aside from individual birds like ostrich or eagle, but not with passerines or songbirds. This seems to indicate that their category of "bird" consists of passerines and songbirds. Menominee children used bird (if at all) basically as a pure superordinate and not to describe a certain class of birds (Ross & Medin, 2000).

To sum up, free-list methods, if applied correctly, can be much more than a tool to elicit items in a domain that we would like to study. Their simplicity makes them a powerful tool for field research, as they are easy to understand and to perform. The tasks can be adjusted easily to particular needs for a given research question as well as to local needs. Note, however, that in the studies with children we did not analyze the actual number of species recalled. This is very important. In this study, children were interviewed in classrooms, and it was hard to control for the interview setting (what's visually available), the time a child spent on this task, and the (individual) stimulation presented to the child. Furthermore, even if we had been able to control these factors, emerging group differences could still be the result of an overall response bias (e.g., the members of one group being less used to these kinds of questions and, therefore, less comfortable in this setting). Still, if properly planned, number recalled can be an important data point in itself, as has been illustrated in the above example of tree generation among Tzotzil Maya adults.

So far, I have described unrestricted and unconditioned free-listing tasks, where the informants are basically asked to generate as many X they can think of. Free-listing tasks can also be (a) restricted (e.g., name X number of animals), (b) conditioned (e.g., tell me all the causes that can lead to disease X), and (c) further elaborated by the use of stimuli material, such as pictures. Antweiler describes restricted free listing as the first step in the *Repertory Grid Method* (see Kelly, 1955) he used to explore the environmental cognition among urban dwellers in Sulawesi (Antweiler, 1993, p. 271). He first asked his informants to describe opposites for three items presented on written cards, pictures, or other stimuli. The aim of this task was to elicit, rather than assume, individual constructs (opposition relations) of the informants for further research. In this case, only the stimuli (written cards) were provided and the informant created whatever seemed to be a meaningful opposition-relationship (Antweiler, 1993, p. 271). When comparing two items, informants were not guided by any attribute of comparison (nice–ugly; colorful–black & white, etc.). Rather, the researcher tried to elicit the relevant opposition relations as applied by the informants. These relation constructs (opposition pairs) constitute elements comparable to the animal species in the task described earlier. The idea is similar: Rather than assuming certain opposition relations to be present, the researcher uses a free-listing task as a tool to elicit these relations from the perspective of the informants. Again, there are almost unlimited possibilities for creating relationships of opposition among a group of three items, and general saliency and informant agreement (cultural relevance) are important features to be explored. This is another example that shows the extension of possible research areas and topics that these methods allow.

Again, all these examples should illustrate that free-listing tasks can be employed far beyond the mere elicitation of as many elements as possible within a given domain (see Berlin & Romney, 1964). In fact, they are well suited for exploring differences in saliency and structure of elements in a given domain across groups (see Trotter, 1981), and as a result they provide us with important information about the domain itself.

However, there are certain drawbacks (see Weller & Romney, 1988, p. 16). For example, it is often difficult to find appropriate generic terms to start the listing process (e.g., the right question); free listing, therefore, generally doesn't provide a fruitful starting point for research. A second disadvantage is the lack of statistical tools to check reliability: When do we have enough informants or elements, and what constitutes the normal distribution and drop off?

Still, the method is too powerful and flexible to be ignored by researchers in the field.

It is clear that once the salient elements of a domain are identified, a series of new questions can be asked. One general question was already asked at the beginning of this section: What are the distinctive features of the individual elements? The feature or componential analysis proved to be efficient in outlining some general semantic differences between individual elements. However, this analysis normally remains superficial because it leaves many open questions about the structure and meaning of the elements explored.

Before I proceed with the description of further research methods, however, I want to draw attention to two different perspectives our analyses can and should take. If we apply rigorous methods in terms of study design and data gathering, we are able to analyze (a) the actual content of the data, as well as (b) the distribution of responses across our informants. This is a crucial issue. The former is built into the early works of cognitive anthropology and has dramatically improved the general standards and perspective of anthropological research methods. This led some anthropologists to call it the "new ethnography" (Sturtevant, 1964). However, it is the study of knowledge distribution that actually led to a paradigm shift in cognitive anthropology and the field in general. Not only did it open a whole new area of research, but it also resolved an old problem of cultural research: Whose knowledge gets represented, and how do we construct our ethnographies (e.g., account for and represent variability within cultures, etc.)? This problem influences how we theorize about and conceptualize culture (see Chapter 3 on this issue).

In the discussion on free listing, we talked about both the analyses of the actual structure of elements, and the comparison of informants according to their level of agreement and disagreement. In our example, this could be done on different levels: the saliency of particular elements, their appearance and ranking in the list, and their clustering. This perspective is rather new in cognitive anthropology and the social sciences, partly because it depends on powerful personal computers to run some of the analyses.

Coming back to our research methods, I will now describe further methodologies that allow us to explore the relationships and differences of the elements under consideration. These methods can be seen as extensions of the feature analysis, although the features explored here might not always be linguistically encoded. This is, for example, the case with causal relationships between elements (similarity in causes).

As will be seen, many of the methods described share common features. These methods are neither exclusive, nor do they only represent different means by which to get to the same goal, the findings. On the contrary, depending on the research question, a combination of several of these methods can prove to be very useful and can provide the researcher with a way of replicating previous data with a different methodology and thereby test the stability of the findings.

One method that is often used to explore causal relationships or similarities based on causal relationships is the so-called question answer frames or sentence frame techniques, to which I now turn.

Question Answer Frames, True/False Questions, and Sentence Frame Techniques

Question answer frames, true/false questions, and sentence frame techniques share some common features in that the informants have to react to clear statements. These statements can be questions to be answered, statements that the informants have to classify as true or false, or statements with blanks that informants have to fill in. These strategies can be helpful to check a list of elements against already established categories: "An eagle is a bird."

These sentences can also be constructed as questions: "Is an eagle a bird?" or as statements with a blank: "An eagle is a type of _____."

While this format is easy to handle in the field, the information gained is often limited compared to the input. Its usefulness also depends on previous elicited data.

In addition, this task can be rather boring for the informants, who might develop a bias toward responding "yes" or "no" regardless of their actual opinion. This effect can be particularly significant if the lists are long and possibly frustrating for the informants. Another way to design this task is to ask informants to fill in blanks within a statement that is either written or orally communicated.

Linda Garro (1986) used the former approach to elicit causes for diseases in a Mexican village. Using two lists, one of diseases (D) and one of causes (C), she asked her informants to state if a given disease (D_{1-nd}) could be the result of a given cause (C_{1-nc}) (YES/NO). Going through all possible combinations, Garro was able to analyze the following:

1. Specific cause–disease relationships

2. Similarities of causes (causing similar diseases) and of diseases (sharing similar causes)

3. Patterns of informant agreement (experts vs. nonexperts)

Similar approaches were applied by Fabrega (1970) with respect to illness concepts in Incanting (Mexico), Boster and Johnson (1989) looking at U.S. expert and novice fishermen, and Weller, Romney, and Orr (1987) looking at corporal punishment. Two things are needed to run this task: a list of elements and a list of features related to the elements (e.g., diseases and causes). Both can be elicited with unconditioned or conditioned free-listing tasks.

These tasks are easy to administer once the right items and features are identified, although the coding of particular responses might not always be as unambiguous as we would wish. Responses like "Yes, but . . ." or further elaborations on differences or special scenarios can force the researcher to make decisions about how to classify a response within a given set of possibilities, making pilot studies and informal interviews prerequisites for all of these methods. Collecting and analyzing justifications normally helps to overcome some of these difficulties. This can prove essential for an in-depth understanding of differences among our informants, as I will describe in detail for pile-sorting tasks later on.

Still, sentence frame techniques can be a crucial tool in establishing essential features of certain items (taste of fish, as in Boster & Johnson, 1989) compared to other features and items in a given domain.

A criticism of this kind of research maintains that the features and items used in the task already define the outcome of the study. However, if we only use items and features previously elicited as culturally meaningful and if the statistical analysis establishes a given finding as reliable (e.g., agreed upon more than chance would predict), then we can assume that the result has some relevance to the individuals studied. This, in fact, applies to most of the methods described in this chapter. Because many of our studies are exploratory in their character, we need to find a clear pattern of informant agreement to establish (post hoc) the meaningfulness of the task itself.

The different sentence frame techniques—if properly applied—can provide us with a rich set of data and are easily managed, even with large numbers of items. They are especially suited for exploring the connections between different dimensions (values, emotions, etc.) and different domains. They are repetitive for informants (Weller & Romney, 1988, p. 61), however, and might include questions that make no sense (Bernard, 1995, p. 244). For example, because we have to include all possible options, questions such as "does a bleeding toe cause heart-attack" might appear on the list. Therefore, it is extremely important to have a well-grounded knowledge about what is acceptable in a given society.

Triad Comparison

In a triad comparison, informants are asked to compare three items at a time with respect to a given question. In general, informants are asked to "put the two things together that are more alike," or "to sort out the one item that is most different" (see Ross, 2001, for an application within the domain of folk-biological taxonomies). Another application is the ranking of three items according to a given attribute. Kelly (1955) developed this methodology, which, as far as I know, was applied for the first time in anthropology by Romney and D'Andrade (1964), exploring English kin terms. Other research that used this tool includes Burton and Kirk (1979) on Maasai models of social identity and on Maasai personality descriptors (Kirk & Burton, 1977), as well as an ethnomedical study looking at treatment choices in two Mexican communities (Young & Garro, 1982).

In triad comparison, as in most of the tasks presented in this chapter, it is important to randomize the order of (a) the trials presented to the informants and (b) the order of the items presented in the individual trials. It is also recommended that this task be introduced with several examples from a different domain to make sure that the informants understand the task the same way the researcher does. The importance of this is usually underestimated. For example, in my own research I found informants sorting picture cards of animals in a pile-sort task (described in the next chapter) according to the colors or the size of the image, rather than their concepts of the animals. For example, informants would sort animals according to size of the image rather than the size of the actual animal, with which the informants were quite familiar. Obviously, this changed the results in unforeseen ways. If examples are used—in fact, there can be a pilot test with each informant—the chosen items have to be from a different domain to avoid introducing criteria that could influence the informant's responses.

In general, the data allow the researcher to make inferences about similarity judgments in a way that does not a priori assume a particular structure of the domain—which is the case for pile sorts, as we will discuss below. Because a triad comparison task involves only three items at a time, it is easy to administer in the field and stimuli material can range from photographs to name cards. The fact that only three items are presented at a time allows the use of written devices even with informants who can't read. In work with the Lacandon Maya, I used name cards (Lacandon names of species) as stimuli, and although most of my informants weren't able to read the words (written in Lacandon Maya), the cards nevertheless served as mnemonic devices (Ross, 2001, p. 159). After shuffling the cards several times, informants were still able to recognize each card as representing a given species (among the three cards). Moreover, the use of words has a big advantage over picture cards, as can be seen in the example given above, because informants base their judgments on their mental representations of the item depicted rather than searching for clues in the pictures themselves. In addition, because pictures are seldom perfect representations of size and color, they can lead to artificial results.

Besides these practical aspects, the task has the further advantage of allowing us to control the processes involved in the judgments. For each trial (individual triad) we can explore the reasons given for the informant's judgment and thereby investigate the "local reasoning strategies." This information can get lost to some extent in tasks that present us only with final results (e.g., pile sorting).

To give one example, I applied this method to explore the multipurpose taxonomic order of animals and plants as perceived by the Lacandon Maya of Mensäbäk. As expected from the literature (see Atran, 1998, and Berlin, 1992), the respective taxonomies share a lot of features with general taxonomies all over the world, as well as with the scientific taxonomy. In this study, however, the triad task allowed me to examine the following more extensively:

justifications given for individual decisions, and

informant agreement across the different trials

Justifications can tell us a lot about the reasoning applied in specific trials, as well as the overall patterns of reasoning strategies applied in a specific domain. In the study referred to, this helped to explore the features deemed relevant by the Lacandones in order to distinguish different species from each other. This can be analyzed on different levels, depending on the coding applied to the judgments (e.g., morphological vs. ecological reasoning, size vs. color, etc.).

In closely controlled comparative studies, these data allow a better understanding of the differences found in the respective taxonomies, and also allowed exploration of conceptual differences that might not be visible in the final taxonomies. Obviously, to do this the individual trials have to be absolutely identical across individuals! Weller and Romney (1988, p. 35) suggest collecting the justifications after the final analysis of the data, which implies going back to the field to discuss the results with the informants. While there is nothing wrong with this approach, it might be expensive and the justifications given might deviate from the ones applied at the time of the original interview and to specific trials.

In the mentioned research, I was furthermore able to calculate informant agreement, which is not as straightforward for other tasks like sorting stimuli cards (Antweiler, 1993, p. 261). This could be done across all the trials and for each trial individually. If a trial reaches high agreement (e.g., most informants agree on the response), we can assume that (a) the response to the trial is culturally salient and (b) that the found response can be taken as representing the culturally correct response. Both results provide us with important data about the structure of the domain, as well as the saliency of certain differences and similarities.

This approach was successfully applied in a task where I intentionally constructed "difficult triads" based on information learned earlier. Results showed the existence of competing models for reasoning (domesticated-wild vs. separation based on life forms) that led to some differences among the informants (Ross, 2001, p. 180).

All this makes the triad task a suitable task for anthropological fieldwork. It can be readily applied across different domains and does not assume a priori a certain structure of the data. Depending on the research questions, it provides a wide array of possibilities for data analysis, in terms of both content and informant agreement. There are some drawbacks, however.

In a *complete* triad task—one that compares every possible constellation of three items—the number of trials rises exponentially with increases in the numbers of elements included in the study. If there are only 8 elements in a complete triad design, the number of trials is 56. This is manageable, but raising the number of elements to 21 means eliciting responses for 1,330 individual trials from every informant (Burton & Nerlove, 1976, p. 250). This puts some limitations on the number of elements that can be included in regular field research.

One solution to this problem is to administer parts of the complete task to different groups of informants. To do this, however, the population studied has to be large enough and fairly homogeneous, unless it would be possible to go back to each informant and split the task over several sessions, which in itself creates some theoretical problems. Splitting the task over several informants has the disadvantage of losing opportunities to explore informant agreement in addition to the agreement pattern within the different groups, allowing for only a general analysis of the content of the underlying models. It also requires a fairly homogeneous group of informants, which has to be established for each of the subgroups of informants separately.

Another approach to avoid this problem is the application of the balanced incomplete block design described by Burton and Nerlove (1976; see also Weller & Romney, 1988, p. 49, and Ross, 2001). In this particular design, trials are created in a way that allows all possible pairs of elements to be compared exactly the same number of times during the interview. Depending on the number of times each pair of elements is compared—each time with a different third element—the task can be dramatically shortened. For example, if each pair is compared only once during the interview ($\lambda = 1$ describes the fact that each pair appears only once in the experiment), only 70 trials have to be conducted for 21 elements. In my own study this proved to be a manageable size, as each interview took between 40 and 60 minutes. Including 25 elements would have required 100 trials (with $\lambda = 1$), and 200 trials if λ were increased to $\lambda = 2$.

However, limiting the number of times each pair is compared creates a structural problem. Consider the following example:

Horse   Trout   Spider Monkey

Using a taxonomic classification that distinguishes "mammals," "birds," and "fishes," individuals probably would have no problem describing the horse as more similar to the monkey (with the trout being the alternative). However, this changes if we switch to the following triad:

Horse   Howler Monkey   Spider Monkey

Here, the two monkeys probably would be seen as similar to each other and the horse would be the element regarded as different. Because only one or the other of these two trials would appear in an incomplete triad design with $\lambda = 1$, it is obvious that the whole structure of our data set would be affected. This problem decreases with an increasing λ and vanishes altogether in a complete triad design. The different designs (how to pick the triads), as well as the number of trials required, can be found in Cochran and Cox (1957).

Given the numbers provided above, which make a complete design almost impossible, it is clear that trade-offs are required and that a compromise between facility of data collection and clarity of results has to be found.

In my own research, I changed the procedure to adjust this method better to the field setting. This was done as a partial remedy for the problem described, and also in response to an informant's unwillingness or uneasiness in responding to some of the trials. In this design, informants are generally "forced" to provide "their best guess," which in itself might give us a good idea of underlying cultural biases. Yet in some of the triads, the elements were so different (e.g., trout, deer, eagle) or so similar that informants often refused to make a judgment (Ross, 2001, p. 160). In order to mediate this problem somewhat, I introduced "all elements different" and "all elements similar" as additional possible responses. Responses were coded as such if an informant could not provide a response even after being asked several times.[6] When that happened, I asked the informants for a reason—for example, whether the elements were too similar or too different. Antweiler (1993, p. 274) made similar changes to a ranking comparison he used. He explicitly anticipated that individuals could not always rank one item over another. This is important to note: In a field setting, informants are generally guided by common sense, to which the requirements of formal methods of data collection are often opposed (see also the preceding section on sentence frames). Our analyses, on the other hand, often depend on a complete data set and people might have to be forced to give an unambivalent response and, as in formal triad tests, to draw distinctions that might not be meaningful locally. At best, these conditions lead to a random distribution of the responses, telling the researcher that the applied methods were not successful.

Triad tasks are very powerful tools for understanding underlying structures of differences and similarities among the elements of a given domain. The data allow us to look both at the content of the data set (similarity of items), as well as at the pattern of informant agreement/disagreement. Different analytical procedures are available for both types of analysis (see Chapter 5). However, the number of elements that can be used is limited due to the large number of trials required, even when we limit the task to an incomplete design. While enhancing the number of items that can be tested, the incomplete design introduces a serious structural problem, as discussed earlier in this chapter. Still, as described by Antweiler, this method is easy to administer in the field because of its simplicity, and it does not put too many demands on the informant. Compared to the pile sort (described below), it does not assume a taxonomical structure (or any structure at all). Test experiments conducted with Northwestern University students showed that the results of both experiments correlated highly for both the resulting order of elements and the pattern of informant agreement.

Pile Sorting: The Hierarchical Sorting of Elements

Pile or card sorting is another way to investigate the similarity structure of individual items in a given domain. In this task, a set of cards (written or illustrated) are laid out in random order in front of the informant, who is then asked to put them together according to a given attribute. As in the triad task, the attribute applied can be "general similarity" (Q: "Please put the items together that are similar, go together, etc.") or any other attribute the researcher is interested in (similar in X way).

In the conditioned version of this task, the researcher presents the informant with the number of possible piles into which to sort the elements (Q: "Please put the items in n piles according to their similarity"). In the unconditioned version, the researcher does not predetermine the number of piles.

This first sorting is recorded as the privileged level of differentiation, and for each pile, the informant might then be asked to create subsorts until individual items are reached or the informant refuses to split the piles further (subsequent sorting). In the next step, the original sorts can be reestablished (privileged-level sort) in order to ask the informant to put the different piles together according to the same attribute (superordinate level). The result is a taxonomical order with each individual item appearing only once on each individual level.

This kind of task was recently applied successfully in studies that included such populations as the Itza' Maya of Guatemala, U.S. tree experts, and U.S. college students that tried to elicit local taxonomies of living things (see, e.g., Atran, 1999; López, Atran, Coley, Medin, & Smith, 1997; Medin, Lynch, Coley, & Atran, 1997).

The elements under study do not have to be individual physical units. Freeman et al. (1981), for example, explored different statements about failure and success in life among individuals in the United States and Guatemala. They then asked informants in both countries to sort these statements according to similarity in a pile sort. This method allowed them to explore differing concepts of success and failure in both countries.

In contrast with the triad task, it is not advisable (and almost impossible) to ask the informants right away for justifications of what they just did. Justifications can still be elicited at the end of the task, however. This proved to be an important source of information in Medin et al. (1997) and Medin et al. (2002). In the latter work, two groups of local (nonprofessional) fish experts (Menominee Indians and Majority Culture participants from central Wisconsin) showed striking differences in how they sorted 44 local fish species in a similarity taxonomy. The differences in justification (e.g., habitat vs. ecology, and goal orientation) were then used to predict outcomes in other tasks. Contrary to the assumption by Weller and Romney (1988, p. 31), this task can indeed be used with illiterate people. Both López et al. (1997) and Atran (1999) provide data based on research with the Itza' Maya of Guatemala who were, despite their inabilities to read and write in Itza' Maya, capable of performing the task with picture cards.

The examples illustrate yet another strength of this approach. In the cited study with Menominee fish experts, 44 fish species were sorted according to their similarity. This large amount would be impossible to handle with a triad format. Yet card sorting still allows analyses, such as the calculation of informant agreement, which proved essential for this particular research project.

One of the drawbacks of this task is the a priori assumption of a taxonomical structure of the data (Antweiler, 1993, p. 261; Weller & Romney, 1988, p. 31). When the data do not have an underlying taxonomical structure, or the researcher does not have a clear notion of the structure, this task is not appropriate.

This problem can be avoided to some extent by allowing the same item to appear in several piles on a given level (see Stefflre, Reich, & McLaran-Stefflre, 1971, p. 86). In the research among Menominee and Majority Culture fish experts, for example, the author and his colleagues applied this strategy to elicit informants' knowledge about the sharing of habitats of local fish species. In this framework, it would have been impossible to constrain each single species to just one pile at each level, because different species are particularly known for their variability with respect to their habitat. As a consequence, we allowed the informants (a) to create as many different sorts as they liked and (b) to place each fish in as many of the different categories (upstream-river, channel, lake, etc.) as they wanted to.

Distances (negative similarity) between pairs of individual species were counted by summing the number of nodes between the two species. These distance calculations could then be used to generate a fish-fish-distance matrix. In the case of multiple entries—two data points of different distances for two species—the shortest distance was used, as this reflected the closest ecological relation (sharing of a habitat) of the two species involved in this study.

In general, data analysis for pile sorting is less straightforward than for a triad task. Particularly in the unconditioned version, a problem known as "lumping versus splitting" can occur (Weller & Romney, 1988, p. 22).

"Lumpers" and "splitters" are individuals with a tendency to lump the items into a few big groups (lumpers) or to do the opposite, to split the groups up to the smallest possible level (splitter). These differences create problems in (a) calculating a general matrix across all individuals and (b) making inter-individual comparisons that go beyond this possibly superficial bias (Weller & Romney, 1988, p. 26) impossible.

Although this task usually is described as allowing a high number of elements to be compared in a single task, I still would like to caution the researcher. It is not yet clear (a) what the impact of large numbers of items is and (b) how readily informants use all items presented in the task when they decide on a given sort. For example, it is conceivable that individuals use local strategies, such as working on one corner at a time, rather than using the whole array of items to decide "what goes together." To single out the latter, moving the cards constantly might be helpful, but that brings up the question of how willing we are to draw attention to the cards we are moving. Still, data are too convincing to be ignored, as in López et al. (1997), who show correlations of different folk taxonomies with the scientific taxonomy and use the elicited taxonomies as a base for predictions for further experiments. Furthermore, comparing data sets elicited with triads and with card sorting showed no significant differences in the results of either content analysis or informant agreement.

Rating Tasks

In rating tasks, informants are usually asked individually to rate a set of items according to given attributes. Ratings are normally done by providing the informants with an attribute and a scale on which to rate the value of each item. In the study of fish experts in Wisconsin, for example, we asked the experts of the two groups to rate each fish according to how well it represents the category "fish," or how typical a fish it is. This allowed us to make an assessment not only about the category "fish" itself, but also about each individual species. Similar studies were done with Itza' Maya in Guatemala, as well as with tree experts in the United States. Results showed some interesting deviations from previous findings on typicality. Experts tend not to see average similarity, but rather particular values as central for typicality (Atran, 1999; Medin et al., 1997). For the Itza' Maya, for example, the wild turkey was the most typical bird, a result that is rather surprising in U.S. culture, where "bird" is generally identified with passerines or songbirds (Atran, 1999, pp. 174-177).

Although this question might appear artificial from the outside, these differences are sometimes even encoded linguistically, as is, for example, the case in the lowland Maya languages with respect to the naviaca, the true snake, *hach kän*, or with the jaguar, the true cat, *hach barum*.

The provided scales can include two (e.g., true/false or agree/disagree statements), three (e.g., none, neutral, very much), or more options, with a higher number allowing for the exploration of more finely graded differences. There are, however, limits to the number of scales applied, because too many might confuse the informants more than help them with their decisions. Scales with between 7 and 11 choices seem to offer a good range and produce stable results (Nunally, 1978, p. 595) that allow us to differentiate levels of agreement/disagreement without confusing the informants.

Scales can be of even or odd numbers; there are advantages to both forms. Odd numbers allow the introduction of a neutral category (neither/nor), which in turn might create a bias for the informants to choose this response. Even-numbered scales do not allow neutral responses (only approximations, as the scales do not have a middle point) that might be the most sensible response to some of the questions. However, this format allows the lumping of responses into a binary format (agree/disagree) and at times can be useful for certain analyses (Weller & Romney, 1988, p. 41).

Data can be in the form of statements or individual elements, and questions can target comparisons (Q: How similar do you think X is to Y?), judgments (Q: How well does X represent Y?), or rankings (Q: How important is X to you?). Obviously, some of these measures allow us to relate the tested items or statements (here X) to each other indirectly. Comparisons, for example, should lead to results comparable to data gained from the triad or pile-sort tasks on similarity. It is a less direct method, however, because the elements are not compared directly to each other, but are rated against an independent attribute. Still, the individual ratings allow comparison of the elements with one another.

At first glance, this seems like an unnecessary complication, but the advantage can be threefold. First, because there is a common target for comparison, individuals rate each element based on the same attribute; something that is not guaranteed in the triad or the pile-sorting tasks. Card sorting in particular does not allow control of the kind of attributes the informants apply. Second, this approach lets us explore the attribute itself and not only the relationship of elements with one another, because we can analyze the fact that some elements get higher on an attribute than others. I used this approach to gain insight into the Lacandon Maya concept of *tukuj*, loosely translated as "thinking." Different amounts and kinds of *tukuj* were attributed to different items (humans, plants, different animals, and artifacts). This approach allowed for a much better understanding of the concept and at the same time gave important information about each item. Third, some domains are too sensitive to be explored directly, evident in Röttger-Rössler's (1989, pp. 77-81) unsuccessful study in which informants in Makasar refused to sort actual individuals according to prestige. The same informants, however, might have been willing to rate each individual on a scale that then would allow the researcher to compare the individuals with one another.

Besides obtaining typicality ratings for fish species, we also asked our informants to rate certain statements according to the degree of their agreement or disagreement. Here a scale of 7 points was used, with response 4 indicating neutrality:

(disagree absolutely) 1 – 2 – 3 – 4 – 5 – 6 – 7 (agree absolutely)

In this task, informants were asked to indicate if they absolutely object to (1) or absolutely agree with (7) a given statement. The task was administered verbally, and the experimenter, showing the scale, filled in the respective answers. Obviously, administering the questionnaires to informants by asking them to write the answers might save time; the drawback is that the data are normally much less reliable because people might mark an answer by mistake or put less thought into their responses. Ratings are easy to apply in the field, and justifications can be selected for each question. Resulting data are easy to analyze because they are already in numerical values and so do not need to be coded.

As Antweiler (1993, p. 262) pointed out, however, informants often tend to use one of the two extreme ends of the scale or the neutral value with only limited variation. What Antweiler called the anchor effect might make the research trivial. As a consequence, we (a) need a larger data set, and (b) have to cross-check our results with differently framed questions.

Frey (cited in Weller & Romney, 1988, p. 42) introduced a variation on the method that avoids the anchoring effect and allows an oral application of the task. Constraining the task to a 4-point scale, the researcher presented the informants with two separate questions: Q1: "Some people think X. Do you agree or disagree with this statement?" This allowed the researcher to locate the response as either 1 or 2 (disagree) or 3 or 4 (agree). Then, the second question was asked, depending on the response: Q2a/b: "Do you agree/disagree strongly or only more or less?" This second question allowed the researcher to classify the informant's response further as either 1 or 2 (or 3 or 4).

Ranking

The aim of ranking is to order a set of items on a given attribute. This can be done indirectly with a triad task, a pile or card sort, a rating method, or directly in a ranking task. Informants are generally asked to order a set of items according to a given attribute—for example, from most X to least X, with X being the attribute under exploration. The attribute can be an inherent part of the element (e.g., typicality rating) or the attitude of the informant toward the elements (e.g., like most to dislike most).

As with other tasks, this approach might be too direct for sensitive issues. However, if applicable it offers a simple and powerful tool to explore the relationship and order of elements in a domain. Hammel (1962) used this task to ask informants in a Peruvian village to compare individuals of the same community according to their prestige. This allowed him to explore the different views of social hierarchy the individuals held. Note, however, that a very similar task didn't work for Röttger-Rössler (1989) in her village in south Sulawesi. This underscores an important point: Our methods have to be chosen for and adjusted according to each setting.

In theory, if one works with stimuli cards, one can administer large sets of data that are then arranged by the informants according to the particular question. Usually 21 items (written cards) are no problem to administer to literate informants, but a large number of written cards might make it difficult for informants to keep track of all the items.

In research conducted in the Petén (Guatemala), we developed a different approach. Instead of presenting each individual with the whole set of elements at a time, we first asked each person to rank only three items. When the next card was introduced, the informant was asked to locate this new item among the first three. Hence, the card was compared to each of the cards already laid out (e.g., is it more X than n1/n2?). This continued until the proper position was determined by the informant. As only a limited number of cards was presented at a time, the procedure allowed the researcher to work with written cards as mnemonic devices and still administer a large set of data. However, there is one drawback to this method. Because the order in which the stimuli cards are introduced has to be randomly selected, we might not have comparable information on justifications, as the individual steps (items to be compared) depend on the order in which the cards are introduced. Still, we are able to perform an overall comparison of justifications, or can ask the informants for post hoc justification for the individual rankings.

The applicability of this task depends on the informant's knowledge of the elements and attributes used in the task (see Antweiler, 1993, p. 263). However, this is not unique to this task, but should be a requirement for any of the methods described so far.

Ranking data provides rich material that can be analyzed for a whole array of aspects, as described for the free-listing task. There is also nothing wrong with allowing an informant to rank two or more items equally (n1 and n2 are the same X). The clear structure of the data allows straightforward analysis, in terms of both the elements of the domain and the pattern of informant agreement. Finally, because the resulting order of items is absolute compared to the rating of the data, the data allow for direct cross-group comparisons.

Eliciting Relationships Between the Elements

So far, most of the tasks target the underlying structure of the domain, looking at aspects of similarity or ranking of the individual elements within a domain. While this might be sufficient for certain studies, at times it can be important to look at the specific relationships between the elements within (and across) domains. In many of my own studies, an element-interaction task has proven to be useful. As always, a number of possibilities for administering this task exist. I will describe only one form that was applied successfully in several different cultural settings.

Two sets of preselected elements (animals and plants) represented on cards (words and pictures) were used in this task. A free-listing task had supplied the researcher with the necessary base and target elements. One card was picked randomly from the base set. Each informant was asked to report all the relationships between this element (the first base card) and any of the elements of the target set. After going through all the elements with one base card, the procedure was repeated with the rest of the elements of the base set. This method was applied in a study looking at cultural models of animal-plant interactions in the Petén, Guatemala. Animals were used as base cards and plants as targets. For example, when the agouti was picked as the base card, each informant was asked, for each plant, whether the agouti had a connection to the particular plant. It is important that this is done individually in a card-by-card fashion (does "A" interact with "B?"), rather than asking the informant to name all the elements that have a relationship with the base. In the latter case, a great deal of information can be lost because informants might not consider all possibilities when reporting the relationships.

Base and targets can either be different sets of items (see Atran et al., 1999; Ross, 2001, 2002a) or the same (see Ross & Medin, 2003). If they are the same, each item serves as both base and target.

In the above-mentioned study, each informant was asked (a) to elaborate on specific types of relationships and (b) to judge whether element A helped or hurt element B. For example, once the informant described a relationship between the agouti and the mamey tree, he was asked to describe the relation (eats fruit) and to judge whether the agouti helped or hurt the mamey tree (e.g., it hurt the tree by destroying its seeds).

This was done for all possible pairs of elements, and questions were asked in both directions (A → B and B → A). (Though the agouti hurt the mamey tree, the mamey tree helped the agouti by providing food.) Note that the questions have to be adapted to the task at hand. Helping or hurting might not always be the appropriate question. All this was recorded with the use of different coding, and the final judgment was marked as + / −.

For each individual, this approach resulted in two element-by-element matrices, each of which described the reported relationship (sometimes more than one) between any given pair. The two matrices were necessary to describe the two directions (A → B and B → A). If there is only one set of elements, only one matrix is necessary, as each relation appears twice (above and below the diagonal). Unknown elements were marked as missing data, and relationships reported as not existing were coded 0.

This design resulted in a very rich data set, providing the informant with many stimuli for thinking about the possible relationships between any two elements of a domain. In various projects, we handled up to 29 different species in each set (see Atran et al., 1999; Ross, 2001), with each task taking between 45 minutes and 1½ hours. Because the informant is asked about possible relationships for each pair of elements individually, the task can be administered orally as well as with the use of stimuli cards, and is easy for informants to comprehend. A design involving 21 elements in each of two sets produces a total of 840 data points per interview. While this allows for a relatively finely graded analysis, the data are produced under considerable time pressure unless the task is split up into a number of sessions. In fact, in the study of fish experts among Menominee and Majority Culture informants in Wisconsin, we found clear cultural differences in the speeded version of this task. These differences disappeared once we scaled the task down to a non-speeded version using only 10 items. This is an important finding: It tells us that (a) cultural differences exist, but that these differences are (b) based on differences in saliency and knowledge organization, rather than on differences in the knowledge base per se (Ross & Medin, 2003).

This task was also used in a study on environmental cognition among the Lacandon Maya of Mexico. The data not only allowed the comparison of the individuals with each other, but also the partial reconstruction of the complexity of forest life as reported by the Lacandones. Structural differences in these relationships could be compared across groups of informants emerging from the task, which helped to understand some of the differences that were revealed (Ross, 2001, 2002a). In this particular case, clear differences were found between the members of the younger and older adult generations. These differences were seen in the number of relationships mentioned by each group, and also in the resulting structure of forest life. It was specifically in individuals' final judgments of impact (helping/hurting) that I was able to detect important group differences. While younger informants readily describe some human or animal actions as harmful to a plant, older informants normally didn't assign any impact at all. The respective reasoning is that plants are created by *hächäkyum*, the highest god in the Lacandon cosmos, to provide for the necessity of animals and humans. Obviously, this kind of data offers us many insights into framework theories, reasoning strategies applied by our informants. In yet another study (Atran et al., 1999; Atran et al., 2002), it was important to distinguish the different directions of the relationships. In this case, it was interesting to see that only the native Maya group had a clear concept of reciprocal relationships, were animals that would actually help plants. I mention these specific examples to illustrate two important features:

> Different coding and questions often allow us to reveal otherwise hidden information.

> The results of these tasks often allow us to make inferences that go beyond what one might expect (e.g., changes in underlying cosmologies).

As this task explores the relationship between elements of different domains, it provides us with important information about the domain itself, and, hence, opens up the exploration of the relationships between different domains.

Induction and Reasoning Tasks

All of these methods explore the elements as perceived by the informants with respect to several features (e.g., similarity, ranking, relationship) and a set of attributes determined in each study.

This allows us to make some inferences about how human beings reason about these issues and the elements involved.

Saying that two items are similar does not necessarily imply that the perceived similarity is actively used to make inferences about the elements, or that this knowledge is applied in reasoning strategies. This is done with another set of studies that explore strategies of inductive reasoning. These studies are concerned with the kinds of beliefs/knowledge that do or do not support inferences drawn from partial knowledge to more general situations (Coley, Medin, Proffitt, Lynch, & Atran, 1999, p. 207; Medin & Ross, 1996, p. 538). For example, if we know that a German shepherd barks, we might infer that all dogs bark. This inference is stronger if we know that both German shepherds and terriers bark (see Osherson, Smith, Wilkie, López, & Shafir, 1990, for a general model).

These inferences are not logical truths, but may reflect the experience of the informants. Induction and reasoning tasks provide a rich field of inquiry because they tell us a lot about the organization of domains and elements within these domains.

In this final section, I will describe some research designs that target these kinds of issues.

Property Projection Task

In this task, informants are told that an element has a certain property as an essential part. The property should be unknown to the informant (a blank property made up by the researcher) to avoid the informants actually reasoning about the property rather than the elements under study. After being introduced to the property and the fact that a base item has this property, the informant is asked to judge if the property also forms part of other items.

Susan Carey (1985) applied this task in her influential work on conceptual change in early childhood. A replication of this task in different cultural settings can be found in Ross et al. (2003).

Two sets of elements are needed for this task: base items and targets. For example, informants are told that Base Item A has *Estro* inside and that all items of the same kind A have *Estro* inside (e.g., "all wolves have *Estro*"). The informant is then asked, for each of the target items as they are individually shown, if he or she thinks that this item also has *Estro* inside. Justifications can be collected right after the response, before switching to the next target card.

This task can be administered verbally even though all the cited studies used picture cards to represent the elements. The task has been successfully used in work with children and adults of different cultures. Albeit its simplicity, it provides important insights into how individuals reason within and across domains, and how they conceptualize larger structures of elements, such as categories.

In our study, for example, we looked at children's understanding of the biological world. The task allowed us to judge to what extent children of different cultures and at different ages use a concept of biological affinity in their reasoning. This was the fact for all children except our youngest group of urban children, who obviously lacked the necessary knowledge. Another question we were able to address in this research explored the extent to which children see human beings as just another animal, or whether they give humans a special position within the system of living kinds. For example, if children were more likely to project from humans to animals than from animals to humans or if they would not project at all from and to humans, we would have a strong indication that they, indeed, separate humans from other animals. Among our three study populations—Menominee Native American, rural Majority Culture, and urban Majority Culture children—we find all three possibilities. Menominee children project just as much from humans to animals as from animals to humans, rural Majority Culture children do not project either from humans or to humans, and urban Majority Culture kids project from humans but not to humans (Ross et al., 2003).

Further analysis can include the extent to which projections are based on similarity (comparing with data from other tasks) or to what extent violations of similarities occur (Carey, 1985). Handling five or six bases and 15 to 20 targets allows for a good sample, but requires about 1 hour per interview (with adults). The task is straightforward, but one shouldn't expect too many justifications. It can be used to test certain hypotheses developed from other tasks. For example, individuals should be more likely to project properties between members of the same category than across categories. When this happens, we can assume that these categories are indeed important for human reasoning strategies.

The lack of justifications, however, introduces a possible problem for this task because the reasoning behind identical answers might differ across informants. Several reasons could lead a person to think that two items share a certain property. Take an example from folk biology: Two animals might share a certain property because they are both members of a certain category (biological affinity) or because they are connected by ecological relations (e.g., a bee stinging a bear and thereby transmitting certain properties). This problem illustrates an earlier point. Experimental research is not fast-track research that replaces long-term fieldwork. On the other hand, tasks like the one just described often share some aspects with other tasks. For example, the question of whether individuals view humans as different from other animals was addressed in our research both with the help of the just-described property projection task and in the free listing of "living things." If the results of both tasks point in the same direction, we have reason to assume that the data in fact represent a meaningful result. These kinds of interactions between different tasks are the real strength of any experimental approach in psychology and anthropology.

Category-Based Reasoning

Another important task that has proven to be rewarding in cognitive research, targets more directly the question of category-based reasoning strategies (Osherson et al., 1990). The question targeted here is whether we use specific elements and strategies for inductions about a category.

This can be important when deciding whether a given group of items (e.g., one elicited with a triad task) represents a category that instructs our thinking, or whether it is only a loose compound of items within a larger category based on general similarity.

Again, an example might help illustrating this point. In a study of Lacandon plant taxonomy, I applied a triad experiment to explore the different groups of plants (life forms) as perceived by my informants. Most of the groups found were also linguistically encoded categories (overt categories), such as trees, grasses, and vines. The task also revealed that the palms formed a group of their own. There is no Lacandon word for palm, however, which might tempt the researcher to assume that the palms form a covert category (linguistically unmarked). Nevertheless, the results of a triad task depend in part on the items chosen in the first place. Hence, the palm-compound could be an artifact of the selection of trees to which they were compared, and to their internal similarity as a special group of trees rather than a separate category of palms.

One way to test this is to use a projection task. One could provide trees and palms as base items and different trees and palms as targets. If both groups were seen as different from each other, one would expect the patterns of projections to differ accordingly.

A more direct way of exploring this question is to explore the informants' judgments of predictions that confirm or contradict the hypothesis that trees and palms indeed form different categories. This task usually takes the following form: Item A is introduced, and the informant is told that the item has property X. The property should be unrelated to any property the informant might know. Two more items (B and C) are introduced, and the informant is asked whether it is more likely that item B or item C also has property X.

Suppose now that A and B are palms and C a tree, or in another instance C is a palm and A and B are trees. This task allows us to see if the informants consistently choose either palms or trees as (exclusively) sharing certain properties. If this is the case, we have strong evidence that the informants indeed separate trees and palms into different categories. (Note that in an ideal scenario one would control for similarity effects.)

Once the categories are known, we can apply the same task to see if certain features, such as typicality ratings of category members, have an impact on our reasoning processes. Here, for example, we can select both an element rated as typical and one rated atypical in a category and compare their power for inductive reasoning instead of posing trees against palms. This proved to be the case for both the Itza' Maya of Guatemala and U.S. Americans for the category bird. For the Itza' Maya, the turkey (high rating for being a true bird) has more inductive power for the category bird than the sparrow does. When Itza' Maya were told that turkeys have a certain property, they were much more likely to project this property onto all birds than when told that sparrows have that property. The opposite is true of U.S. Americans. Here, sparrow not only receives a much higher rating for being a true bird, but also serves as a better inductive base to the category bird (Atran, 1999, p. 175; Rosch, 1975). Both groups then seem to apply the same basic strategy, but based on different underlying concepts of true or typical.

Another reasoning strategy that can be tested within this paradigm is the question, "Which two (or more) elements serve as a better base for induction into the category?" Instead of looking at individual measures (e.g., typicality), one intends to explore to what extent the coverage of a category as provided by the two elements predicts inductive power. For example, informants could be asked if it is more likely that all mammals have a certain property if dolphins and bears have that property or if tigers and lions have that property. Here, the idea is to see if coverage (base items being very different from each other, and, therefore, covering a large part of the category; dolphin: bear) predicts the inductive power of an argument (see López et al., 1997).

All these tasks are highly flexible in their application, and analyses are straightforward. The kinds of questions and their specific wording, however, are crucial.

So far, I have described methods to test the existence and the use of categories for processes of induction. However, if we know the categories already, we can use the methodology to acquire information about specific properties. This might have happened by chance in the scenarios described by López et al. (1997). Here, the researchers used unknown diseases as properties. In their paper, the authors claim that Itza' Maya use ecological reasoning strategies rather than a diversity principle (based on a taxonomy) to reason about how animals share a given disease. However, it is not clear to what extent Itza' Maya reasoned about the animals in the task rather than the diseases (the property). In this particular case, the authors had to choose a property that was not known to the informants but still something they could relate to, otherwise the Itza' Maya would refuse to participate. This is an important limitation on all methods that introduce unknown properties. Still, once controlled, we can use the tool to elicit the underlying models people attribute to some properties—such as disease.

Interested readers might consult the excellent review article by Osherson et al. (1990). The methods described are innovative from an anthropologist's perspective and allow for an in-depth understanding of some of the underlying characteristics of the elements, categories, and domains studied. They are flexible and can be applied in a variety of settings. They put a relatively high demand on the informants, however, because the informants are forced to reason about unreal properties. Still, findings so far seem to be rather stable across different tasks and populations.

In this chapter, I have presented different methods or research designs for exploring the elements of a domain, as well as the domain's underlying structure as perceived by the informants. These methods are just a sample of the possibilities, and their final applicability has to be determined within each field setting. As discussed in Antweiler (1993), these methods have to be adjusted to particular research questions and to the people we are studying. While some tasks can be administered verbally, others cannot; this could pose some serious restrictions, especially with respect to the populations often studied by anthropologists.

Some of these tasks might not be appropriate for use in certain cultural or social settings. This might force the researcher to abandon certain methods or, even worse, it might lead to an unnoticed distortion of the data. Alternative methods are usually available, however, so eliminating formal approaches does not seem to be justified. These alternative methods are also necessary to replicate our findings and to test their validity, which makes them important tools for confirming or rejecting hypotheses.

From the discussion so far, it should be clear that formal approaches are important tools for anthropologists. Their importance becomes even more salient when we look at the possibility of combining different methodologies. This not only allows us to replicate our findings, but also to connect different tasks and ask different questions. This often extends an individual tool's usefulness and results in new insights. Kelly (1955) did this when he developed the *repertory grid technique* (as described in Antweiler, 1993). The procedure combines an innovative form of free listing of opposition pairs using stimuli cards; the pairs are then used as attributes in a rating task. In this example, the free-listing technique is an essential point of departure for the other tasks.

When using these approaches, we must always be careful not to guide our informants with leading tasks or questions or with a priori assumptions that might be unnoticed in the research design.

The three most frequent sources of errors—and probably the most delicate issues—are (a) the selection of elements to be studied, (b) the selection of questions to be asked (including implicit meanings, translation problems, etc.), and (c) the coding applied to responses if coding is used. All three allow for ample opportunities to introduce (unnoticed) the researcher's preferences and values.

Especially when selecting and translating questions, and also when coding, it is advisable to take the time for independent individuals to check each step—translate and back-translate each question, for example—and code each response independently. Once the data are gathered and the coding is done, there is usually no way to detect errors that occurred prior to the analysis. As returning to the original data (or even to the field) might prove to be impossible or at least very costly in both time and money, spending some extra time at the beginning and during the data-gathering process is worth the effort.

All this has some repercussions on how we present our written results. With these methods, we are not only able to present our data and interpretations of the topic, but we also can provide our readers with an exact description of the methods used, the informants chosen, especially how and why we chose them, and the results. This separation allows replication and makes room for productive criticisms and discussions that can eventually lead to improvements in the quest to understand human cognition, culture, and behavior.

Before turning to the next chapter, on data analysis, I want to outline some possibilities for how these methods can be connected with methodologies from other fields. It is the formality of the approaches that allows for these connections.

Cognition and Observational Studies

Cognitive data elicited with the above methods can provide us with important insights into how people think about certain issues and how they reason within certain domains. Often, however, these data leave us with two problems: (a) do the data represent simply an observed reality (as opposed to a mental construct)? And (b) to what extent does the way people think about certain issues influence their behavior (this is often assumed rather than shown).

For example, if we are interested in how individuals or a group of individuals organize living things taxonomically (Atran, 1999; Berlin, 1992; López et al., 1997), it might be important to compare the extent to which these taxonomical orderings correlate not only with one another, but also with the scientific taxonomy. In the latter case, we might infer with Brent Berlin (1992) that people judge these relations on the basis of overall similarities (see López et al., 1997, for a more detailed version of this hypothesis).

Other approaches might make it necessary to learn more about the actors involved to understand some of the differences encountered. This approach was taken in my study among the Lacandon Maya of Mexico (Ross, 2001). The formal approach allowed me to correlate individual responses with the following:

personal attributes (e.g., age)

the number of plants each person planted in his agricultural plot

the distance of each household's location from the village center

the distance of each person's household from that person's agricultural fields

These analyses provided a rich set of data that allowed a thorough understanding of the ongoing changes in the village. They showed that older individuals lived farther away from the village center and closer to their agricultural fields, in which they planted significantly more crops. They also held much more complex models about the forest ecology than younger Lacandon adults, in terms of both the number of relationships reported and of the structure in which these relationships were ordered.

A somewhat different approach was taken in our work in the Petén, Guatemala (Atran et al., 1999, 2002). One of the focal points targeted the role of individual plant and animal species and their role in forest ecology. Two tasks exploring the relationships between the forest species allowed us to calculate an index of ecological importance for each species according to the cultural model of each of the three populations studied (native Itza' Maya and two migrant groups).

The Itza' Mayas' list of ecologically important plants, calculated from the task, correlated highly with the species that the members of this group reported, protecting the most because of their value. The format of the data allowed us to correlate these data with data from an actual tree count conducted in the forest plots of the community (random samples of the plots were taken). The finding was quite striking: If we controlled for fast-growing or weed trees, the ecological importance and the protection index predicted the frequency with which a certain species was encountered in these plots. This indicates that the Itza' Maya model of ecologically important species predicted the Itza' Mayas' attitude toward these trees, which were found more frequently in their plots than the less important ones.

The opposite was the case for one of the migrant groups: The most valuable trees were the ones that were most damaged by the members of the group, according to both actual tree counts and individual reports. Furthermore, we asked each individual to rank-order a set of trees based on (a) how important each tree is to EGO, (b) how important each tree is to God, and (c) how important each tree is to the forest spirits, a concept known to all three groups. The rankings for God and the forest spirits were introduced first, to understand the role of both in the resource management and second, to provide the informants with the opportunity to value these species in an additional dimension, different from their utility value. Obviously, utility value (construction wood, fire wood, medicine, etc.) dominated the rankings for both EGO and God. Because God is seen as looking after the humans He created, He places a higher value on the species that serve human beings. For both migrant groups, forest spirits had the same rank order as EGO and God. For the Itza' Maya, and only for them, rank-ordering by forest spirits was predicted best by the ecological importance of a plant (as calculated from the previous task). This indicates that ecological importance plays an important role in how Itza' Maya think about living things and how the Itza' Maya act upon the environment (Atran et al., 2002).

Because of the formal approaches in these studies, observational and experimental data could be connected with each other to provide new insights that otherwise would have remained hidden. Because the informants were selected randomly and a strong consensus was found (see Chapter 5), it was not necessary in the second study to use the same individuals for the experimental task and the observational study. This can be an important feature in certain field settings.

Social Network Analysis and Informant Agreement

I have mentioned the two perspectives on data analysis that can be applied to the data elicited by the methods described above:

a focus on the content of emerging cultural models, and

a focus on the distribution of agreement patterns among the members of a culture or cross-culturally

This possibility opens some important new fields in anthropological theory (see Chapter 2). I call this shift toward the exploration of informant agreement a paradigm shift within cognitive anthropology and the cognitive sciences in general.

The analysis of informant agreement allows us to tackle two major problems:

To what extent are certain aspects of knowledge shared among the members of a group?

How can we explain the emerging agreement pattern?

Both points are important if we want to study the processes that lead to shared cultural knowledge, the underlying processes of knowledge acquisition and transmission, and the maintenance and loss of knowledge in different domains.

Not much work has been done in this field, and I won't be able to describe the whole array of possibilities.

The Network Perspective

In a sense, the social network perspective was introduced into anthropology by Radcliffe-Brown's (1940, 1952) concept of social structure. This perspective conceives of the individual as embedded in repeated relationships that create and maintain a certain pattern of organization: the social structure (Schweizer, 1996a, p. 14; Wasserman & Faust, 1994, p. 3). These relationships include systems of friendship (Ross, 2001, 2002a, 2002b); reciprocal exchange of gifts, as done among the !Kung (Schweizer, 1996b); or any other type of repeated interaction, whether direct or indirect, among individuals.

For example, institutions can play an important role in connecting people in voluntary or nonvoluntary ways (Schweizer, 1996b). A school might provide nonvoluntary connections among students that can be further differentiated by voluntary connections, such as friendship circles. These different kinds of relationships can lead to different types of social networks among individuals.

Much more could be said about this perspective[7]; however, for the purpose of this chapter, the important point is that at its heart lies the identification of clusters of individuals or items that are in repeated exchange (relationships) with one another. In this perspective, the unit of analysis shifts from the individual to a collection of individuals and their linkages among one another (Wasserman & Faust, 1994, p. 5).

If we combine the perspective of patterns of social interaction and relationships with the paradigm of patterned informant agreement, we have a whole array of research questions ahead of us. *How are certain kinds of information transmitted? Are individuals who agree highly with each other more closely connected with one another than with individuals they agree less with? How (if at all) does social interaction translate into an agreement pattern? And finally, How does the density of a network interact with the formation of strong versus weak agreement?*

With the help of powerful PCs it is now feasible to address these questions, and others yet to be asked, in actual research projects. It is obvious that their answers are of great importance in the study of culture and cognition.

Boster (1986b) identified kinship relationships as an important source of information among Aguaruna manioc planters in Peru. Coleman, Katz, and Mentzel (1957) studied the diffusion and adoption of innovations, a topic also targeted by Rogers (1979). Research in Guatemala (Atran et al., 1999, 2002) suggests that friendship and social interactions can serve as possible information channels even across different cultures. And finally, data show similar changes in interaction pattern (social activity) and environmental cognition among the members of the two adult generations among the Lacandon Maya (Ross, 2002a).

These studies and more that could be named (see Wasserman & Faust, 1994, p. 6, for a small collection) target a better understanding of the relationship of social interaction and the formation of agreement among individuals. Within this field of inquiry, a network approach can serve to identify and explore

the internal structure of groups of individuals who

agree with one another (actor attributes) and

the overall structures that lead to these groups (network structure)

In a sense, these questions look at the general problem of knowledge transmission and acquisition, and, hence, the respective methods should form an essential part of the tool kit of any cognitive scientist.

Social Network Concepts and Eliciting Methods

Wasserman and Faust (1994) and Schweizer (1996a) both provide extensive overviews and descriptions of the different concepts and methods in the field of network analysis. My intention is not to explain particular methods in detail, but to draw attention to certain possibilities that are opened up if network analysis is included in our research.

Wasserman and Faust (1994, pp. 35-40) define three different modes of networks:

One-mode networks that explore the relationships of one set of actors with one another (e.g., the interactions of a set of friends)

Two-mode networks that explore the relationships between the actors of two sets (e.g., gift exchange between members of two families—not within one family)

Two-mode networks that describe the relationships of one set of actors with one set of events (e.g., individuals attending the same school)

We can elicit three different kinds of data with a network approach:

Relational data: these data tell us about the kinds and frequencies of relations of a given pair of individuals.

Structural data: while the relational data focus on the individual actor, structural data are concerned with the overall structure of the network. For example, how many relationships exist (density)?

Actor attributes: data referring to the individual actors, such as gender, age, occupation, and more (Wasserman & Faust, 1994, p. 29)

All three kinds of data can be of interest in cognitive research to explore the distribution and emergence of patterns of agreement.

To explore relational data, one can ask which kinds of network relations best predict the identified agreement pattern. A possible analysis could look at the correlation between informant agreement and network distance of the individuals involved, because individuals who are closer to each other in the network might agree more with one another.

Obviously, not all relationships are equally likely to produce informant agreement in a given domain. Therefore, the selection of what *kinds of networks* we explore depends on the general research question. It is important to have clear rationales for the kinds of networks selected in the study, because if we test a large number of different networks, we might expect at least one to "predict" the agreement pattern simply by chance.

In the Petén study (Atran et al., 1999, 2002), we looked at friendship relations as a possible predictor of the agreement we found for environmental cognition within populations. No correlation was found, but this does not necessarily mean that this kind of information is not shared and transmitted within friendship circles. It could simply mean that our tools were not powerful enough or that other kinds of relations and different modes of learning interfere with such a direct approach. Our expertise networks, however, were able to predict agreement patterns across cultures. Migrant individuals who mentioned native Maya as forest experts agreed significantly more with the Itza' Maya model than did their peers who didn't mention native Maya experts.

Structural data can help us identify subgroups of a given population that agree more strongly with one another than with the members of other subgroups. The general approach in this analysis is similar to the one taken above, but instead of looking at direct agreement patterns, we compare two or more subgroups of agreement with each other. However, this approach bears some dangers of misinterpretation. In a study of Lacandon Maya, a network task looking at friendship relationships showed two components (unrelated subgroups; Wasserman & Faust, 1994, pp. 109-110) that suggested that men and women almost never interact with each other outside the household (Ross, 2001). Women and men also differed significantly on their environmental knowledge. Explaining these differences as a consequence of the different network relations would be misleading, because women have much less experience with the forest. Still, it could be interesting to explore the data further to determine whether women who are related to forest experts (identified independently) might show a greater knowledge than women who are not.

Finally, we can collect data on informant attributes—information about the informants themselves. In the study of Lacandon environmental cognition a second network task was applied, asking each individual to name seven forest experts. These data helped to establish my prior findings on group differences in environmental cognition as a difference in expertise recognized by the community members themselves. The findings allowed understanding these differences as an expression of the ongoing cultural change, connecting changes in social interactions to changes in environmental cognition.

In all the network approaches cited, individuals were asked to name other individuals related to them. The resulting networks are called EGO-centered networks (Wasserman & Faust, 1994, p. 41) because they have several EGOs as their point of departure. If all individuals have an equal chance of appearing in these listings, we can combine the data to reveal a network that can be analyzed on the different features described above (Wasserman & Faust, 1994, p. 42). These kinds of network data are probably the most suitable for anthropologists, although network data can also be acquired in observational studies (who interacts with whom) or other types of network experiments (see Wasserman & Faust, 1994, and Schweizer, 1996a, on this point). For all these tasks, it is important to understand that (a) network data can be based on different attributes, such as friendship, work relationship, exchange of goods, and (b) that there is no limit on the types of interactions, such as by phone, over the Internet, or in-person communication. These decisions depend entirely on the objectives of the individual research project.

One of the basic assumptions that drives combining a network approach with research on informant agreement is that consistent and frequent contact among individuals should lead to stronger cohesion among the individuals (Schweizer, 1996a, p. 116). This cohesion might lead to a stronger agreement between the involved individuals because of fast and repeated information exchange. Because this chapter is not intended to replace the books on concepts and methods in network analysis, I will conclude by mentioning only some of the features that might be important for improving our understanding of the distributions of individual cognitions:

Network Position. The calculation of *individual distances within a social network* can be explored with respect to specific patterns of agreement among the informants. This, however, might prove to be too idealistic. Further studies should be done with respect to *different subgroups* within the network as was described. The *centrality* of certain actors might also play a crucial role. For example, in the study in the Petén, the researchers tried to locate the forest experts in each group within the friendship network for each community. If experts are the central players in the social network, then information might be readily available to all the members of the network, which leads to a higher consensus. In one of the migrant communities we studied in Guatemala (Atran et al., 1999, 2002) all the named forest experts were located outside the friendship network (members of the government, of NGOs, etc.). Is it surprising that essential knowledge is not readily available in this community? Proximity to an expert (or several of them) might also lead to increased competence with respect to the cultural model, which can also be tested with the above-described methods (see also Chapter 5).

Network Density and Components. Besides individuals' positions in the network, we can also look at a more abstract level. To what extent does a dense network, one with many relationships among the individuals, ensure a strong consensus, improving the flow of information (repetition, etc.) and increasing general agreement? To what extent are different components (not connected subgroups) responsible for certain patterns of informant agreement due to a lack of exchange of information?

Many of these points are rather speculative. However, my aim is to stimulate research in this direction by describing some basic methods and outlining some possibilities for research projects.

Some results are available that describe a relationship between pattern of social network relations and the patterned distribution of human cognition. However, to pursue these tasks we need sound methods that guide the collection and analysis of our data. I explore the analysis of data in the next chapter.

It was the purpose of this chapter to describe a set of formal methods that will help to understand human cognition in the context of culture. From the preceding chapters, it should be clear that these methods are not meant to replace more qualitative approaches. On the contrary, both approaches are needed to reinforce one another, to elaborate hypotheses that can then be confirmed or rejected with the help of independent methods. Also, these formal approaches allow us to arrive at a finer understanding of our data and the specific cognitive processes and strategies used by our informants. It is a mistake to judge these methods based on their design. Although these tasks are very formal, they still provide the informant with ample space to respond to the questions. For example, applying a triad task (comparing animals and plants) with Lacandon Maya children, I was able to collect Lacandon Maya mythology and oral history that they used in their justifications. Just as in more informal talks, we still have to provide our informants with stimuli to talk to us. It is the kinds of stimuli chosen—for both formal and informal methods—that make our efforts successful or not. Still, I hope that the elaborations in this chapter illustrated the importance of integrating formal approaches in anthropology.

Notes

1. Note, however, that psychology still continues to "randomly" select most of their subjects among college students at major research institutions. Given that the data are most often used to make universal claims, it strikes one as rather odd to call these samples "random" (see Medin et al., 2002).

2. See Bernard (1995, p. 51ff) for a more detailed discussion of research designs, problems of validity, and confounds.

3. Ross et al. (2003) suggest a further strategy; the triangulation of three populations, each possible pair overlapping on certain features but not others (see Chapter 2 for further discussion).

4. It is not an accident that many cultural groups name themselves the *true or autochthonous* people.

5. In some stories, the bat transforms from a bird to a mouse and back.

6. After an informant declined to answer, the respective triad was put aside to be asked again at a later point in the interview.

7. The two most important introductory works are Wasserman and Faust (1994) and Schweizer (1996a). Schweizer is shorter and presents a reduced set of methods in a more accessible way (for German readers), while Wasserman and Faust describe the various methods in much more detail.

5

Patterns of Informant Agreement

Some Analytical Implications

This chapter deals predominantly with the possibilities and problems of data analysis for the data-gathering methods described earlier. Formal methods are but one type of instrument in any successful anthropological endeavor. Due to their central role in any scientific research and cognitive research in particular, however, I concentrate on these kinds of data (see, e.g., Bernard, 1995; Holstein & Gubrium, 1995). This is not to say that more informal types of inquiry are irrelevant; this was discussed in previous chapters.

Although informal methods are important, it is the formal approach that allows us more detailed observations, tests our intuitions, and elaborates on connected data sets, as described at the end of the preceding chapter. Given that any two groups differ on an infinite number of traits, cultural research has to be guided by theory and a good hypothesis is needed to start exploring cultural differences and their effects (see Ross, Medin, Coley, & Atran, 2003; van de Vijver & Leung, 1980, pp. 260-261). While it is the informal approaches that often lead us to formulate theories and hypotheses, we need formal research to confirm or reject these hypotheses.

For both data analysis and research design, social scientists depend increasingly on sophisticated software packages for their PCs (e.g., ANTHROPAC). In principle, there is nothing wrong with these programs; they can be useful and help to save time (Antweiler, 1993, p. 282). Unfortunately, they often come with an implicit illusion of clean methods that are universally and mechanistically applicable, blinding us to the intricacies of data collection and analysis. Thus, we often ignore important decisions. This problem is not inherent in these programs, but their accessibility and user friendliness often blinds us to less obvious possibilities. Also, different types of data require different treatments, which is often overlooked.

Obviously, the objective of this chapter is not to provide a complete guide to data analysis, nor do I claim that the methods of data analysis presented are applicable in all instances of research. The assumption of such universal methods themselves—often the case in cross-cultural psychology—is contrary to the purpose of this book. Rather, the intention of this chapter is to provide detailed enough descriptions of different methods and approaches to data analysis to explore their limits and possibilities and to encourage (and force) the researcher to search for further options and possibilities.

Although all research should finally aim at revealing patterns in the structure of our data (e.g., a content analysis), this part of the analysis is not the focus of this chapter. This is for three reasons.

First, depending on the data gathered, there are a multitude of different analyses that can be useful. Because problems often occur in the details of a research design, no adequate overview could possibly be given. Just to briefly note, methods can range from simple one-way ANOVAs, correlations, and frequency lists to correspondence analysis. This, however, is the easy part. To apply these procedures often requires previous preparation of the data. These preparations are essential and bear on the kinds of analyses that can be applied and, again, vary from case to case.

Second, many books and articles on the topic are available (e.g., Bernard, 1995; Hartwig & Dearing, 1979; Lewis-Beck, 1980; Weller & Romney, 1988, 1990), and ideally each research article includes a section on data preparation and analysis.

Third, the content of our data can often not be understood without taking into account its distribution, or parts of it, within and across the populations we are studying. Unfortunately, this aspect often receives little attention in research (see Chapters 1, 2, and 3 on this issue). Yet it is essential in order to (a) understand our findings and (b) elaborate our theories in both cross-cultural and cultural research (see Chapters 4 and 6). Suppose, for example, that the mean group response on a given task is 0.5 (on a range of possible answers from 0 to 1). In the extreme case, this could mean that half of the individuals responded 1.0 and the other half 0.0. Obviously, in this case the mean is not an adequate way of describing the group's response. Rather, the group's response should have been described as two different response patterns within one group, which would allow for further analyses of differences between the members of the two subgroups. Later in this chapter, I will describe an analytical tool that allows a closer look at group responses with respect to their agreement pattern.

The preceding chapter should have made it clear that all formal methods of data gathering have to be adapted to each individual research context. This means that changes of design are frequently needed to provide the best possible results. However, to create a meaningful research design, one needs to consider *what type of data* can be subjected to *what kind of analysis*, producing *what kind of results*.

Nevertheless, rather than assuming statistical methods to be the center-piece of data analysis, I view them as basic tools that allow us to confirm, reject, or verify certain trends found in the data and to test the extent to which observed trends are significant beyond chance. After all, once we rule out the existence of subgroups, the mean still is the best descriptor of a group's response pattern.

Statistical analysis can also be used as an *exploratory tool* that helps to detect any structure in the data by making the pattern more visible to the researcher. Both types of analyses are different in their approach and their results. Again, the already cited literature and statistic handbooks give insight into all kind of methods (e.g., MDS, cluster analysis, etc.).

Most of anthropological research and research in cognition has so far concentrated on the question of knowledge content. This is, for example, the case in the truly groundbreaking study by Berlin, Breedlove, and Raven (1973, 1974) on Tzeltal Maya plant taxonomy. The authors astonished many readers with their documented richness of traditional folk-biological knowledge among this highland Maya group in Chiapas. However, this astonishment led some readers to wonder 30 years later whether, for example, every single individual in the group shared all of the knowledge represented in these studies. Obviously, this question has some serious implications for our theories of culture, cultural processes, and cognition (see discussion in Chapter 3).

Consider the design of a cross-cultural study. Data are aggregated across the subjects of each group to successively compare the two emerging cultural models and naïve theories. In complex data sets this might pose a problem, for we often do not know the extent to which the informants of each group agree with one another more than with members of the other group. This is important because it tells us whether we are actually allowed to aggregate (average) across the individuals of the groups and if we can indeed compare the two groups as separate entities. This has strong repercussions for our interpretations of the findings. Imagine a gender split, dividing our informants into two different sets of responses that go unrecognized. These differences are ignored in the aggregation of the data, which, as a consequence, might result in an erroneous cultural model. The consequence is a skewed cross-cultural comparison. The study by Choy and Nisbett (2000), for example, lacks this attention to within-group differences and general within-group agreement. This does not necessarily mean that their results are wrong, but unless we analyze these kinds of differences, we simply do not know. As discussed in more detail in Chapter 6, the authors did not explore or even describe the gender differences within their sets (or any other attribute of the informants), nor did they inform us about other differences within their samples. As a result, readers are left on their own when it comes to interpretation of the authors' findings.

In a similar vein, the study of agreement pattern can shed some light on cultural processes, such as the emergence of cultural knowledge (Boster, 1986a) or cultural change (Ross, 2001, 2002a, 2002b). In the latter study, informant-agreement was calculated across different tasks that sometimes involved more than 400 questions. No informal approach is able to detect or even keep track of differences and similarities in the response pattern for such a database.

Rather than just assuming that certain features or types of knowledge are shared across and within cultures, an analysis of informant agreement allows us actually to explore the distribution of cognitions not only across but also within cultural groups.

This means that we have to establish whether the members of a group under investigation—our informants—agree strongly enough with one another for us to assume a common cultural model that will allow ascribing meaningful content to the model. A statistical model (Romney, Weller, & Batchelder, 1986; described below in "Cultural Consensus and Informant Agreement") is available that allows us to test for levels of agreement among a set of informants. This model allows us to determine whether we are justified in aggregating the responses of our informants (i.e., whether they share a common model). Furthermore, this model provides us with a tool to assess the existence of subgroups that differ in some aspects of their responses.

By now, it should be clear that the analysis of an agreement pattern among our informants also has important implications for the analysis of content. The distribution of knowledge helps us to understand the social dimensions, as well as the content of the knowledge under study. This is best illustrated in case studies that target the distributions of cognitions, such as the studies conducted by Garro (1986, 2000) and Ross (2001, 2002a). In each of these, the emerging pattern of distribution led to different interpretations of the content analysis. Garro, for example, examined the existence of a cultural model of disease in a Tarascan village in Mexico and found the existence of a general cultural knowledge that is further developed by the specialists (here, village curers). Curers and noncurers seemed to share the same general model; however, the curers proved more knowledgeable in the domain. Her formal approach allowed her to decide between competing hypotheses:

Curers and noncurers have different models of disease.

Members of one group share a model that is not shared by the members of the other group.

Both groups share the same models and have about the same knowledge.

Finally, both groups share a model with one group possessing a more elaborated version of it (Garro's final finding).

Obviously, the different hypotheses have different implications for social theory and even application, as they tell us very different stories with respect to the distribution of folk-medical knowledge in this particular community. Thus, learning about these distributions is a necessary tool for understanding the construction of meaning from individual cognitions. In this view, culture is no longer treated as a quasi-objective set of meanings, rules, and norms that somehow affect human beings (see Chapter 3 on this topic). On the contrary, culture is treated as an emergent product located in individual cognitions. Viewed like this, culture consists of shared patterns of knowing and of seeing things, the emergence of which—along with its effects—can and must be the subject of further studies in both cross-cultural and cultural approaches (see Chapter 2).

To summarize briefly: The analysis of agreement pattern is important for two reasons: (a) Unless we know we are dealing with a cultural (shared) model among our informants, we cannot know whether we are justified in aggregating our informants' responses into a single model for further analysis. (b) A well-developed analysis of agreement pattern has an important bearing on the interpretation of our findings, because it allows us to formulate more accurate research designs in both cross-cultural comparisons and cultural studies. It is for these reasons that I focus in this chapter on the exploration and analysis of informant agreement.

Informant Agreement/Disagreement

The Basic Analysis

Any analysis of informant agreement also necessarily explores the disagreement between the informants. One cannot be detected or identified without the other. Because complete agreement is limited to few domains and informants, we find complex patterns of informant agreement/disagreement in our data, the understanding of which depends on our methods of data gathering and analysis. (Often we might not detect patterns, but might be confronted with a random distribution or a distribution that cannot be explained, or detected, with the methods applied.)

Most of the methods described in Chapter 4 provide us with numerical values or with data that can easily be transformed into numerical values. Transforming nonnumerical data into numerical data (coding) often requires additional work, such as applying a previously elaborated coding system or post hoc coding by "blind" coders. Blind coders are individuals who have no knowledge of the theories and hypotheses guiding the research. Coding is a tricky issue, especially in borderline cases where researchers have to decide which coding best fits the response. Having several blind coders normally provides the best protection against unconscious biases. I will not elaborate on this problem further, except to remind readers to take coding seriously and to pay attention to the differences that occur with different ways of coding the data.[1]

Tasks such as free listing, individual rankings, and scaled judgments may often be compared directly across populations with the application of statistical procedures like ANOVAs or t tests. In many instances, however, we must compare individual's responses across a series of questions rather than one at a time. This is especially important if we are interested in describing group response patterns.

Consider a list of 50 statements that elicit "true" or "false" responses from 20 informants. We could code the responses as 1/0 and compare each trial individually across each pair of informants. This is rather time-consuming and would yield little insight into the underlying structure of a response pattern. To explore a response pattern, it is more informative to compare all informants on all their responses. This is not only more informative, but allows avoiding serious misjudgments about our data. Again, take the list of 50 statements as an example. Suppose that for each statement 70% of the informants reach consensus—that is, agree on their response. If the answers conform with our hypotheses, we might take this as evidence in favor of our theory. This might well be true if the remaining 30% are randomly distributed across the informants. However, what happens if these 30% constitute a subgroup of 30% of the informants who usually disagree with the majority? It is here that our theory gets into trouble as it seems to hold for only one group of the informants, while the opposite seems to be the case for a second group of informants. Obviously, in these cases analyzing agreement across informants and responses provides us with a much more detailed understanding of our data.

Table 5.1   Informant-by-Response Matrix

	Inf 1	Inf 2	Inf 3	Inf 4	Inf 5
Quest 1	1	1	1	1	1
Quest 2	0	1	0	0	0
Quest 3	1	1	0	1	0
Quest 4	1	1	0	0	0
Quest 5	0	1	0	0	1
Quest 6	1	0	0	1	0

The first step in analyzing agreement is to create an informant-by-response matrix, with the columns representing the informants and the rows representing the responses—in this case, 50. In this matrix, each cell represents an individual informant's response (column) to a given question (row). Table 5.1 illustrates this kind of matrix with five informants and six questions.

In Table 5.1, Question 1 represents each individual's (Inf1–Inf5) judgment of whether the respective statement is false or true (in this illustration, all informants judged it to be true, "1"). Looking at all the questions, we can see that there are remarkable differences in the responses of the individual informants that could provide some important insights into the distribution of knowledge of the particular domain and, hence, knowledge about the domain itself. Obviously, this kind of analysis makes sense only if the questions are on a single domain and are related to one another.

To analyze the differences and similarities of the informants with respect to their individual responses, we can use this table to calculate the *raw agreement*, also called the *observed agreement*, between each pair of informants. The raw agreement is the ratio of agreed answers and total number of answers given. Calculating this (matched pair) agreement for all possible pairs of informants will result in an informant-by-informant matrix. Table 5.2 shows this matrix for our example.

The entries in Table 5.2 represent the average agreed-upon responses between two informants. Note that the matrix in this table is symmetrical because the agreement between informants 1 and 2 has to be the same as the agreement between informants 2 and 1. The main diagonal always has a value of 1 (or "." for missing data), representing the agreement of EGO with him- or herself. In this example, informants 1 and 2 agree in 50% of their responses. Informant 1 also agrees in 50% of the responses with informant 3, who agrees in 33% of the responses with informant 2. The final row (AVER) represents the average agreement of each informant with all the other informants.

Table 5.2   Informant-by-Informant Agreement Table

	Inf 1	Inf 2	Inf 3	Inf 4	Inf 5
Inf 1	1	0.5	0.5	0.83	0.33
Inf 2	0.5	1	0.33	0.33	0.5
Inf 3	0.5	0.33	1	0.67	0.83
Inf 4	0.83	0.33	0.67	1	0.5
Inf 5	0.33	0.5	0.83	0.5	1
Aver	0.63	0.53	0.67	0.67	0.63

These data show the first result of this procedure. Informants 3 and 4 have the highest across-informant agreement, meaning that they show the largest overlap with all the other informants. It is interesting to note that they do not show the highest agreement with one another. This suggests that both individuals share different subsets of responses with different informants. Again, one can easily imagine that insights like this would be hard to acquire in informal interviews, especially for a large number of informants and questions.

For example, in a study among Tzotzil Maya of Zinacantán I interviewed (supported by local assistants) 130 men and women of the community on several occasions (Ross & Medin, 2003). On another occasion, Atran et al. (1999, 2002) compared 36 informants from three different cultures on more than 800 questions. Obviously, an informal approach would not have been able to manage the amount of data reported in each interview, let alone across 36 informants!

An agreement calculation like this is straightforward, especially because the example has only binary responses (Yes/No) represented by "1" and "0," respectively. Binary responses are not necessary in agreement calculations, however. The method can also capture different kinds of answers. For example, Medin, Ross, Atran, Burnett, and Blok (2002), Medin, Ross, Atran, Cox, and Coley (2003), and Ross and Medin (2003) used this approach to calculate informant agreement between fish experts of two cultures with respect to their folk-ecological models about freshwater ecology. In one of the tasks, individuals were asked to report relationships between a series of pairs of fish species (see Chapter 4, "Eliciting Relationships Between the Elements," for a description of the technique). Coding included as many as 18 different relationships described by the informants. This means that different pairs of informants could agree on different responses for the same pair of species. Even if a number of different responses are included, a binary distinction between agreement and disagreement is made.

This means that this method is not sensitive to relative similarities in responses. This is important to keep in mind if the data are informants' ratings on a scale (see Chapter 4, "Rating Tasks"). Obviously, in these cases a binary calculation of agreement would be inappropriate, because it is exactly the different rates of similarity of the individuals' ratings that are important here. Consider three informants rating the importance of a specific fish species on a scale from 1 to 7, with responses of "1" for individual one, "4" for individual two, and "5" for individual three. The procedure just described would show the three individuals disagreeing equally with each other and ignore the fact that responses from individuals two and three are very similar. Two approaches are available that will result in an informant-by-informant matrix similar to the one shown in Table 5.2. Before describing them, however, it is important to note that in agreement calculations only the cells for which both informants give a response are counted. Again, this can lead to substantial errors. Suppose one informant responds to only 1 of the 10 questions and another responds to all 10 questions. If they agree on the single question they both answered, their raw agreement would be 1, indicating 100% agreement between the two informants. However, if both informants respond to all 10 questions and actually agree in 9 responses (disagreeing on 1), their raw agreement would be lower—0.9 or 90%. Obviously, constellations like this can create problems and have to be taken into account in each research setting.

One way to avoid these artificial results is to weight the actual agreement score between two informants by the number of cells used for the calculation, but eyeballing the data is often enough to ensure that the results are not due to such artifacts. Again, this can best be illustrated with an actual research example. In a study of plant names among two groups of Q'eqchi' Maya in the highlands of Guatemala, we guided individuals along a plant trail and asked them (individually) to name previously determined plants (Collins & Ross, n.d.). In a first analysis, we found a strong (negative) correlation between age and the number of plants for which a person didn't know a name. In a second step, we calculated informant agreement. In this procedure, we treated a not-known/not-provided name as a missing data point. At first, this seemed to make sense because our goal was to compare the actual knowledge of the individuals. This resulted, however, in the more difficult plants—those culturally less salient to our informants—being ignored in the calculations as agreement was calculated only for the species known by both individuals. This created a problem, because the people who identified the fewest plants also had the highest average agreement with all the other informants. Due to their higher average agreement, individuals identifying fewer plants were assigned higher competence scores (see "Cultural

Consensus and Informant Agreement," below) compared to informants who provided more names. This has two important drawbacks: First, higher average agreement with all the other informants can no longer serve as an indicator for higher cultural competence (knowledge of what's known in a group). Second, lacking an objective measure of cultural competence (with respect to the questions at hand) inhibits our weighting individuals' responses toward establishing the "cultural truth." This, however, was one of the ideas of this study. In order to identify the "culturally correct" names for these plants, we needed to weight individuals' responses based on their competence (e.g., give more weight to individuals who showed more knowledge in the naming task; see Romney et al., 1986, on this point). To be clear, we used this approach because for some species more than 10 different names were recorded across the different informants. It is highly unlikely that these names are all equally valid or salient in a community, which led us to ask *whether a "culturally true name" exists, what it is,* and *which individuals report this name.*

In order to avoid this problem, we conducted a second analysis, coding "don't know" as a case of disagreement. The rationale is simple: If person "A" does not know plant X, he or she cannot agree with any other informant with respect to this particular plant. With this coding scheme, the individuals with the least number of responses showed the lowest average agreement with all other informants. This solution is clearly not a fix-all, and it applies to only certain kinds of questions and data.

Our first analysis was not useless, but we have to know exactly what the data stand for. Two things can be gained from our first analysis: First, it reconfirmed an assumption of the cultural consensus model, namely that easily accessible knowledge is widely shared. After dropping the less well-known plants from the analysis, all individuals agreed strongly with one another, indicating that all individuals agree highly on the names of a small set of plants.[2] Second, in a way this first approach captured a type of consensus that was ignored in the second calculation method. For this group of informants, the culturally correct response—the one on which most informants agreed—for some of the plants might well be "I don't know." In this case, only a few people might have had access to more specific plant knowledge. Given the way plant knowledge is distributed in the United States, this is not at all unusual—as most of us probably would not be able to identify more than 10% of the plants surrounding us. This kind of approach allows us to overcome some of the traditional mistakes made in anthropology, where knowledge systems—assembled by the researcher by adding up individual responses into a coherent system—were often described as if they were completely known and shared across all members of a culture. In this specific case—as among U.S. adults—the default answer to naming certain specific plants might just as well be "I don't know." Of course, this is different from saying that the culture or the language does not provide a name for these plants, a fact that can be tested by a walk to whatever botanical garden. All individuals do not necessarily possess the complete knowledge, and only a minority of individuals might in fact share parts of the knowledge. Naturally, a finding like this opens the way for a whole new study: exploring the causal mechanisms underlying this kind of pattern of knowledge distribution.

In a sense, this brings us back to the problem of sampling, discussed in Chapter 4. In all our analyses we have to be very conscious of *who our informants are* and *which sector of their society they represent.*

The differences between the two sets of data analyses presented for the Q'eqchi' naming data illustrate some important points for data analysis in general.

Data analysis is usually not as straightforward as it might appear at first sight, and we need to put much more thought into it than is usually assumed. Second, the existence of alternative ways of analyzing data makes it imperative that our research, including the analysis, is guided by clear theories that allow us an informed choice of analysis methods. Third, a variety of different analyses often have to be conducted to best describe the content and distribution of our data.

Correlational Agreement Analysis

The correlational agreement analysis is one of the two options mentioned above that account for relative agreement (e.g., some responses being more similar to each other than others). In this approach, informants' responses are correlated over all the trials (all responses). This has the advantage that informants are compared with one another looking at their general response pattern (e.g., items with high vs. low ratings). However, in this approach, it's the agreement in the general response patterns rather than actual agreement in individual responses that is measured. This means that two informants can reach absolute agreement (correlation $r = 1$) without actually agreeing on a single response. Consider the rating series for three different informants shown in Table 5.3.

The correlation among all three informants' responses would be 1 (100% agreement) even though only informants 1 and 3 have given exactly the same responses. This can have some serious implications for the data analysis. Correlational analysis might often be the only choice, however, as is the case with the analysis of data on taxonomical orderings

Table 5.3   Informant Responses, With Full Agreement in the Response
Pattern

Inf 1	Inf 2	Inf 3
1	2	1
2	3	2
3	4	3
4	5	4
3	4	3
6	8	6

(see López et al., 1997) elicited in a pile-sorting task (see Chapter 4, "Pile Sorting: The Hierarchical Sorting of Elements").

At first glance, this might seem to be a huge drawback for this approach, but under certain circumstances it is a strength. Consider a rating task in which informants have to rate an object on a scale from 1 (not important) to 7 (very important). Can we easily assume that rating 5 means the same for all the informants? A correlational analysis of the informants' responses mediates this problem because it does not calculate direct agreement (two informants reporting "5"), but rather relative agreement (e.g., both rate item 4 one point higher than item 3). In other words, each individual rating is compared across all responses. It is, therefore, in the context of all responses that individuals are compared to each other. Again, consider the responses in Table 5.3. Here, informants 1 and 2 do not agree on a single response, but in the context of all their responses, they have very similar judgments with respect to the individual items. Each response has the same status relative to all others: Their first response is not only lower than all the other responses, but the difference from all the other responses is exactly the same. In this case, informant 2 might simply have a response bias toward higher numbers, although his overall appreciation of the questions (compared to each other) seems to be in essential agreement with the ratings reported by informants 1 and 3.

Tables 5.4 and 5.5 show a set of possible response patterns with the respective informant-by-informant agreement matrix.

Again, the resulting agreement table is symmetrical, with the main diagonal representing the agreement of an informant with him- or herself. Note that informants 1 and 2 agree 100% without actually agreeing on a single response. It is interesting to note that informants 2, 3, and 4 share 50% of their actual responses, yet this has no influence on the correlational agreement calculations.

Table 5.4   Informants' Responses

	Inf 1	Inf 2	Inf 3	Inf 4	Inf 5
Resp 1	1	2	3	2	1
Resp 2	2	3	4	4	3
Resp 3	3	4	4	6	2
Resp 4	4	5	5	5	4
Resp 5	2	3	3	3	6
Resp 6	5	6	2	8	4

Table 5.5   Agreement Table for Table 5.4, Calculated With Correlations

	Inf 1	Inf 2	Inf 3	Inf 4	Inf 5
Inf 1	1.00	1.00	−0.06	0.92	0.34
Inf 2	1.00	1.00	−0.06	0.92	0.34
Inf 3	−0.06	−0.06	1.00	−0.18	−0.11
Inf 4	0.92	0.92	−0.18	1.00	0.14
Inf 5	0.34	0.34	−0.11	0.14	1.00

Again, depending on the original data, this can be an advantage or a disadvantage. For the purposes of this book, however, this example should make one point clear: Not all methods of data analysis are suitable for all tasks, and one must decide which method to apply to which data, anticipating the different influences these methods might have on the results. Obviously, in order to anticipate the different influences we need to know the analyses techniques applied! This is not only important for conducting our own research, but also for evaluating the work of our peers.

If we want to distinguish exact matches from similarity measures without losing the strength of a similarity analysis, we have to apply a third analysis, which weights the individual agreement scores.

The Weighted Similarity Measure

Weighted similarities, like correlational agreement calculations, take relative agreement into account. The difference is that, in this approach, agreement is further weighted by the number of absolute matches. In the first step, we calculate the difference between the responses for each pair of informants across all items. As shown in Table 5.4, the differences between two informants' responses are the result of subtracting one informant's answers from the other's.

Table 5.6   Weighted Similarity

Inf 2	Inf 3	Difference
2	3	1
3	4	1
4	4	0
5	5	0
3	3	0
6	2	4
		Average: 1

The differences between informants 2 and 3 in Table 5.4 are shown in Table 5.6. Note that in this measure the difference is always calculated as the absolute value of the differences.

Depending on the task, a further weighting of the data could be introduced by differentiating the number of times an absolute agreement occurred. That is beyond the scope of this chapter, however, so I won't go into more detail.

The average value in row 7 represents the weighted agreement between the two informants, or rather the weighted difference between their responses. Rather than being a similarity measure, it is the inverse, an index of difference. If we calculate the agreement for all informants in Table 5.4, the average differences shown in Table 5.7 emerge.

Again, the matrix is symmetrical and entries show differences, not similarities, between the responses of two informants. To convert these data into similarity data comparable to the data obtained with the previous measures, we first have to reverse the value of each entry by multiplying it by –1. This converts all our data into similarity data with negative values. To convert the resulting matrix into one with positive entries ranging between 0 (no agreement) and 1 (absolute agreement), we first add the highest possible value a difference can take (maximum possible distance) and divide the resulting numbers by the same value. Doing this converts the maximum distance to 0, and the distance of 0 becomes a similarity of 1.

Let our initial distance measure be D; the maximum distance (average over individual maxima of all responses) between two informants Md; and the calculated similarity measure S. The following equation expresses the transformation described above:

$$[(D * -1) + Md] / Md = S$$

Let's assume that an informant's responses can range from 1 to 8 (highest possible rating is 8, lowest is 1). In that case, Md, the largest possible difference

Table 5.7   Average Difference Among Informants

	Inf1	Inf 2	Inf 3	Inf 4	Inf 5
Inf 1	0.00	1.00	1.67	1.83	1.17
Inf 2	1.00	0.00	1.00	0.83	1.50
Inf 3	1.67	1.00	0.00	1.50	1.83
Inf 4	1.83	0.83	1.50	0.00	2.33
Inf 5	1.17	1.50	1.83	2.33	0.00

is 7 (for each response as well as for the average). The conversion would lead to the similarity matrix shown in Table 5.8.

Not surprisingly, the resulting agreement matrix correlates highly ($r = 0.64$) with the agreement matrix based on correlation. The differences between the two matrices are due to the fact that they both evaluate individual differences differently.

Up to this point, we have seen three different approaches to calculating agreement between pairs of informants. More could be found and might be needed, depending on the particular tasks and questions asked. All three approaches have in common that they intend to establish an overall agreement between two informants on a set of given questions/tasks. In all three cases, the outcome is an informant-by-informant matrix that can tell us about the agreement (and, hence, disagreement) pattern between the individual informants. The ways this informant agreement is calculated are quite different from one approach to another, and it logically follows that they cannot simply be substituted for each other. In each case, we need to justify selecting a specific analysis. Still, the final product of all these measures is a similarity matrix describing the response pattern of our informants.

This is an important measure that can provide us with insights into the distribution of knowledge across informants. However, some further work and elaborations are needed.

Adjustment for Guessing

Suppose a task involves a question-answer frame technique where individuals are asked only to confirm or reject a set of statements. Given that the format has two choices, we would expect any pair of informants to agree in 50% of the cases just by chance. This is to say that if both informants randomly picked their responses (e.g., flipping a coin), they would still show relatively high agreement (50%). Guessing might occur if informants do not know a response

Table 5.8   Similarity Matrix Calculated for Table 5.4

	Inf1	Inf 2	Inf 3	Inf 4	Inf 5
Inf 1	1.00	0.86	0.76	0.74	0.83
Inf 2	0.86	1.00	0.86	0.88	0.79
Inf 3	0.76	0.86	1.00	0.79	0.74
Inf 4	0.74	0.88	0.79	1.00	0.67
Inf 5	0.83	0.79	0.74	0.67	1.00

but are forced to choose from two options, or if they simply do not understand the task, which, of course, says more about the researcher than the informants.

Given the amount of chance agreement we can expect (up to 50%), it is obvious that guessing can lead to important differences in our data and the resulting interpretations. Consider Linda Garro's (1986) study on intracultural variation in folk-medical knowledge. Garro studied a Tarascan village in Mexico, comparing curers and noncurers on a set of beliefs about diseases. Using a sentence frame technique (see Chapter 4, "Question Answer Frames"), she calculated agreement between informants to explore the question of intracultural differences. In a rather elaborate analysis (for the time), she tested two hypotheses: (1) curers and noncurers have two different belief-systems, and (2) curers and noncurers share one belief-system, with the curers being more knowledgeable about the domain. The null hypothesis was that no difference existed between the members of the two groups. Hypothesis 1 would produce two groups of informants (curers vs. noncurers), with the members of each group agreeing with each other but less so with members of the other group. Hypothesis 2 would produce an agreement pattern where curers agreed strongly with each other because they had the relevant knowledge, but agreed less with noncurers, who also wouldn't agree as strongly with each other as the curers did (Garro, 1986, p. 357). Garro's findings support the second hypothesis, as indicated in a two-dimensional scaling of the informant distance (p. 360). There is a potential problem in her original analysis, however: The question-answer frames used in this study asked informants to respond with "Yes" or "No." This means, save other biases, two informants will agree on 50% of their responses just by guessing (e.g., if each responded by flipping a coin). At the time, Garro did not consider guessing to be a problem, and there is no indication of any adjustment for it in the original paper. This brings up the question of the extent to which the noncurers of her sample agreed with each other and with the curers just by chance. If this happened, then the correct interpretation would be quite different from the one set forth in the original paper (Garro, 1986). In this scenario, curers might share a common model that is not shared by noncurers, who themselves seem not to adhere to any particular model. Fortunately, in a later paper, Garro provided a new analysis, now with the data adjusted for guessing. The patterns she originally described hold even after the adjustment procedure (Garro, 2000, p. 282).

As this example illustrates, it is important to take into account the possibility of guessing when calculating informant agreement.

In general, two different approaches can be taken, with two very different implications. In the first approach, informant-by-informant agreement is adjusted by considering only chance agreement based on the number of responses possible (e.g., flipping a coin for two possible responses). This approach ignores the possibility of an individual's general response bias. However, guessing might not always occur in a random manner. Individual preferences (biases) might lead a person to guess more in one direction than the other (e.g., saying "Yes" rather than "No"). This can be important if person A shares a particular guessing bias with person B but not with person C. Obviously, this is important if culture has an impact on these kinds of biases, because cultural differences might be due to these guessing differences alone, rather than to actual differences in the knowledge base (members of culture A might for some reason prefer to say "No" rather than "Yes").

The second approach addresses this issue by including individual preferences in the adjustment calculations. For each person, the likelihood of giving one response over another is calculated and taken into account.

Both ways of adjusting for guessing have their advantages and disadvantages. Accounting for individual biases in guessing can be an important tool if we want to go beyond biases in differences and similarities to explore actual differences in the knowledge base (see Medin et al., 2003). Suppose, however, that cultural differences in guessing biases exist and culture influences the way we guess (on certain issues). These might be important data points in a cross-cultural study that should not simply be "adjusted away," but that might become the focus of certain analyses.

Depending on the kind of adjustment to be done, one of two basic formulas can be used to adjust an informant-by-informant agreement matrix. The first one is taken from Romney et al. (1986), and adjusts only for guessing as a function of the number of possible responses.

Let A be the number of possible responses, and L the observed (raw) agreement. In this case, the formula to adjust for guessing is

$$(A * L-1)/(A-1)$$

In the case of three possible responses, the way to calculate agreement adjusted for guessing would be

$$(3 * L\text{-}1)/2$$

See Romney et al. (1986) for a more detailed explanation.

The second way of adjusting agreement takes into account the probability of each individual giving a certain response (e.g., each individual's response bias).

Let i and j be informants 1 and 2, with RAi,j the raw agreement observed between these two informants. Ppi is the probability of informant 1 giving a positive answer ("Yes"), and Pni is the probability of informant 1 giving a negative answer ("No"). This probability measure is the ratio of positive (or negative) responses divided by all responses. Ppj and Pnj are calculated in the same way and represent the corresponding probabilities for informant 2.

In this case, the following formula can be used to calculate Aai,j, the agreement between the two informants 1 and 2 adjusted for guessing:

$$RAi,j = AAi,j + (1 - Aai,j) * (Ppi * Ppj + Pni * Pnj)$$

As described, this latter procedure not only excludes chance agreement, but also agreement that might be due to cultural or individual response biases. Again, the possibilities emerging from this kind of differentiation are immense. If cultural differences are only found using the first adjustment measure (for chance) but not the second (response biases), we can reasonably assume that these differences are due to a cultural bias in guessing and not due to actual differences in consensual knowledge (see Medin et al., 2003). Although the example case accounts for only two possible responses, the formula can easily be adjusted for more complicated formats.

A final note on these adjustment procedures: In several instances, agreement data cannot (or should not) be adjusted for guessing. This is the case when agreement calculations are based on correlations (e.g., the pile-sorting task described in Chapter 4, "Pile Sorting: The Hierarchical Sorting of Elements"). There is no clear structure that would allow for an adjustment (e.g., no clear number of possible responses because the agreement calculation is not based on paired matches). In other tasks, like free listing, the same logic applies and an adjustment for guessing is neither possible nor plausible, as the number of possible answers is infinite.

Obviously, the existence of two different methods that lead to different outcomes indicates the need for a clear concept of (a) why we adjust for guessing and (b) what kind of biases we want to address with our adjustment calculations. This is important, because otherwise we might unintentionally exclude (or include) differences, such as cultural response biases, from the outset of our analysis.

So far, the procedures described have led us to calculate informant-by-informant agreement and to adjust these measures for both possible influences of guessing and response biases. The entries in this matrix represent a conservative measure of the degree to which our informants agree with one another. It is a conservative measure because the possibility of guessing has been ruled out. The correction for guessing can produce quite some difference in our data. Linda Garro (2000, p. 382) describes this fact. In one of her data sets, average informant agreement with the consensus (see below) was as high as 84% before the guessing procedure, dropping down to 68% after the adjustment. Again, this is obviously an important step in the process of analyzing our data. It also shows the strength of formal approaches of data collection and analysis. Guessing can and probably does occur even within informal (qualitative) interviews. However, unless we have a clear theory and method developed to account for it, guessing might just go unnoticed. It should be clear from the discussion and examples that this can have a severe impact on our findings and how we interpret them.

Agreement Pattern and Residual Analysis

All the above procedures led us to calculate a matrix of inter-informant agreement adjusted for guessing. At several points, I hinted at possible ways to analyze this matrix. One way might be a multidimensional scaling (MDS) of the informants as a function of their agreement. The idea behind this task is to represent the agreement between two informants in two-dimensional space (more dimensions are rather complicated to visualize and interpret). In this case, the inverses of the entries in the agreement table are taken as the entries for the MDS because high agreement should be expressed as proximity (rather than high distance). Garro (1986) used this strategy to reveal patterns of informant agreement. There is a huge body of literature on the mathematics of MDS easily accessible to the interested reader, so that I won't go into more detail.

While the scaling method proved to be very useful for analyzing patterns of agreement, it still does not tell us the extent to which we can assume that our informants agree with one another. This agreement is an important issue in cultural studies because it is here that we can develop a formal justification for aggregation of the individuals' responses into a single set of data, the cultural model.

Cultural Consensus and Informant Agreement

The topic of how much sharing is needed to identify a set of responses as representing a cultural model was originally addressed by Romney et al. (1986)[3] in their seminal paper "Culture and Consensus: A Theory of Cultural and Informant Accuracy." Because it was published in *American Anthropologist*, it didn't come to the notice of psychologists for a long time (and still has only minor recognition in the field), and at the same time— probably due to its technicality—anthropologists didn't pay much attention, either. This is unfortunate, for their model points out some important issues anthropologists have struggled with for a long time. The model addresses two important issues at once: (a) How many informants do we need to make safe assumptions about the cultural knowledge of a domain? And (b) how do we identify the culturally correct responses? These questions are essential for overcoming one of the major obstacles in the field: namely, how do we know for sure that our descriptions (and intuitions) capture a consensus of our informants? (See Chapter 3 for further discussion.) Furthermore, once we have identified a consensus, we can explore patterned deviations from the consensus.

Consensus theory uses the pattern of agreement—the consensus—among informants to make inferences about each individual's knowledge of the answers to the questions. One central assumption of the model is that the extent to which two informants agree with one another is a function of both informants' knowing the "culturally correct/salient" response (Romney et al., 1986, p. 316; Weller & Romney, 1988, p. 75; see also Garro, 2000). In this theory, then, two informants agree more with each other if they are more knowledgeable about the domain in question. Note that it is important that we are dealing with clearly defined domains of knowledge, because across domains, individuals might have different expertise and competencies (see below).

In Garro's study, curers in the Tarascan community agree more with each other than with the less knowledgeable noncurers. Boster (1986b), in a rather innovative approach, showed that among Aguaruna manioc planters in Peru, the informants that agreed most with all the other informants (see measure of average agreement) were also the most reliable informants. Reliability was operationalized with the help of a repeated interview. Here, the informants that agreed the strongest with all the other informants (in the first round) agreed in the second interview (several days later) more strongly with their own previous responses than did the informants who showed less average agreement in the first interview. This indicates agreement with other informants reflects the competence of an informant with respect to the knowledge that is available within a group of informants. I refer the interested reader to the literature cited and to Kimball Romney's Web page at the University of California, Irvine, for a list of applications.

The centerpiece of the model is a principal component factor analysis over the inter-informant agreement table (adjusted for guessing). The rationale for this analysis is to determine whether a single underlying model (one-factor solution) can describe the agreement pattern of the informants. If this is the case, then there is enough agreement on what the culturally correct answers are to infer that the informants are responding similarly to each other (see Garro, 2000, p. 282).

Three criteria can be singled out for this to be the case. (a) The ratio of the *eigenvalue* of the first and second factors is 3 to 1 or higher, (b) a substantial amount of the variance is explained by the first factor, and (c) all individual factor loadings on the first factor are highly positive. If these criteria are met, then we can safely assume that a high agreement between the informants exists, captured by the first factor. In this case, an individual's first factor loading can be treated as his or her competence score with respect to the consensus, the general agreed-upon model.

Let me try to clarify this important concept with a rather intuitive description. Factor analysis is a method of reducing complex data sets into simpler structures. The way it is used in the model (conducted over the informant agreement), the analysis tries to construct an ideal informant (the first factor) who agrees as strong as possible with all the informants of the study. If such a factor is found (and the above criteria are met), this factor represents the ideal cultural response. Note that this "ideal informant" is a formal representation of the key informants often used in anthropology. However, the ideal informant is not key in that it represents an expert's knowledge, but rather in that it represents the average knowledge of our informants.

The one-factor solution indicates that agreement is strong enough to assume the existence of one underlying (response) model that explains the high agreement among the informants. If we think of this first factor as the "ideal informant," then we can treat each individual's loading on this factor as the agreement with this ideal informant (the cultural model). If agreement is taken as representing the cultural truth—that which is shared—then it is reasonable to take the factor loading of each informant as a measure of his or her competence score with respect to the domain under exploration.

In this sense then, the model gives us (a) a measure of the extent to which the knowledge of a domain is shared (one-factor solution), and (b) a measure of each individual's competence score with respect to the model. This applies only if the necessary criteria are met.

Consequently, if no single-factor solution is found, we cannot assume that one model exists among our informants. This might be due to several reasons, such as a lack of informants, the sampling method, or the domain under investigation.

If the criteria of this model are met, then we can reasonably assume the existence of a cultural model among our informants, and, hence, aggregate the data across all informants into a single set of data points, the *modal responses*. This is an extremely important feature for cultural and cross-cultural research (see also Chapter 2). From what has just been said, it should be clear that the confidence levels (percentages of allowed errors) and the number of informants needed depend on the level of agreement between the informants. Again, this is a common truth in anthropology, although never formalized. The more informants agree with each other (i.e., the more widely spread the knowledge is), the fewer informants we need to gain a reasonable understanding of the domain under exploration. The model provides clear indices of confidence, as well as the number of informants needed for the different levels of confidence (as a function of the informant's competence). For a technical description, including summary tables, see the original paper by Romney et al. (1986, p. 326). Indeed, the number of informants we might need can be surprisingly small (p. 333).

Informant Competence and Residual Analysis

In the previous section, I introduced the concept of an informant's competence as agreement with the cultural model, the first factor. In the model, this competence is expressed in the informant's loading on the first factor. Due to the procedures of the analysis, individuals who agree strongly with all the other informants are said to have a high competence with respect to the shared cultural knowledge, a fact that is logically true. This makes it necessary to remind the reader of two underlying assumptions of the model: (a) that culture is socially transmitted and, hence, (b) shared among relevant participants (Romney, 1999, p. 104). A third assumption was also mentioned, that only relevant questions from a single domain be included in the study. However, this has some theoretical implications we have to keep in mind.

If cultural knowledge is defined by what is shared, then we have to be careful about the selection of our informants. Suppose that out of a set of 15 informants, one individual stands out as an expert in the domain under investigation. When we calculate the modal response and the individual competence scores, it is likely that this person will stand out by showing a very low competence score. As consensual knowledge is basically average knowledge—or *what everyone knows*—there is a good chance that one expert, if surrounded only by relative novices, would fail to participate strongly in the consensus (recall the discussion of research on plant naming among the Q'eachi' Maya). Of course, it would still be interesting to see if this expert showed positive *factor loadings* and, thereby, still agree with the novices.

This means it's necessary to know *who* our informants are and how far we can generalize the notion of cultural consensus from our data (see Chapter 3 for a discussion of this point). Also, it is important to note that a *competence score* should not be treated as an evaluative term, only as a measurement of participation in the consensual model of the participants of the study. In the above example, the expert would be less competent with respect to the novice model, which is just another way of saying that he differs from the novice participants in the task. Of course, such a finding would call for further explorations, including the incorporation of more informants and, particularly, more experts in the study.

The competence scores (if we find consensus) frequently range between 0.4 and 0.9 (e.g., Garro, 2000, p. 382), indicating that informants agree between 40% and 90% with the consensual model. Obviously, this still leaves ample space for between-informant agreement that is not based on participation in the consensus. This type of agreement is called *residual agreement*, and it describes the agreement that is left if we factor out agreement based on what everybody knows. Note that if all informants agreed completely with one another, there would be no pattern of agreement except the one based on the general consensus. This is almost never the case in our studies, however, which makes exploring the pattern of residual agreement an important tool.

Recall that in Table 5.2 informants 1 and 2 agree in 50% of their responses. Informant 1 also agrees with 50% of the responses from informant 3, who agrees with 33% of the responses from informant 2. Informants 3 and 4 show the highest across-informant agreement, indicating that they show the largest overlap with all other informants. Although we might expect these two informants to have the highest competence scores, they do not show the highest agreement with each other. Again, this indicates that they share different subsets of responses with other informants. This example illustrates the fact that the modal responses (the consensus) are not equally distributed among all members and that there might be considerable agreement between two informants who agree on a set of responses different from the consensus.

To calculate this residual agreement and to test for its existence, several related possibilities exist. First, if we have reason to assume a certain pattern of knowledge distribution, we can test this hypothesis by comparing the loadings for our informants on the first two factors (if the second factor is nontrivial). If we expect that different individuals (experts/nonexperts, women/men) have different access to the knowledge under exploration, then we might predict significant differences in their competence scores. In a similar vein, we can explore the individuals' loadings on the second factor as well. If there is a significant submodel (expressed in the residual agreement), then there is a good chance that it is captured by a nontrivial second factor. These patterns are often distributed across both factors (and maybe others), however, and are, therefore, not easily detected. In this case, the next step is to calculate residual agreement directly.

Nakao and Romney (1984) developed a procedure based on each individual's agreement with the consensus/modal responses. This agreement is described by the loadings on the first factor of each informant and allows us to calculate the *predicted agreement* between each pair of informants (as the product of their loadings on the first factor). The idea behind this procedure is simple. If informant 1 agrees in 70% of his responses with the general model and informant 2 agrees 60% with this model, then informants 1 and 2 have to agree in at least 42% of their responses with each other (based on each person's participation in the consensus). Calculating this predicted agreement for all pairs of informants gives us a matrix of predicted inter-informant agreement.

Subtracting this predicted agreement (for all informants) from the observed agreement (adjusted for guessing) results in a matrix representing the residual agreement among all informants. Again, this residual agreement represents the agreement between two informants that is not explained by their participation in the consensus. For example, the observed agreement between informants 1 and 2 might be 60%, which is considerably higher than the 42% predicted by their agreement with the general model. In this example, their residual agreement would be 18%. However, to test the residual agreement for pattern, we need a firm hypothesis. If we expect gender to make a difference, then we might predict that women agree more with one another than with men (and vice versa) in their residual agreement (this test has to be done on the standardized residual agreement matrix).

This can be easily calculated by comparing (a) the average agreement among women, with (b) the average agreement of each woman with all the men (and vice versa). A simple one-way ANOVA is sufficient to test the difference for significance. Different possibilities exist. First, we may find that both men and women show a higher within-gender residual agreement than across gender. In this case, both groups share a common base (the consensus), but each group holds a submodel (differing across groups) beyond the commonly shared model. Second, one group shares higher within-gender residual agreement, but not the other. In this case, both groups share a general consensus, with one group holding a specific submodel, not shared by the other group. This might be the case for the curers in the Tarascan community studied by Garro. Finally, we might not find differences in residual agreement, indicating that both groups share a common model without further differentiation. Obviously, depending on the outcome of these analyses, our explanations and further explorations will take very different directions.

At this point, I would like to take up again the discussions in Chapter 4 from "Cognition and Observational Studies" to "Social Network Concepts and Eliciting Methods." In these sections, I attempted to show how different methods (observational studies and social network studies) might be combined with a genuine cognitive approach using these kinds of analyses. One important contribution of methods, such as social network analysis, is the development of clear theories of how certain kinds of knowledge might be distributed within a culture. This was the case in one of my studies among the Lacandon Maya in Chiapas. Concerned with generational differences in environmental cognition, I collected network data asking each male adult in the community to nominate the people who knew most about the forest. These peer nominations could be translated into frequency lists, rank-ordering the members of the community with respect to how often they were reported as an expert. These frequency data were then compared with the agreement pattern emerging from a cognitive experiment targeting the environmental models of the group members. The distribution of the loadings on both the first and the second factor could be predicted by how many peers nominated a person as an expert. At the minimum, these data showed that the experiment covered a good part of what is locally perceived as expertise in forest knowledge.

On a different level, Boster (1986a) explored similar effects in his work with Aguaruna women, who cultivate many different species of manioc. In his analysis, Boster was able to show that kinship relations and the exchange of manioc species helped to communicate knowledge about manioc species. Both types of relations predicted a higher residual agreement between any pair of women with respect to the knowledge of manioc names. Women who exchanged manioc frequently and women of one kin group showed significantly higher within-group agreement than women who didn't share either of the two relationships.

The potential of these analyses depends on the appropriate application of the models described—and I do not claim to have exhausted the list of possibilities. However, before I continue, it is important once more to highlight several points: The procedures of data analysis described in this chapter stand and fall with the data to which they are applied. The best data analysis procedure cannot (or very rarely) compensate for poor sampling or unreliable methods of data collection. These procedures can be applied in a meaningful way only if they are embedded in a broader research framework. First, as indicated in Chapter 4, we need data-gathering methods that are adequate to the question and the population we are studying. Second, we need to know who our sample informants are. Third, for most of the analyses of agreement pattern, we need a clear hypothesis about which informants we expect to agree more with each other. The best analytical methods are meaningless if we do not know what to look for or how to explain emerging results. Although the emphasis here is clearly on formal methods, these methods have to be embedded in a sound ethnographic approach to become sensitive instruments in cultural research. When this is done, they provide insights that would otherwise go undetected by the observer's eye.

Notes

1. See, for example, Medin, Ross et al. (2003). In this work, the researchers use different coding schemes to analyze their data. The schemes differ with respect to their level of abstractness.

2. Of course, this can be easily calculated by looking at the percentage of agreement for each plant.

3. For a short and less technical description of how the model works and what it does, see Weller & Romney (1988, 72-78).

6

Combining Strengths

Toward a New Science of Culture

Implicitly, one of the concerns of this book has been the combination of two disciplines, anthropology and psychology, into a research program that targets the cognitive study of culture, as well as (cross)-cultural studies of cognition. These studies, however, can only be meaningful if we define, first, what we mean by the term *culture,* and second, if we go beyond simple statements like culture A differs from culture B. On the other hand, going beyond such simplistic descriptions implies exploring the notion that culture might indeed represent an important aspect in the formation of human thinking and behavior by shaping how and what people think, for example, individuals' cognitions. As seen in the previous chapters, exploring culture in this sense forces us to go into more detail by looking at social processes that led to groups we often distinguish as being of different cultures. In this kind of approach, culture has to be seen as a starting point for understanding social processes and their effect on individuals' cognitions and their distribution across social groups.

Cultural studies must be concerned with cognition for two reasons. First, unless we think of culture as an entity existing outside human beings, we have to explain culture as emerging from an individual's cognitions (see Strauss & Quinn, 1992). Second, this perspective requires that we explore the exact context in which these individual cognitions are formed. *How individuals of a certain group model the world, or certain aspects of it, and what they know about these aspects surely has an impact on how they act upon this world.* An exploration of these individual models and knowledge allows us (in part, at least) to explain emerging patterns of agreement (the cultural effects) as well as deviances therefrom. These emerging patterns can then be explored with respect to their origin and the kind of knowledge involved. Boster (1987b), for example, distinguishes between a "particle model" and a "wave model" of cultural knowledge, with the particle model representing independent knowledge bites that become accumulated (or not). The wave model focuses more on knowledge that is related to other knowledge by (often) invisible rules and theories.

Both types of knowledge are relevant. The latter, however, might be of particular importance because it allows us to understand how members of a social group acquire tremendous amounts of knowledge similar to each other's when bit-by-bit learning seems implausible (see Atran et al., 2002). One way to visualize this type of learning is the "cultural epidemiology" described by Sperber (1985, 1996). In this view, learning is no longer (only) an item-by-item process (imitation), but can take place through inferences, according to rules and theories.

The study of how individuals handle novel situations and introduce new ideas and concepts into their existing frameworks is of great importance here. These possibilities and their implications are by no means solved yet, and much empirical work remains to be done: exploring different types of knowledge, their acquisition, transfer, and transformation. For example, developmental studies can reveal much about ongoing processes and how they guide or influence the acquisition of cultural knowledge, versus universal patterns of development trajectories. See the controversy between Carey (1985), Ross, Medin, Coley, and Atran (2003), and Bloch, Solomon, and Carey (2001).

On the other hand, within-group differences might represent an ongoing process of cultural change (Ross, 2001, 2002a, 2002b) or differential access to information, often coupled with interest or professional necessity (e.g., Boster, 1986a; Garro, 1986, 2000; Medin, Lynch, Coley, & Atran, 1997; Ross & Medin, 2003).

Obviously, this kind of research agenda poses different kinds of challenges for anthropologists and psychologists. And it is in this sense that the two shouldn't have been separated in the first place (see Shore, 1996) and that each field developed strengths and weaknesses that seem to complement the other (Medin & Atran, 1999).

Given the individualistic ontology of the discipline (Bruner, 1996), psychologists always had a problem in conceiving of culture as an important factor in understanding human cognition and behavior. In fact, psychologists often do not know what to make of anthropology's "cultural representations" (Medin & Atran, 1999, p. 6), a problem I will deal with a little later on in this chapter (see also Wassmann, 1995).

As a result, psychologists were often satisfied with the convenient study of college students. As their focus, they tried to understand all cognitive parts of the human from the "inside out" (Bruner, 1996). If culture was considered at all, it was in the simplistic way of differentiating the students according to their ethnicity, with African Americans, for example, including everyone from recent immigrants from different countries to third-generation U.S. citizens (Fish, 2000). Aside from the implicit racism of this approach (Fish, 2000), this kind of selection has additional problems. Think of studies that are concerned with the identification of cognitive universals, an important part in the psychologist's quest. Even if we test college students across different ethnicities, the differences we find are probably relatively small compared to the diversity of the world's population (consider education, income, status, age, as well as ambitions and exposure to "Western" concepts). To be sure, this does not necessarily change if we choose our study participants from universities abroad, a newer trend in cross-cultural psychology to get around some of these problems (see, e.g., Kitayama, Markus, Matsumoto, & Norasakkunkit, 1997, or Choy & Nisbett, 2000).

Of course, one could argue that if we find cultural differences among college students, our findings should be even more significant because college students probably share many traits across countries. However, U.S. college students do not provide a representative sample of the U.S. population, and a similar point can be made for other countries. Indeed, here the issues might become even more complicated. First, different selection processes might influence who our subjects are in different places. For example, in some places income, social status, or gender play direct or indirect important roles in selecting students (e.g., U.S. psychology students are predominantly female). Second, if only college students are targeted, we generally lack the basic ethnographic information about our subject pool (activities, interests, etc.). Even if we control for obvious issues, such as time in the United States, we normally don't have sufficient information about each participant to allow a meaningful explanation of the responses. Yet, even time in the United States is very rarely accounted for in psychological studies (Fish, 2000). Similarly, psychologists have very little knowledge about American subjects, either. What is their background, what are their values, beliefs, and interests? These questions are almost never asked. Third, responses of American students from different ethnic groups can often reflect their minority status in the United States rather than the model of the culture from which they receive their often hyphenated names (such as "Asian-Americans," "Mexican-Americans," if these are indeed to be identified as cultures). In these cases, the question becomes to what extent we should consider these students an extension of their "home culture," as is often assumed in these kinds of studies. The discussion in Chapter 3 suggests that we should not simply assume this overlap, and that we have yet to understand the effects of the particular situation of these individuals (as a group)—being brought up in an environment that includes two very different cultural settings. Multiculturalism (Hong, Morris, Chui, & Martinez, 2000)—for example, a person maintaining two (or more?) cultures—is only one possible outcome, and much more research in the field is needed with respect to its depths and limits.

This leads to the next problem. If we think of science as a peculiar cultural outcome of "Western thought" rather than a universal feature (see Atran, 1998), then the same problem holds true for university students in different cultures. *To what extent did their knowledge of and in these institutions shape and change their cognitions and worldview?* Or to put the question differently, *what makes a university education a goal for some people but not others in a given culture? How does this goal limit access to or interest in other kinds of knowledge?* Again, these processes and conditions have yet to be studied to understand the responses we receive from our student subjects. Until then, we might still use college students as informants, but we won't be able to extend our findings beyond this particular population, and we will not know what our data really mean (note that it is often difficult to replicate findings from one university to the next, using the student-subject pool).

This seems a high price: Researchers compromise the validity of their findings for the convenience of running the studies from their offices. Finally, let me turn to one more point against the use of college students as participants. By now, it is well established that experts in a domain show different patterns of reasoning than novices do. On a structural level, at least, experts from different cultures might be even more similar to each other in their reasoning pattern than they are to novices of their own culture (see Bailenson, Shum, Atran, Medin, & Coley, 2002; Coley, Medin, Proffitt, Lynch, & Atran, 1999; Medin et al., 1997; see Medin, Ross, Atran, Burnett, & Blok, 2002, for an overview). This has direct consequences for our study samples. For example, studying folk-biological reasoning by looking only at college students (who are normally not exactly experts in the domain; see Coley et al., 1999) would definitely misrepresent how humans in general conceive and reason within the domain of folk biology. It is like studying the English language by interviewing individuals who have only a limited knowledge of the English language to start with. While the latter might be an interesting study in itself, we have to be aware of the limitations (and peculiarity) of such an approach with respect to understanding the English language. Again, a good example of this mistake is the work by Susan Carey (1985, 1995, 1999), who proposed the theory that children learn folk biology from a previously developed folk psychology—what they know about humans. Carey, however, did not test this hypothesis in different cultural settings or even among rural children, who might be more likely to possess some kind of expertise on the matters of animals and plants. Instead, she trusted the results of studies with children in an urban U.S. setting. Recent cross-cultural research indicates that the patterns found by Carey are rather peculiar to her study sample. Urban U.S. children seem to lack essential knowledge about animals and plants, forcing them to use what they know about human beings as a base for reasoning about animals (Ross et al., 2003). The use of novices has yet another disadvantage, because we are often faced with additional constraints on the stimulus material we can use. Novices, for example, might not be familiar with certain stimuli we are interested in using, such as specific animals and plants (Medin & Atran, 1999, p. 3).

Still, the selection of research participants is only one part of the problem. While systematic controlled experiments are definitely one of the strengths of cognitive psychology (Greenfield, 2000), this strength can create some potential problems within cultural research. One previously mentioned example is the study by Yager and Rotheram-Borus (2000) on social experience among adolescents from different ethnic groups in the United States. In their study, the researchers attempted to control for as much as possible, and, therefore, sampled African American, white, and Hispanic high school students based on similar family incomes. If anything, this method probably biased the sample toward poor white families and rich Hispanic families (relative to the average income of the respective ethnic groups). It is more than likely that this kind of bias influenced the findings or at least limited the extent to which they can be generalized to other contexts. The researchers' intention is clear. They tried to control for everything but ethnicity (which they set equal with culture). Yet in their ill-guided attempt, they probably created more confusion than clarity. This problem stems from the general lack of methodological flexibility (Medin and Atran pointedly call this *rigor mortis;* 1999, p. 7) and theoretical grounding. As discussed in Chapters 2 and 3, cultural and cross-cultural studies have to be firmly based in theory and clear predictions. This connects to another problem. Unless we have clear theories and prior knowledge about the cultures that we study, we do not know if the methods we are using are appropriate and comparable across cultures (see Cole, 1996, for examples). This problem seems to be the case, for example, with Craig Anderson's (1999) cross-cultural study on depression. Contrary to previous work, Anderson found that Chinese are more prone to depression than Americans. The difference, however, might lie only in the fact that Anderson used a measurement tool that was developed based on Western individuals, including some basic assumptions that might not hold true across cultures. This is important for the argument here. Despite a huge body of literature about the differences in self-construction among Americans and Chinese (see the review by Markus & Kitayama, 1991), Anderson did not feel the need to adapt (or at least to question) his methods for different cultural contexts.

These problems are all expressions of the lack of a clear conceptual framework that includes both culture and cultural differences. This lack stems from a widely unchallenged ethnocentrism in the field that often leads to cultural studies that are suspiciously little concerned with culture and cultural processes and that often ignore the wider field of related studies (see Chapter 2 for some examples). Again, this is not to say that there are no exceptions, and I have mentioned many works throughout this book. Still, the majority of studies suffer from at least one of these malaises.

In a sense, anthropology went in the opposite direction. Instead of focusing on the cognitive part of culture and exploring issues, such as the extent to which certain aspects are shared in a culture, the field took a more holistic approach: describing observations, narratives, with a focus on local generalities (at best). Anthropologists' virtue was and is to "put things in their place," to see knowledge in its context; something that psychologists not only ignored, but often actually even tried to avoid in their studies (Bruner, 1996). This led to a huge body of ethnographic studies that gave detailed descriptions of locally learned and prescribed systems of action (D'Andrade, 1995, p. 7). Most of the early studies targeted cultures as "natural systems," where behavior emerged out of an institutional framework and the incentives and ideas created by it. This approach is probably as close as anthropology ever got to behaviorism. The history of anthropology, however, shows a clear shift in the 1950s toward systems of ideas, values, and so on—hence, culture as systems of meaning (D'Andrade, 1995, p. 12; see Clyde Kluckhohn's, 1949b, work on Navajo concepts and values for an example). Cognitive anthropology and symbolic anthropology were the offspring of this shift, both trying to locate and identify meaning within the context of culture. Yet while cognitive anthropology originally identified culture as *what one needs to know to behave properly* (Goodenough, 1956), symbolic anthropology treated *culture as a system of meaning* (see Geertz, 1973).

Identifying meaning within the context of culture allows us to (a) locate and specify meaning within its specific context and, therefore, (b) understand individual cognition in a wider context. However, both symbolic and cognitive anthropology failed to explore the processes that lead to the systems of shared knowledge or meaning called culture (see Ross, 1997; see Roseberry, 1989, for a critique of Geertz). In particular, the symbolic approach never answered (or even asked) the question of where cultural meanings are located. Because the individual as carrier of these meanings was rejected (see Strauss & Quinn, 1997), differences between actors, through both time and situational context, were almost by necessity ignored (see Roseberry, 1989). Disagreement between informants was simply seen as the lack of cultural knowledge among groups of the informants (see Garro, 2000, for a similar point).

All of this had broad implications. For example, phenomena such as cultural change are hard to conceptualize within such a framework—other than resorting to the introduction of yet another "natural system" that somehow miraculously replaces at least parts of the first one (e.g., Vogt, 1967). Because agreement was basically seen as a given, anthropologists often did not pay much attention to developing a clear methodology, and rare is the anthropological paper that clearly describes the methods applied in the research (e.g., compare the publications in major psychological and anthropological journals). Because content is seen separate from the individuals, ethnographic observations are often written in summary form, where the "cultural representations," the "facts," and "knowledge" are like free-floating entities waiting for the (native) individual to draw on them or for the anthropologist to pick them up. Most often, the reader of these ethnographic descriptions is left on his or her own with respect to *whose knowledge/ models are actually represented* (sampling method) or *what methods were used to elicit this knowledge* (eliciting methods).

This mistake is implicitly introduced even in Bernard's book, *Research Methods in Anthropology* (1995). Describing the elicitation of ethnographic decision models, Bernard (p. 373) encourages his readers to aggregate data from one informant to the next and to add, "until you'll stop getting new decisions, reasons and constraints" (p. 376).[1] In principle, there is nothing wrong with the general task of eliciting individual decision models. In certain circumstances, it might indeed be instructive to explore all possible decisions, reasons, and constraints that can be found among a group of people. We might want to start our research by looking at the whole pool of possibilities, or we might conduct a pilot study to discover the kinds of responses we can expect. As discussed in Chapters 2, 3, and 5, an approach like the one proposed by Bernard should not blind us to the existence of individual differences and potential subgroups of informants sharing certain features. Otherwise, our results implicitly assume either that every member of a group holds (and uses) every possible bit of knowledge (decision alternatives), or that the differences between our subjects are based on different levels of competence (see Garro, 2000).

In Chapter 3, I discussed the consequences of this approach for the field in general. Because replications are impossible, so are constructive criticisms, improvements, and subsequent advances in our knowledge. As a result, anthropologists tend to accept an argument if (a) similar evidence is available from other areas or (b) if the argument makes intuitive sense. Both ways of establishing scientific knowledge are very dangerous because they are not independent of the original process of coming up with the research project. (What if my research intuition is guided by previous findings? If this is the case and my intuitions get in the way of my perceptions of the situation, a match between my "data" and previous findings is a logical consequence.) One effect of this approach was that the validity of the whole academic endeavor was questioned, both from the field and from other fields; see Greenfield, 2000, for a similar point.

Ignoring clear methods has further consequences. As indicated in Chapters 4 and 5, understanding the content of individual informant's responses is only one step toward an understanding of who they are with respect to our research. In the quest to understand culture, we need to explore each individual's response in the light of the responses of all other informants. It is only in this context of inter-informant (dis-) agreement patterns that the content begins to make sense to us.

In Chapter 5, I elaborated on the cultural consensus model developed by Romney, Weller, and Batchelder (1986). This model provides us with an unambiguous tool to assess the existence or nonexistence of an underlying model that explains the variance and commonality among our informants. Furthermore, it allows us to estimate the agreement (and, hence, the deviations) of each individual. Of course, this tool is not a magical cure-all, for we are still left with deciding who we will interview and what kind of questions to ask. Still, *using* some creativity, we can get around most of the problems and limitations Garro (2000) mentions, a point to which I will return.

As pointed out in Chapters 2 and 5, calculating agreement is an important step in justifying the aggregation of data across informants (see Romney et al., 1986), which helps avoid the problem of whose knowledge we are describing and how this knowledge is distributed.[2] This approach, which requires looking across all informants individually, allows further exploration of patterns of residual agreement that go beyond what is shared by our informants based on their general agreement on a common model. Naturally, this is invaluable information for understanding not only each individual's responses (in their context) but also the content of the knowledge, the differentially shared representations (Hutchins, 1995). Obviously, sound methods and a clear theory are needed to detect these similarities and differences. This seems to be missing in Jürg Wassmann's (1995) approach. While he rightfully points out the advantage of experimental data, he nevertheless underestimates their power and use for an ethnographic approach and for a deeper understanding of the relevant processes. Not only does Wassmann's approach lack a well thought out and detailed study design, because there is no analysis of the informant agreement pattern it also seems to lack theoretical grounding (see Lawrence, 1995, for a similar critique).

Understanding these patterns shines a new light on the processes that created the differences, which in turn allows us a much better qualification of the content data as well. An example discussed earlier might help to illustrate this point:

Garro (1986, 2000), in her study of folk healers in a Tarascan community in central Mexico, explored the within-group differences in individuals' beliefs about disease. Exploring the knowledge and beliefs of relative novices and of curers in the community, she compared possible models: (a) curers and noncurers share one single model of beliefs (or share no system at all); (b) curers and noncurers share one common model, with the curers having some special knowledge, e.g., agreeing more with each other; and (c) curers and noncurers hold independent models.

It is clear that each of the three hypotheses describes the knowledge bases of curers and noncurers and by inference the processes of their formation in very different ways. Model 1 basically does not find any differences between the two, while model 2 sees the curers as more experienced on a continuum of increasing knowledge. Model 3, on the other hand, describes the knowledge base of the two groups as substantially different, presenting the curers' knowledge as independent and separate from that of the rest of the community, which shares a model of its own. Within these different contexts, each individual response receives a different meaning and evaluation, and, obviously, we expect different processes to be involved in the creation of each of these models.

Of course, a researcher might get a "good feeling" for what goes on in the field. But how do we actually know that our perceptions and intuitions are not biased by our theories?[3] Garro's (1986, 2000) data clearly show that both groups share a common model with the curers being more knowledgeable (model 2). This example is even more instructive for our purpose if we consider the potential impact that guessing and agreement resulting from guessing can have on our data and the resulting theories (see Chapter 5). The problem of guessing is an issue not just for formal methods, but it is only here that we have the opportunity to control our data for the potential influence of guessing (see Chapter 5).

Formal methods have even more advantages. In many cases, we need to make abstractions from individual (and often idiosyncratic) responses to larger patterns in order to understand the content of our data. For example, to understand how children acquire their knowledge of a special domain (see Ross et al., 2003) we need to go beyond the individual child to test for general patterns across age groups. In fact, this is true for all cross-cultural work (e.g., Atran et al., 1999, 2002; Medin et al., 2002). Besides, many important patterns simply cannot be elicited in semistructured interviews. Referring again to research among the Lacandon Maya of Chiapas might serve as an illustration. Like many Maya languages, Lacandon-Maya does not have a word for "palm" (tree). However, in a triad comparison of different plant species, it became obvious that Lacandon Maya perceive palms as more similar to each other than to other plants (Ross, 2001). These covert life forms are fairly common in folk biology (Berlin, 1992, p. 176) and have been reported by Harold Conklin (1954, p. 94). Obviously, since no term exists that represents the groupings of these items, an elicitation based on informal interviews is rather difficult (for further examples, see López, Atran, Coley, J., Medin, & Smith, 1997; Wassmann, 1995). These examples illustrate and strengthen the critique of early cognitive anthropology's focus on linguistic terms and expressions (see Wassmann, 1995).

For all the above reasons, anthropology has a lot to gain from embracing systematic controlled comparisons and clear methodology. This is not to say that our task is simply to take psychological methods to populations other than college students. Although this often seems to be implied (Antweiler, 1993; Wassmann, 1995), Cole (1996) could show that one and the same method can produce very different results among members of two different cultures and, hence, a direct comparison is not always possible or even recommended (Greenfield, 1997).

Again, this problem goes beyond informants not being willing to do "strange tasks," as described earlier (see also Antweiler, 1993; Wassmann, 1995). While this might present a problem, at least we become aware of the problem right away and are not led to wrong conclusions. But what if different groups respond differently to the same task, such as when the results show a general response bias? It is here that we have to be extremely careful in our analyses and their interpretations, because there are no obvious indications of what might have produced the results. Finally, our studies have to be embedded in a framework of clear theories and built around a clear concept of culture. This demands a sound ethnographic knowledge of the culture under study. Again, data from the Lacandon Maya serve as an example (Ross, 2001, 2002a, 2002b). The data show clear differences in the knowledge bases of the members of the two living adult generations in the community. The group of older men appears to know more (e.g., have more complex knowledge). Therefore, one could think that the data simply describe development from novices to experts. However, given other converging data and the ethnographic context of an ongoing cultural change, the resulting data reveal the loss of knowledge among younger Lacandones. Data confirming this conclusion came from an array of different methodologies and domains, including an individual's dependence of the forest, choice of household location, and economic decision-making processes. Further evidence was the difference in general framework theories (see below), including religious aspects. Here, both groups had fundamentally different views with respect to the forest and the role of humans and animals. These additional data were necessary to conclude that the results do not describe an ongoing process of learning, but rather the opposite— the probably irreversible loss of knowledge as part of a larger process of cultural change (Ross, 2001, 2002a, 2002b).

In an ideal world, final proof would come from a longitudinal study. This would mean a restudy of the location, which would have to be interpreted in a new context, and the resulting processes. Still, the study provides the necessary information about informants and the methods applied that would be needed to conduct a restudy. Given that the results were predicted by the hypothesis developed prior to the study, I am fairly confident that a restudy (in 20 years) would basically confirm the findings.

More generally, the point is that if cultural research and cross-cultural studies are not guided by theory, we could get lost in the middle of a forest of differences that might conceal a view of the broader landscape.

All this should make another point clear: Some of psychology's methodological rigor is definitely needed in cultural studies. Not only does it enhance the quality of our data, but it also allows the individual researcher to systematically question his or her own intuitions and other researchers' findings.

As mentioned several times throughout this book, it is astonishing how little culture is reflected within cognitive studies. However, it is at least as astonishing how little anthropology participates in the respective debates.

Schemata, Cultural Models, and Consensus

In recent years, cognitive anthropology has moved toward the use of schema theory (D'Andrade, 1992, p. 47; 1995, p. 122) for an adequate description of cultural symbols (see Medin & Ross, 1996, p. 297, for schema theory in psychology). In this line of research, schemata are seen as "simplified interpretative frameworks used to understand events" (D'Andrade, 1992, p. 48).[4] This approach emerged partly as a critique and an extension of previous approaches in cognitive anthropology that were more concerned with the semantic structure of lexical domains, such as what one needed to know to label pieces and portions correctly (Quinn & Holland, 1987, p. 14).

A schema, on the other hand, does not just consist of some set of facts, but includes how these facts are related (Medin & Ross, 1996, p. 298). It is an organizing framework for objects and relations that is to be filled with concrete detail (D'Andrade, 1995, p. 124). The fact that we constantly use unstated schemata is maybe best illustrated in an example:

> The bell went off. Peter gathered his stuff together and left the classroom.

Although the two sentences seem to be connected to each other, no such relationship is stated in either of them. In fact, to understand the phrase we have to activate relevant information about the organization of schools; classrooms, including a timing bell that indicates the end of the hour; and more. This implies activating default assumptions (what information is most likely to fit) as well as restrictions (what information would not be appropriate; Medin & Ross, 1996, p. 299).

Intuitively, these kinds of examples seem to make two things clear: First, we couldn't possibly perform the necessary calculations, including all possible inferences and interpretations, every time we hear a phrase or a sentence. Second, it therefore seems that we perceive and understand certain units of knowledge and inferences together (Medin & Ross, 1996, p. 297). If this is the case, it seems logical to argue that an understanding of the organization of cultural knowledge cannot be based solely on the semantic structure of lexical domains.[5]

So far, different kinds of schemata have been proposed (see D'Andrade, 1995; Shore, 1996), based primarily on the influential work of George Lakoff (1987). Although the general idea is very plausible and convincing, there are several problems with this approach that have to be mentioned. First, it is not entirely clear how people actually implement the different properties of a schema (the various default inputs). We might think of this "missing information" in a schema as slots that have to be filled with appropriate details. But how do we select the right input information for a slot? This gets even more complicated when we think of schemata whose slot values are dependent on each other. For example, consider a general schema for a restaurant visit with the details to be determined by facts such as the type of the restaurant (fast food vs. fancy restaurant; Italian vs. Thai, etc.).

In addition to these problems, several authors suggest a nested embeddedness of different schemata (D'Andrade, 1995, p. 124). This adds the further complication of how individuals decide which is the appropriate schema in a given context.

Yet another problem is that of novel situations and how to account for "messy situations," such as those exemplified by Holland (1992) who describes a peculiar situation that obviously poses problems for an account based on schema theory. Conducting interviews at a field station in a community in Nepal, the author and a doctoral student interviewed individuals from different castes on the second-floor balcony of the field station. Because the author and his assistant were generally seen as akin to high-caste members, visiting the field station posed quite a challenge to many members of the lower castes. In this cultural setting, it is normally not appropriate for lower-caste persons to enter the houses of members of higher castes. This was even more problematic as the house had to be entered through the kitchen. Food is seen as particularly vulnerable to pollution, so members of the lower castes are generally kept away from kitchens (Holland, 1992, p. 70). On this particular instance, a low-caste woman came for a scheduled interview. Even though one of the researchers went downstairs to greet and welcome her, this woman—who was in her 50s—took pains to scale the vertical outside wall to the second-floor balcony in order to avoid passing through the kitchen (p. 70). Obviously, the whole context violated her schemata (lower-caste members do not visit the houses, much less enter the kitchens, of higher-caste individuals), challenging her to find a novel solution.

So far, no clear theory has emerged that embraces all these different instances. This task seems to become even more difficult as researchers stress the flexibility of schemata in general. Roy D'Andrade (1995), for example, states, "it would be more accurate to speak always of *interpretations with such and such a degree of schematicity*" (p. 142). If he is correct, then the next question becomes *whether* and *how* we can measure the degree of schematicity. A vicious circle, it seems, that questions the usefulness of the whole approach.

In a sense, these points indicate that the discussion of schemata moved in the wrong direction. This is further confirmed if we look at recent applications that are stripped of much of the vagueness pointed out. Some of these applications seem to embrace a different approach—often keeping only the name and a certain amount of theoretical confusion; for example, Garro's (2000) recent publication in which she supposedly compares consensus theory with schema theory.

To begin with, it seems that the decisive turn away from traditional research topics in cognitive anthropology (it seems that almost everyone had to take a stance on that) was flawed from the very beginning, for it underestimated the power of these more traditional methods when applied in creative new ways.

For instance, two major criticisms have been brought against the elicitation of taxonomic models as described in Chapter 4, "Pile Sorting: The Hierarchical

Sorting of Elements."[6] First, according to the critics, taxonomies often seem to be a product of the methods rather than representing meaningful structures of informants' knowledge (D'Andrade, 1992, p. 51; 1995, p. 101). Second, such an approach ignores the varying amounts of information people have at the various taxonomic levels (D'Andrade, 1992, p. 51). It is no doubt important to be aware of both critiques when we apply these methods to investigate a taxonomic structure within a domain (see Chapter 4 on pile sorts). However, we should not ignore important research that has shown that taxonomic structures are an appropriate way of representing certain types of informants' knowledge in domains. Folk biology and the "natural" ordering of species in multipurpose taxonomies is one such a domain (see Atran, 1998; Berlin, 1992). Linguistic evidence can often serve as good indicators for the existence of a taxonomical structure (e.g., the terms *tree, oak tree,* and *white oak* indicate this kind of hierarchical structure). More important, however, are recent findings on category-based induction (see López et al., 1997; Medin et al., 1997) that clearly show that within the domain of folk biology, taxonomic order can indeed explain and predict individuals' reasoning strategies (see Osherson et al., 1990, for a general model). The ability to predict behavior (here reasoning pattern) from elicited taxonomies assures us that the taxonomic order is something that the informants actively use to order and understand the world (see Chapter 2 for the research strategy of predictive models). This is not to be confused with saying that taxonomical structures are the only way or always the best way of ordering information.

In addition, and contrary to the second critique mentioned above, ongoing research usually does not assume that an equal amount and/or kind of information is encoded in the different levels of a taxonomy (tree vs. oak) or even that these distributions are constant across different cultures. In fact, comparing individuals' preferences across cultures and expertise for using certain taxonomic levels in reasoning and in exploring the different amounts of information encoded on these levels is a major line of research (Coley, Medin, Proffitt, Lynch, & Atran, 1999; Rosch, Mervis, Gray, Johnson, & Boyes-Braem, 1976; see also Medin, Lynch, & Solomon, 2000, p. 128). Beyond that, researchers have also found that different levels of taxonomies do serve different functions (Murphy & Wisniewski, 1989). Again, much of this work has been done either in psychology (Murphy & Wisniewski, 1989), often ignoring the impact of culture and expertise, or in cross-disciplinary approaches. Unfortunately, this kind of work and topics are rather exceptional in anthropology.

Obviously, this kind of research goes beyond simply establishing culturally correct labels, or rules, which was the focus in many previous anthropological accounts. It goes a long way in exploring these "rules" themselves. What we often discover are "silent rules" or theories, of which the individuals are often not even aware (such as the underlying dimensions of taxonomic systems; see Medin, Ross, Atran, Cox, & Coley, 2003). These rules can be preferences, goals, or values (see Atran et al., 2002), or entail theories about the relationship between the items of a domain and the domain in general.

Understanding these *theories* seems to be a more rewarding way to understand an individual's interpretations of the world than to turn to schemata. In fact, many of the schemata evoked might be better conceptualized as naïve theories. This is the case for D'Andrade's (1995) "germ-schema" (p. 126). What D'Andrade describes are underlying reasoning patterns based on causal theories of germs and diseases. Turning to schemata as an explanation is neither the obvious thing to do nor is it particularly useful; on the contrary, it seems to obscure more than it explains.

In a sense, the notion of *naïve theory* extends the concept of schemata because it explores the existence of a coherent body of knowledge that involves causal understanding (Hatano & Inagaki, 1994, p. 172). These theories provide us with and are embedded in explanatory frameworks for understanding (and simplifying) our environment. As such, they help the individual to make inferences as well as to incorporate novel knowledge and situations (Carey, 1985; Murphy & Medin, 1985; Medin et al., 2000). These *framework theories* differ across domains of experience. A framework theory for understanding and predicting the behavior of physical objects necessarily differs from one that allows us to predict the behavior of sentient beings.

Again, this approach differs greatly from D'Andrade's (1995) definition of a schema as an organized framework of objects and relations, which has yet to be filled in with detail (p. 184).[7] To be sure, this is not to assume that naïve theories are organized in a "building block fashion," as criticized by Keller (1992, p. 63). However, neither are they incoherent, chaotic, or randomly variable. Goal orientation and values, for example, play a distinct role and interact with these theories and the resulting behavior in ways that are not yet obvious. Research done so far seems to make two points clear: Mental models clearly interact with behavior (see Atran et al., 1999) and are not to be seen as independent from values and goals (Atran et al., 2002). The latter is seen in the different ways Menominee Native American and Majority Culture fish experts of rural Wisconsin classify freshwater fish in a multipurpose taxonomy. While Menominee consistently show an orientation toward ecological reasoning, Majority Culture experts show a tendency to sort the species in accordance with the individuals' goals (game fish vs. "garbage" fish; Medin et al., 2002). Interestingly, Menominee nonexperts are similar to the experts in their group, while the goal orientation of Majority Culture experts seems to be acquired with increasing expertise (e.g., pursuing the activity). This once more shows the interrelation of activity, goals, and cognition (see Keller & Keller, 1996, for other examples).

In general, mental models can be described as simplified representations of the world that allow us to interpret observations, generate novel inferences, and solve problems (Gentner & Stevens, 1983; Johnson-Laird, 1983). Their ability to help individuals in solving problems is particularly interesting because it responds to some of the problems identified in schema theory. Dorothy Holland (1992), for example, describes how schema theory might be able to explain individuals' *avoiding certain behaviors*. According to Holland, "it is not difficult to imagine that a child comes to have a schema of fire that includes keeping his or her body out of the flames" (p. 74). Granted, it is not impossible, but is it plausible? If we follow Holland, would the child then need a different schema that includes keeping her clothes, toys, and her pets out of the flames? Would she need different schemata for types of fire (burning houses vs. kitchen fire) and locations? And how could the child always decide which is the right (relevant) schema to apply (see Medin & Ross, 1996, p. 306, for a similar critique).

It seems much more plausible that the child develops a theory of fire and its effects on physical bodies, allowing him or her to make inferences (e.g., what happens if . . .). This kind of view would more easily incorporate novel solutions in messy and not-so-messy situations (see Holland, 1992, p. 71, who raises this question). Following this line of reasoning, we are in a much better position to make sense of the lower-caste woman scaling the house wall to reach the balcony for an interview.[8] Our woman would "simply" bring different theories and models together (appropriate behavior; how to get into a house; climbing a wall; meeting the researcher's demand, etc.) with which she was faced at the time, combining them with certain goals and values. This view includes the possibility for change (incorporating novel knowledge and handling "messy situations") and might go a long way toward explaining processes of cultural change (see Ross, 1994, for an example, although not related to naïve theories or schema theory).

In fact, from this perspective, situations like those described by Holland (1992) cease to be messy and become a rather normal state of affairs within a constantly changing environment.

To be sure, in certain instances, the difference between a schema, a naïve theory, and a mental model might be only name preference. Janet Keller (1992, p. 60), for example, finds three basic properties for schemata: they (a) simplify experience, (b) facilitate inference, and (c) are potentially evoked by and made up of goals. Each of these three properties can also apply to naïve theories. Interestingly, in recent years, many researchers switched (back it seems) to the term *model* rather than *schema* (see Garro, 2000; Strauss & Quinn, 1997; Shore, 1996).

Some of the evoked schemata do not have the status of theories, however, such as those on the family described by Keller (1992, p. 61) based on a U.S. sample. Statements like "family is permanent" or "family is always in transition" seem to *describe certain instances of* rather than being *theories about* family. They seem more like instantiations of personal experiences and expectations that might eventually build up into a theory about family (see above for goals and values) or represent the informants' effort to come up with "silent rules" as described above. It is not surprising that it is on this level that researchers find many contradictions—between and across informants—in their data (Keller, 1992).

Again, all this is not to say that theories always form a coherent body and/or that an individual cannot hold more than one theory. Besides, not all theories have equal status. I have already introduced the concept of framework theories. Framework theories are theories that entail ontological commitments producing causal understanding of real-world phenomena (see Medin et al., 2000, p. 136) that allow and inspire the development of more specific theories. However, they do so by defining the domain of inquiry in the first place (Wellman & Gelman, 1992, p. 342). Interesting debates about the innateness of these theories are going on (see Atran, Medin, Lynch, Vapnarsky, & Ucan Ek', 2001; Bloch et al., 2001; Carey, 1985; Ross et al., 2003), but to go into this topic would lead us away from the present discussion. Instead, I just want to give a brief example: Many researchers have proposed that a framework theory for biology is innate in human beings (Atran, 1998; Atran et al., 2001; Hatano & Inagaki, 1994). For Hatano and Inagaki, this theory entails three main points: First, the individual must know which objects biology applies to (e.g., animals vs. pencils). Second, it entails a mode of inference that can produce consistent and reasonable predictions for attributes and behaviors of biological kinds (e.g., reproduction leads to offspring that are similar to the parents). Third, a nonintentional causal explanatory framework for behaviors is needed for individual survival and bodily processes (e.g., a person *can* move not because it has the intention to move, but because it has the ability to do so; Hatano & Inagaki, 1994, p. 173).

Obviously, it is not always clear how to solve these three issues on which most research converges. Carey (1985) and her associates, for example, deny young children a nonintentional causal framework because children often do not know the physiological mechanisms involved. Still other research indicates that this does not mean that children apply an intentional causal framework to biological processes (see Atran et al., 2001; Hatano & Inagaki, 1994, p. 176).

Besides, it is not at all clear whether adults are actually aware of the exact physiological mechanisms involved and how specific and detailed this knowledge would have to be to qualify. Again, these points are still up for discussion, but a discussion that seems to point in the right direction, enhancing our knowledge along its course.

Overall, it seems that a theoretical framework that focuses on naïve theories can go a long way toward explaining consistencies and at the same time explain inconsistencies and the appropriation and incorporation of novel knowledge. In fact, the consistencies might explain (or cause) the different levels of systemacity of schemata observed by D'Andrade (1995, p. 142). Having a theory about a cat creates clear pattern of behavior across contexts—a rather schematized description, one would think.

Several consequences follow from such a view: First, individuals do not necessarily draw on isolated bits of information, but rather actively construct knowledge along the general lines of underlying theories that are themselves often subject to change (see Boster, 1987a). Second, this means that we should expect different patterns of agreement depending on the level of specificity of these theories, from domain-defining framework theories to idiosyncratic models. We, therefore, have to adjust our methods and interpretations to these different levels. While this might be quite a challenge at times—two informants might give the same response for different reasons—it is definitely not an impossible task.

In Chapters 4 and 5, I described some tools for exploring and detecting individuals' theories, as well as the culturally shared aspects of these theories and models. Of course, when exploring those issues we have to be careful not to forget the level of specificity of our data, as Garro (2000, p. 306) correctly reminds us. The more specific we are in our explorations, the more differences we should expect between individuals' responses. Of course, this always depends on the domain of inquiry. Furthermore, as discussed above, we should not assume that only one correct model exists for a given group of people. Differences such as expertise or social position of the individuals might lead them to have very different understandings of an issue. Any discrepancies should, therefore, not be treated as informant error, but as differences that, if co-occurring among several individuals, might lead us to a better understanding of the epidemiology of cultural knowledge (see Chapters 2, 3, and 5 on this point). This is what Garro (2000, p. 311) seemed to have in mind for her research. Unfortunately, she confused good tools with bad applications (see Chapters 2, 3, and 5), misinterpreting the conditions and conclusions that could be drawn when the cultural consensus model is used as an exploratory tool (see Chapter 5).

It is exactly the confusion of specificity that brings Garro (2000) to reject the cultural consensus theory in favor of a cultural model theory, identified as schema theory (p. 307). Garro reports from her fieldwork on concepts of diabetes among the Anishinaabeg (Native Americans also known as Ojibway), stating that "individuals may have knowledge of these widely shared explanatory frameworks but, on the basis of their personally and socially situated experiences, they may reject specific or interrelated causal relationships as not having relevance for explaining diabetes" (p. 307). It is exactly here that the theory approach can help us: Do individuals agree on a single theory of diabetes, and if so, on what level of abstraction? Who rejects what kinds of causal relationships, and what do they replace them with (if anything)? These questions have to be included in the research plan outlined in Chapters 3 and 4 and can be connected to a theoretical approach known as naïve theory.

To be sure, this approach is meaningful only if it allows us to explore (a) commonalities without masking differences, and (b) a focus on different dimensions that might produce shared meanings (see Strauss & Quinn, 1997; see also Chapter 2). It permits us, however, to explore individual mental models and test the extent to which they are shared (again, on different levels) among the members of a group. In the mental model theory, cultural theories or cultural models would be mental models that are shared across the members of a group under study (see Kempton, Boster, & Heartley, 1995, p. 11).

With this in mind, I proposed a study of culture as a process, rather than a unit, looking at (a) the various degrees to which certain models are shared within a group and (b) their distribution among the members of a group. This view allows us to go beyond the simplistic version of cultures as independent entities (see D'Andrade, 1995, p. 250; Strauss & Quinn, 1997, p. 7) and to explore these processes across social groups.

This brings up another point: If culture is not an entity outside human beings, but rather a process of meaning making (taking into account outside stimuli, experiences, etc.), then the locus of its study has to be the individual as he or she participates in a larger context. It is here that psychology's focus on the individual, as well as the respective methods, become important (see Antweiler, 1993; Wassmann, 1995). At the same time, however, the psychological paradigm of tightly controlled experiments fails. If all of the above is correct, then we could never understand an individual's mind and ways of creating meaning outside its context, and we should assume essential differences in the respective processes from context to context. This is not breaking news to anthropologists. Psychological research, however, is often based on the opposite assumption (Bruner, 1996).

In the preceding chapters, I outlined some of the dangers and possibilities of cognitive research embedded in culture and cultural research that is informed by cognitive processes. In this final chapter, in particular, I have tried to make evident the irony with which anthropology and psychology complement each other in both their strengths and weaknesses. Moving away from questions raised in this book, as well as from the larger scientific discourse, anthropology turned into what Barrett (1996, p. 179) pointedly calls a no-name anthropology suffering from extreme theoretical fatigue (Cerroni-Long, 1999, p. 15). This might come to a surprise to many readers because anthropology seems to be full of theories. Most anthropological theories, however, are applied at a meta level (if at all) and are often concerned only with their academic field (see D'Andrade, 1999, p. 222). To a large extent, however, the field has ignored basic issues of human thinking and behavior with respect to culture and turned away from what should be anthropology's role in the social science: THE STUDY OF HUMAN CULTURE AND ITS RELATION TO THOUGHT AND BEHAVIOR.

It is only recently that this topic has regained importance (and publicity, including in the *New York Times*), but anthropology has been conspicuously absent from recent discussions.

While this is mostly due to a lack of interest, it is also the consequence of methods that are incompatible with those applied in other fields of the cognitive sciences.

Leaving the field to psychology didn't really solve the problems, either. On the contrary, it just created new ones. While most psychologists approach their topics with clear methods, the use of these methods, the basic assumptions (including choice of informants and strategies), and the underlying theories often proved to be major obstacles to a better understanding of the issues at hand. In order to avoid all these pitfalls, a sound research strategy is needed that combines the strength of the two disciplines and overcomes their individual weaknesses.

Several pieces of research show that this can be achieved. However, this kind of work is tedious, expansive, and time-consuming. Still, if we want to understand processes of culture and cognition, it is probably the only way to go.

A New Ethnography and an Enhanced Cognitive Science

Back in the 1960s, when cognitive anthropology experienced its heyday, the term *new ethnography* was coined (Sturtevant, 1964). It was meant to describe the improved methods that would enhance the ethnographer's task with respect to objectivity and clarity. It was thought that clear methods could provide the researcher with better insights into specifics that otherwise would be left undetected.

While anthropology still is in dire need of clear methods, new importance has recently been given to such an approach (see Antweiler, 1993; Wassmann, 1995). In the cognitive sciences, it becomes increasingly evident that to gain a true understanding of human thinking and behavior, a comparative science that takes controlled experiments into the field is needed (Medin & Atran, 1999; Shore, 1996). Many problems have been detected along the way. If we take culture as an important aspect of cognition and the human mind (see Shore, 1996), then a clear understanding of cultural processes and their effect on thought processes has to be one of our priorities. This includes sound ethnographic work combined with clear experimental designs for testing our hypotheses and exploring the cognitive dimensions of these domains.

I have described the need for detailed developmental studies that explore how cultural knowledge emerges and is maintained, albeit not unchanged. This research should also help to find possible universals, for these might be easiest to be detected among young children. This is important because it is possible that children are able to overcome an innate theory of biology based on their cultural upbringing (see Hirschfeld, 1996, p. xii). This is indicated in the example of an 8-year-old Lacandon boy in my studies. When asked in a triad task to pick the two items that were most similar, he placed the Lacandon Maya together with howler monkeys rather than with Tzeltal Maya settlers. His justification was quite simple. According to his grandfather, the howler monkeys originally were Lacandones whom the gods converted into howler monkeys as a punishment for their misbehavior. Developmental studies can take place at (almost) all different ages, including different topics such as looking at children's naïve theories, parental input, and the workings of a standardized school system. All these factors are highly relevant in understanding how culture is shaped, and also how it shapes our thoughts.

Historical studies can further provide some important evidence (see Wolff, Medin, & Pankratz, 1999), especially if combined with studies of cultural change (see Ross, 2001, 2002a, 2002b; Ross & Medin, 2003). Of course, we have to be careful not to be too quick to assume causal connections, and we must be aware that these changes can take very different routes. They can be spearheaded both by experts in a domain or by novices; another distinction that is important to consider (see Medin et al., 2002).

These are all important aspects of understanding culture as a process and its impact on cognition. Before I conclude, however, let me touch briefly on a subject that hasn't been mentioned yet, but that is likely to become an important research topic in the near future:

If culture makes a difference for the way we think, then we have to explore the processes of acculturation and the cognition of individuals who are exposed to different cultures. Biculturalism is a newly coined term, describing instances when individuals supposedly hold models from two cultures that emerge upon priming (Hong, Morris, Chui, & Martinez, 2000). This intriguing field is definitely undertheorized, and we have yet to understand the processes at work and the depth of features to which it applies. Furthermore, no clear data are available exploring how different social and historical processes play out in the cognitive makeup of a person (time of contact, language abilities, economic situation, and kinds of cultures evolved, to name just a few).

This lack of research is particularly unfortunate at a time when migrants make up large parts of the populations in many countries. Interestingly, although anthropology has tackled issues of migration for quite some time now, no clear theory has yet emerged. It seems that rich fields for further exploration of the connections between culture and cognition exist. I hope this book will contribute to the field by helping to combine two different approaches—anthropology and psychology—channeling both toward the same aim: to understand human culture, cognition, and behavior and their interrelations.

Notes

1. To be fair, in his book, Bernard pays attention to issues such as sampling methods as well as informant agreement. Most of the methods he proposes also allow clear replications. In this sense, he definitely proposes a better view than one might guess from this particular discussion.

2. Let me note a point to the critics: the model (and its mathematical properties) is well described in several papers, which allows further analysis (and criticism) of its assumptions and usage. If nothing else, at least with this respect it presents a real advance in the scientific endeavor.

3. This was, in fact, a discussion in the 70s in anthropology whether it is better for a researcher to go to the field without any previous knowledge or whether he/she should be prepared with respect to theory and ethnography.

4. For an overview, see Casson 1983.

5. Examples of cultural schemata and the difficulties they might pose to anthropologists are frequent. For example, in narratives it is very common that certain information is encoded particularly for the outside anthropologist so that he can

understand the reference made (see Ross 1997a). However, if this information is not provided, anthropologists are often at a loss in understanding the "message."

6. A taxonomic relation occurs when one segregate or taxa includes other segregates or taxa (D'Andrade 1995:34; see also Frake 1962). An example would be the two segregates "tree" and "vine" each having different subsegregates, such as "oak-tree" and "strangler vine."

7. D'Andrade's idea of schemata seems more to be related to Bourdieu's concept of habitus.

8. While this is a remarkable example of innovation, it bears the question if there was, indeed, a need to test this informant's innovativeness forcing her into this new framework.

References

Abu-Lughod, L. (1991). Writing against culture. In G. Fox (Ed.), *Recapturing anthropology: Working in the present* (pp. 137-162). Santa Fe, NM: School of American Research Press.

Abu-Lughod, L. (1999). Comments to Brumann. *Current Anthropology, 40,* 13-15.

Anderson, C. (1999). Attributional style, depression, and loneliness: A cross-cultural comparison of American and Chinese students. *Personality & Social Psychology Bulletin, 25,* 482-499.

Anglin, J. (1970). *The growth of word meaning.* Cambridge, MA: MIT Press.

Anglin, J. (1977). *Word, object, and conceptual development.* New York: Norton.

Antweiler, C. (1993). Universelle Erhebungsmethoden und lokale Kognition am Beispiel urbaner Umweltethnologie in Süd-Sulawesi/Indonesien. *Zeitschrift für Ethnologie, 118,* 251-287.

Appadurai, A. (1996). *Modernity at large: Cultural dimensions of globalization.* Minneapolis: University of Minnesota Press.

Argyrou, V. (1999). Sameness and the ethnological will to meaning [with commentaries]. *Current Anthropology, 40,* 29-41.

Atran, S. (1990). *Cognitive foundations of natural history.* Cambridge, MA: Cambridge University Press.

Atran, A. (1998). Folk biology and the anthropology of science: Cognitive universals and cultural particulars. *Behavioral Brain Science, 21*(4), 547-609.

Atran, A. (1999). Itzaj Maya folkbiological taxonomy. In D. Medin & S. Atran (Eds.), *Folkbiology* (pp. 119-203). Cambridge, MA: MIT Press.

Atran, S., Medin, D., Lynch, E., Vapnarsky, V., & Ucan Ek', E. (2001). Folkbiology doesn't come from folkpsychology: Evidence from Yukatek Maya in cross-cultural perspective. *Culture and Cognition, 1,* 3-42.

Atran, S., Medin, D., Ross, N., Lynch, E., Coley, J., Ucan Ek', E., & Vapnarsky, V. (1999). Folkecology and commons management in the Maya Lowlands. *Proceedings of the National Academy of Sciences, 96,* 7598-7603.

Atran, S., Medin, D., Ross, N., Lynch, E., Vapnarsky, V., Ucan Ek', E., Coley, J., Timura, C., & Baran, M. (2002). Folkecology, cultural epidemiology, and the spirit of the commons: A garden experiment in the Maya Lowlands, 1995-2000. *Current Anthropology, 43,* 421-450.

Aunger, R. (1999). Against idealism/contra consensus. *Current Anthropology, 40,* 93-101.

Bailenson, J., Shum, M., Atran, S., Medin, D., & Coley, J. (2002). A bird's eye view: Triangulating biological categorization and reasoning within and across cultures and expertise levels. *Cognition, 84,* 1-53.

Barsalou, L. (1989). Intraconcept similarity and its implications for interconcept similarity. In S. Vosniadou & A. Ortony (Eds.), *Similarity and analogical reasoning* (pp. 76-121). Cambridge, UK: Cambridge University Press.

Barnett, H. G. (1953). *Innovation: The basis of cultural change.* New York: McGraw-Hill.

Barrett, S. (1996). *Anthropology: A student's guide to theory and method.* Toronto: University of Toronto Press.

Bartlett, F. C. (1932). *Remembering.* Cambridge, UK: Cambridge University Press.

Bartlett, F. C. (1937). Psychological methods and anthropological problems. *Africa, 10,* 401-419.

Bechtel, W., Abrahamson, A., & Graham, G. (1998). The life of cognitive science. In W. Bechtel & G. Graham (Eds.), *A companion to cognitive science* (pp. 2-104). Malden, MA: Blackwell.

Berlin, B. (1992). *Ethnobiological classification.* Princeton, NJ: Princeton University Press.

Berlin, B., Breedlove, D., & Raven, P. (1968). Covert categories and folk taxonomies. *American Anthropologist, 70,* 290-299.

Berlin, B., Breedlove, D., & Raven, P. (1973). General principles of classification and nomenclature in folk biology. *American Anthropologist, 74,* 214-242.

Berlin, B., Breedlove, D., & Raven, P. (1974). *Principles of Tzeltal plant classification.* New York: Academic Press.

Berlin, B., & Kay, P. (1969). *Basic color terms.* Berkeley: University of California Press.

Berlin, B., & Romney, K. (1964). Some semantic implications of Tzeltal numeral classifiers. *American Anthropologist, 66,* 79-98.

Bernard, H. R. (1995). *Research methods in anthropology.* Walnut Creek, CA: AltaMira Press/Sage.

Berry, J., Poortinga, Y., & Pandey, J. (Eds.). (1997). *Handbook of cross-cultural psychology* (Vol. 1). Needham Heights, MA: Allyn & Bacon.

Berry, J., Poortinga, Y., Segall, M., & Dasen, P. (Eds.). (1992). *Cross-cultural psychology: Research and applications.* Cambridge, UK: Cambridge University Press.

Bloch, M., Solomon, G., & Carey, S. (2001). Zafimaniry: An understanding of what is passed from parents to children: A cross-cultural investigation. *Culture and Cognition, 1,* 43-68.

Borofsky, R. (1994). Rethinking the cultural. In R. Borofsky (Ed.), *Assessing cultural anthropology* (pp. 243-249). New York: McGraw-Hill.

Boster, J. (1986a). Exchange varieties and information between Aguaruna manioc cultivators. *American Anthropologist, 88*(2), 428-436.

Boster, J. (1986b). Requiem for the omniscient informant: There's life in the old girl yet. In J. Dougherty (Ed.), *Directions in cognitive anthropology* (S.177-S.197). Urbana: University of Illinois Press.

Boster, J. (1987a). Agreement between biological classification systems is not dependent on cultural transmission. *American Anthropologist, 89,* 914-920.

Boster, J. (1987b). Introduction. In Intracultural Variation [Special issue]. *American Behavioral Scientist, 31(2),* 150-162.

Boster, J. (1991). The information economy model applied to biological similarity judgment. In L. B. Resnick, J. M. Levine, & S. D. Teasley (Eds.), *Perspectives on socially shared cognition.* Washington, DC: American Psychological Association.

Boster, J., & Johnson, J. (1989). Form or function: A comparison of expert and novice judgments of similarity among fish. *American Anthropologist, 91,* 866-889.

Boster, J., & Weller, S. (1990). Cognitive and contextual variation in hot-cold classifications. *American Anthropologist, 92,* 171-178.

Bourdieu, P. (1977). *Outline of a theory of practice.* Cambridge, UK: Cambridge University Press.

Bourdieu, P. (1991). *Language & symbolic power* (J. B. Thompson, Ed.). Cambridge, MA: Harvard University Press.

Brightman, R. (1995). Forget culture: Replacement, transcendence, relexification. *Cultural Anthropology, 10,* 509-546.

Brumann, C. (1999). Writing for culture: Why a successful concept should not be discarded. *Current Anthropology, 40,* 1-27.

Bruner, J. (1996). Introduction. In B. Shore (Ed.), *Culture in mind.* New York: Oxford University Press.

Burt, R. S. (1992). *Structural holes: The social structure of competition.* Cambridge, MA: Harvard University Press.

Burton, M., & Kirk, L. (1979). Sex differences in Maasai cognition of personality and social identity. *American Anthropologist, 81,* 841-873.

Burton, M., & Nerlove, S. (1976). Balanced designs for triad tests: Two examples from English. *Social Science Research, 5,* 247-267.

Burton, M., & Romney, K. (1975). A multidimensional representation of role terms. *American Ethnologist, 2,* 397-407.

Cancian, F. (1972). *The innovator's situation.* Stanford, CA: Stanford University Press.

Cancian, F. (1992). *The decline of community in Zinacantán.* Stanford, CA: Stanford University Press.

Carey, S. (1985). *Conceptual change in childhood.* Cambridge, MA: MIT Press.

Carey, S. (1995). On the origin of causal understanding. In D. Sperber, D. Premack, & A. J. Premack (Eds.), *Causal cognition: A multidisciplinary debate.* New York: Oxford University Press.

Carey, S. (1999). Sources of conceptual change. In E. Scholnick, K. Nelson, S. Gelman, & P. Miller (Eds.), *Conceptual development: Piaget's legacy.* Mahwah, NJ: Lawrence Erlbaum.

Casson, R. (1983). Schemata in cognitive anthropology. *Annual Review of Anthropology, 12,* 429-462.

Cerroni-Long, E. (1999). Comment on Brumann. *Current Anthropology, 40,* 15-16.

Chomsky, N. (1959). Review of Skinner's *Verbal behavior*. *Language, 35,* 26-58.

Choy, I., & Nisbett, R. (2000). The cultural psychology of surprise: Holistic theories and recognition of contradiction. *Journal of Personality and Social Psychology, 79*(6), 890-905.

Clifford, J. (1988). *The predicament of culture: Twentieth-century ethnography, literature, and art.* Cambridge, MA: Harvard University Press.

Cochran, W., & Cox, G. (1957). *Experimental design.* New York: John Wiley.

Cole, M. (1995). Culture and cognitive development: From cross-cultural research to creating systems of cultural mediation. *Culture and Psychology, 1,* 25-54.

Cole, M. (1996). *Cultural psychology: A once and future discipline.* Cambridge, MA: Belknap Press.

Coleman, J. S., Katz, E., & Mentzel, H. (1957). The diffusion of an innovation among physicians. *Sociometry, 20,* 253-270.

Coley, J. (2000). On the importance of comparative research: The case of folkbiology [Special issue]. *Child Development, 71*(1), 82-90.

Coley, J., Medin, D., Proffitt, J., Lynch, E., & Atran, S. (1999). Inductive reasoning in folkbiological thought. In D. Medin & S. Atran (Eds.), *Folkbiology.* Cambridge, MA: MIT Press.

Collins, D., & Ross, N. (n.d.). *What's its name: Patterns of plant identification among two Q'eqchi' Maya groups in Guatemala.* Unpublished manuscript.

Conklin, H. (1954). *The relation of Haunóo culture to the plant world.* Doctoral dissertation, Yale University.

D'Andrade, R. (1989). Cultural sharing and diversity. In R. Bolton (Ed.), *The content of culture: Constants and variants* (pp. 349-362). New Haven, CT: HRAF Press.

D'Andrade, R. (1990). Culture and human cognition. In J. Stigler, R. Shweder, & G. Herdt (Eds.), *Cultural psychology: Essays on comparative human development* (pp. 65-129). Cambridge, UK: Cambridge University Press.

D'Andrade, R. (1992). Cognitive anthropology. In G. Schwartz, M. White, & C. Lutz (Eds.), *New directions in psychological anthropology* (pp. 47-58). Cambridge, UK: Cambridge University Press.

D'Andrade, R. (1995). *The development of cognitive anthropology.* Cambridge, UK: Cambridge University Press.

D'Andrade, R. (1999). Comment to Brumann. *Current Anthropology, 40,* 16-17.

D'Andrade, R. (1999). The sad story of anthropology, 1950-1999. In E. L. Cerroni-Long (Ed.), *Anthropological theory in North America.* Westport, CT: Berin & Garvey.

Diamond, J. (1993). New Guineans and their natural world. In S. Kellert & E. O. Wilson (Eds.), *The biophilia hypothesis* (pp. 251-271). Washington, DC: Island Press.

Diamond, J., & Bishop, K. D. (1999). Ethno-ornithology of the Ketengban people, Indonesian New Guinea. In D. Medin & S. Atran (Eds.), *Folkbiology* (pp. 17-45). Cambridge, MA: MIT Press.

Driver, H. (1970). Statistical studies of continuous geographical distributions. In R. Naroll & R. Cohen (Eds.), *A handbook of method in cultural anthropology* (pp. 620-639). New York: Columbia University Press.

Driver, H., & Kroeber, A. (1932). Quantitative expression of cultural relationships. *University of California Publications in American Archaeology and Ethnology, 31*, 211-256.

Dürr, E. (1991). *Der Aufstand der Tzeltal (1712-1713), Analyse einer evitalisations Bewegung im kolonialen Mesoamerika.* Münster: Lit Verlag.

Dürr, E. (1998). Finalidades y cambios en el desarollo procesal de la sublevación de los Tzeltales (1712-1713) en los Altos de Chiapas, México. *Memorias del Tercer Congresso Internacional de Mayistas* (Julio, 1995), Chetumal (pp. 773-787). Mexico: UNAM.

Evans-Pritchard, E. E. (1940). *The Nuer: A description of the modes of livelihood and political institutions of a Nilotic people.* Oxford, UK: Clarendon Press.

Fabian, J. (2000). To whom it may concern. *Anthropology Newsletter, 41*(4), 9.

Fabrega, H. (1970). On the specificity of folk illness. *Southwestern Journal of Anthropology, 26*, 305-314.

Fischhoff, B. (1975). Hindsight ≠ foresight. The effect of outcome knowledge on judgment under uncertainty. *Journal of Experimental Psychology: Human Perception and Performance, 1*, 288-299.

Fish, J. (2000). What anthropology can do for psychology: Facing physics envy, ethnocentrism, and a belief in race. *American Anthropologist, 102*, 552-563.

Frake, C. (1962). *The ethnographic study of cognitive systems.* Washington, DC: Society of Washington.

Freeman, D. (1983). *Margaret Mead and Samoa: The making and unmaking of an anthropological myth.* Cambridge, MA: Harvard University Press.

Freeman, L., Romney, K., Ferreira-Pinto, J., Klein, R. E., & Smith, T. (1981). Guatemalan and U.S. concepts of success and failure. *Human Organization, 40*(2), 140-145.

Friedman, J. (1994). *Cultural identity and global process.* London: Sage.

Garro, L. (1986). Intracultural variation in folkmedical knowledge. A comparison between curers and non-curers. *American Anthropologist, 88*(2), 351-370.

Garro, L. (2000). Remembering what one knows and the construction of the past: A comparison of cultural consensus theory and cultural schema theory. *Ethnos, 28*(3), 275-319.

Geertz, C. (1973). *The interpretation of cultures.* New York: Basic Books.

Gentner, D., & Stevens, A. (1983). *Mental models.* Hillsdale, NJ: Lawrence Erlbaum.

Gil-White, F. (2001). Are ethnic groups biological "species" to the human brain? Essentialism in our cognition of some social categories. *Current Anthropology, 41*(4), 515-554.

Gingrich, A. (1999). Commentary to Brumann, C. *Current Anthropology, 40*, 17-18.

Goodenough, W. (1956). Componential analysis and the study of meaning. *Language, 32*, 195-216.

Goodenough, W. (1964). Cultural anthropology and linguistics. In D. Hymes (Ed.), *Language in culture and society* (pp. 36-39). New York: Harper and Row.

Goodenough, W. (1981). *Culture, language, and society.* Menlo Park, CA: Cummings.

Greenfield, P. (1997). Culture as process: Empirical methods for cultural psychology. In J. Berry, Y. Poortinga, & J. Pandey (Eds.), *Handbook of cross-cultural psychology* (Vol. 1, pp. 301-346). Needham Heights, MA: Allyn & Bacon.

Greenfield, P. (2000). What psychology can do for anthropology, or why anthropology took postmodernism on the chin. *American Anthropologist, 102*(3), 564-576.

Greenfield, P., & Childs, C. (1978). Understanding sibling concepts: A developmental study of kin terms in Zinacantán. In P. Dasen (Ed.), *Piagetian psychology* (pp. 335-358). New York: Gardner Press.

Gumperz, J., & Levinson, S. (Eds.). (1996). *Rethinking linguistic relativity*. Cambridge, UK: Cambridge University Press.

Hammel, E. (1962). Social rank and evolutionary position in a coastal Peruvian village. *Southwestern Journal of Anthropology, 18*, 199-215.

Hannerz, U. (1992). *Cultural complexities: Studies in the social organization of meaning*. New York: Columbia University Press.

Hannerz, U. (1999). Commentary to Brumann, C. *Current Anthropology, 40*, pp. 18-19.

Harris, M. (1975). *Culture, people, nature: An introduction to general anthropology* (2nd ed.). New York: Crowell.

Hartwig, F., & Dearing, B. (1979). *Exploratory data analysis*. Beverly Hills, CA: Sage.

Hatano, G., & Inagaki, K. (1994). Young children's naïve theory of biology. *Cognition, 50*, 171-188.

Henley, N. (1969). A psychological study of the semantics of animal terms. *Journal of Verbal Learning and Verbal Behavior, 8*, 176-184.

Hirschberger, W. (1988). *Wörterbuch der Völkerkunde*. Berlin: Reimer Verlag.

Hirschfeld, L. (1995). Do children have a theory of race? *Cognition, 54*, 209-252.

Hirschfeld, L. (1996). *Race in the making*. Cambridge: MIT Press.

Hobsbawm, E., & Ranger, T. (Eds.). (1983). *The invention of tradition*. Cambridge, UK: Cambridge University Press.

Hollan, D. (2000). Constructivist models of the mind, contemporary psychoanalysis and the development of culture theory. *American Anthropologist, 102*(3), 538-550.

Holland, D. (1992). The woman who climbed up the house: Some limitations of schema theory. In T. Schwartz, G. White, & C. Lutz, (Eds.), *New directions in psychological anthropology* (pp. 68-79). Cambridge, UK: Cambridge University Press.

Holstein, J., & Gubrium, J. (1995). *The active interview*. Thousand Oaks, CA: Sage.

Hong, Y., Morris, M., Chui, C., & Martinez, V. (2000). Multicultural minds: A dynamic constructivist approach to culture and cognition. *American Psychologist, 55*, 709-720.

Hunn, E. (1985). The utilitarian factor in folk biological classification. In J. Dougherty (Ed.), *Directions in cognitive anthropology* (pp. 117-140). Urbana: University of Illinois Press.

Huntington, S. (1993). The clash of civilizations? *Foreign Affairs, 72*(3), 22-49.

Huntington, S. (1996). *The clash of civilizations and the remaking of world order*. New York: Simon & Schuster.

Hutchins, E. (1995). *Cognition in the wild*. Cambridge, MA: MIT Press.

Inagaki, K. (1990). The effects of raising animals on children's biological knowledge. *British Journal of Developmental Psychology, 8,* 119-129.

Ingold, T. (1993). The art of translation in a continuous world. In G. Pálsson (Ed.), *Beyond boundaries: Understanding, translation, and the anthropological discourse* (pp. 210-230). Oxford, UK: Berg.

Johansen, U. (1992). Materielle oder materialisierte Kultur? *Zeitschrift für Ethnologie, 117,* 1-15.

Johnson, K. E., Mervis, C. B., & Boster, J. S. (1992). Developmental changes within the structure of the mammal domain. *Developmental Psychology, 28,* 74-83.

Johnson-Laird, P. N. (1983). *Mental models: Towards a cognitive science of language, inference, and consciousness.* Cambridge, MA: Harvard University Press.

Keesing, R. (1981). *Cultural anthropology: A contemporary perspective* (2nd ed.). New York: Holt, Rinehart and Winston.

Keller, C., & Keller, J. (1996). *Cognition and tool use: The blacksmith at work.* Cambridge, UK: Cambridge University Press.

Keller, J. (1992). Schemes for schemata. In T. Schwartz, G. White, & C. Lutz (Eds.), *New directions in psychological anthropology* (pp. 59-67). Cambridge, UK: Cambridge University Press.

Kelly, G. (1955). *The psychology of personal constructs* (2 Vols.). Cambridge, UK: Cambridge University Press.

Kempton, W. (1987). Variation in folkmodels and consequent behavior. *American Behavioral Scientist, 31*(2), 2013-2018.

Kempton, W., Boster, J., & Heartley, J. (1995). *Environmental values in American culture.* Cambridge, MA: MIT Press.

Kirk, L., & Burton, M. (1977). Meaning and context: A study in contextual shifts in meaning of Maasai personality descriptors. *American Ethnologist, 4,* 734-761.

Kitayama, S., Markus, H., Matsumoto, H., & Norasakkunkit, V. (1997). Individual and collective processes in the construction of the self: Self-enhancement in the United States and self-criticism in Japan. *Journal of Personality and Social Psychology, 72*(6), 1245-1267.

Kluckhohn, C. (1949a). *Mirror of man: The relation of anthropology to modern life.* New York: Whittlesey House.

Kluckhohn, C. (1949b). The philosophy of the Navajo Indians. In F. Northrop (Ed.), *Ideological differences and world order.* New Haven, CT: Yale University Press.

Knorr-Cetina, K. (1993). Anthropologie und Ethnomethodologie: Eine theoretische und methodische Herausforderung. In J. Stagl (Hg.), *Grundfragen der Ethnologie* (pp. 167-182). Berlin: Reimer Verlag.

Köhler, U. (1977). *Chonbilal Ch'ulelal. Grundformen mesoamerika-nischer Kosmologie und Religion in einem Gebets-text auf Maya Tzotzil.* Wiesbaden: Steiner Verlag.

Köhler, U. (1989). Schamanismus in Mesoamerika? In B. Illius & M. Laubscher (Eds.), *Circumpacifica, Festschrift für Thomas Bartels* (pp. 257-275). Frankfurt am Main: P. Lang.

Kokot, W., Lang, H., & Hinz, E. (1982). Current trends in cognitive anthropology. *Anthropos, 77*, 329-350.

Kuper, A. (1994). Culture, identity and the project of a cosmopolitan anthropology. *Man, 29*, 537-554.

Lakoff, G. (1987). *Women, fire and dangerous things*. Chicago: University of Chicago Press.

Lang, H. (1998). Kultur und Evolutionstheorie. *Zeitschrift für Ethnologie, 123*, 5-20.

La Torre-Cuadros, M., & Ross, N. (2003). Secondary-biodiversity: Local perceptions of forest habitats, the Maya of Solferino, Quintana Roo, Mexico. *Journal of Ethnobiology*.

Lawrence, J. (1995). Requiem or recognition: Not omniscient and not plain informants. *Culture & Psychology, 1*, 215-225.

Le Vine, R. (1984). Properties of culture: An ethnographic view. R. Shweder & R. Le Vine (Eds.), *Culture theory: Essays on mind, self and emotions* (pp. 67-87). Cambridge, UK: Cambridge University Press.

Lewis-Beck, M. (1980). *Applied regression: An introduction*. Beverly Hills, CA: Sage.

Lewis, O. (1951). *Life in a Mexican village: Tepoztlán restudied*. Urbana: University of Illinois Press.

Linger, D. (1994). Has culture theory lost its mind? *Ethos, 22*, 284-315.

Linton, R. (1936). *The study of man: An introduction*. New York: D. Appleton-Century.

López, A., Atran, S., Coley, J., Medin, D., & Smith, E. (1997). The tree of life. Universals of folkbiological taxonomies and inductions. *Cognitive Psychology, 32*, 251-295.

Lounsbury, F. (1956). A semantic analysis of the Pawnee kinship usage. *Language, 32*, 159-194.

Madrigal, L. (1998). *Statistics for anthropology*. Cambridge, UK: Cambridge University Press.

Mahalingam, R. (1999). Essentialism, power and representation of caste: A developmental study. *Dissertation Abstracts International: Section B: the Sciences & Engineering. Vol. 60(2-B), Aug. 1999, 0856. Cary, NC: University Microfilms International*.

Manners, R., & Kaplan, D. (1968). Notes on a theory and non-theory in anthropology. In R. Manners & D. Kaplan (Eds.), *Theory in anthropology: A sourcebook*. Chicago: Aldine.

Markus, H., & Kitayama, S. (1991). Culture and the self: Implications for cognition, emotion and motivation. *Psychological Review, 98*(2), 224-253.

Masuda, T., & Nisbett, R. (2001). Attending holistically versus analytically: Comparing the context sensitivity of Japanese and Americans. *Journal of Personality and Social Psychology, 81*(5), 922-934.

McGee, J., & Warms, R. (1996). *Anthropological theory: An introductory history*. Mountain View, CA: Mayfield.

Medin, D., & Atran, S. (1999). Introduction. In D. Medin & S. Atran (Eds.), *Folkbiology*. Cambridge, MA: MIT Press.

Medin, D., Lynch, E., Coley, J., & Atran, S. (1997). Categorization and reasoning among tree experts: Do all roads lead to Rome? *Cognitive Psychology, 32,* 49-96.

Medin, D., Lynch, E., & Solomon, K. (2000). Are there kinds of concepts? *Annual Review of Psychology, 51,* 121-147.

Medin, D., & Ross, B. (1996). *Cognitive psychology.* Fort Worth, TX: Harcourt Brace College.

Medin, D., Ross, N., Atran, S., Burnett, R., & Blok, S. (2002). Categorization and reasoning in relation to culture and expertise. *The Psychology of Learning and Motivation, 41,* 1-41.

Medin, D., Ross, N., Atran, S., Cox, D., & Coley, J. (2003). *The role of culture in the folkbiology of freshwater fish.* Manuscript submitted for publication.

Moore, C., Lizeth, R., & Rusch, C. (2001, April). *Measuring intra- and inter-cultural variation among free lists: An example from English and Spanish emotion terms.* Paper presented at the Culture and Explanation Workshop, Northwestern University.

Morgan, L. H. (1871). Systems of consanguinity and affinity of the human family (*Smithsonian Contributions to Knowledge,* Vol. 17, No. 218). Washington, D.C.

Murphy, G. L., & Medin, D. (1985). The role of theories in conceptual coherence. *Psychological Review, 92,* 289-316.

Murphy, G. L., & Wisniewski, E. (1989). Categorizing objects in isolation and in scenes: What a superordinate is good for. *Journal of Experimental Psychology: Learning, Memory and Cognition, 15,* 572-586.

Nakao, K., & Romney, K. (1984). A method of testing alternative theories: An example from English kinship. *American Anthropologist, 86,* 668-673.

Narrol, R. (1962). *Data quality control, a new research technique: Prolegomena to a cross-cultural study of culture stress.* New York: Free Press of Glencoe.

Nunally, J. (1978). *Psychometric theory.* New York: McGraw-Hill.

Olson, D., & Torrance, N. (1996). *Modes of thought: Explorations in culture and cognition.* Cambridge, UK: Cambridge University Press.

Osherson, D., Smith, E., Wilkie, O., López, A., & Shafir, E. (1990). Category based induction. *Psychological Review, 97,* 85-200.

Ostrom, E. (1990). *Governing the commons: The evolution of institutions for collective action.* New York: Cambridge University Press.

Ostrom, E. (1998). A behavioral approach to the rational choice theory of collective action. *American Political Science Review, 92,* 289-316.

Paarup-Laursen, B. (1989). The meaning of illness among the Koma of Northern Nigeria. In A. Jacobson-Widding & D. Westerlund (Eds.), *Culture, experience and pluralism.* Uppsala, Sweden: Almqvist & Wiksell.

Quinn, N., & Holland, D. (1987). Culture and cognition. In D. Holland & N. Quinn (Eds.), *Cultural models in language and thought* (pp. 3-40). Cambridge, UK: Cambridge University Press.

Radcliffe-Brown, A. R. (1940). On social structure. *Journal of the Royal Anthropological Society of Great Britain and Ireland, 70,* 1-12.

Radcliffe-Brown, A. R. (1952). *Structure and function in primitive society.* Glencoe, IL: Free Press.

Redfield, R. (1930). *Tepoztlan, a Mexican village: A study of folk life.* Chicago: University of Chicago Press.

Rogers, E. M. (1979). Network analysis of the diffusion of innovations. In P. Holland & S. Leinhardt (Eds.), *Perspectives on social network research* (pp. 137-164). New York: Academic Press.

Romney, K. (1994). Cultural knowledge and cognitive structure. In M. Suárez-Orozco, G. Spindler, & L. Spindler (Eds.), *The making of psychological anthropology* (Vol. 2, pp. 254-283). Fort Worth, TX: Harcourt Brace College.

Romney, K. (1999). Cultural consensus as a statistical model. *Current Anthropology, 40,* 103-115.

Romney, K., Boyd, J., Moore, C., Batchelder, W., & Brazil, T. (1996). Culture as shared cognitive representations. In *Proceedings of the National Academy of Sciences* [USA], *93,* 4699-4705.

Romney, K., & D'Andradé, R. (1964). Cognitive aspects of English kin terms. *American Anthropologist, 68,* 146-170.

Romney, K., Moore, C., & Rusch, C. (1997). Cultural universals: Measuring the semantic structure of emotion terms in English and Japanese. *Proceedings of the National Academy of Sciences, 94,* 5489-5494.

Romney, K., & Weller, S. (1989). Systemic culture patterns and high concordance codes. In R. Bolton (Ed.), *The content of culture: Constants and variants* (pp. 363-381). New Haven, CT: Yale University Press.

Romney, K., Weller, S., & Batchelder, W. (1986). Culture as consensus: A theory of culture and informant accuracy. *American Anthropologist, 88,* 313-338.

Rosaldo, R. (1989). *Culture and truth: The remaking of social analysis.* Boston: Beacon.

Rosch, E. (1975). Cognitive representations of semantic categories. *Journal of Experimental Psychology, 104,* 192-233.

Rosch, E., Mervis, C., Gray, W., Johnson, D. Boyes-Braem, P. (1976). Basic objects in natural categories. *Cognitive Psychology, 8,* 382-439.

Roseberry, W. (1989). *Anthropologies and histories: Essays in culture, history and political economy.* New Brunswick, NJ: Rutgers University Press.

Ross, N. (1994). Die Entwicklung der Blumenindustrie in Zinacantán. *Zeitschrift für Ethnologie, 119,* 59-73.

Ross, N. (1997). *Nutz Lok'el li Kaxlane. Die Vertreibung der Ladinos aus San Andrés Larraínzar, Chiapas, Mexico. Von Geschichten, einem Ereignis und Geschichte.* Münster: LIT Verlag.

Ross, N. (2001). *Bilder vom Regenwald: Mentale Modelle, Kulturwandel und Umweltverhalten bei den Lakandonen von Mexiko.* Münster: LIT Verlag.

Ross, N. (2002a). Cognitive aspects of intergenerational change: Mental models, cultural change and environmental behavior among the Lacandon Maya of southern Mexico. *Human Organization, 61,* 125-138.

Ross, N. (2002b). Lacandon Maya intergenerational change and the erosion of folkbiological knowledge. In J. Stepp, F. Wyndham, & R. Zarger (Eds.),

Ethnobiology and biocultural diversity: Proceedings of the Seventh International Congress of Ethnobiology (pp. 585-592). Athens: University of Georgia Press.

Ross, N. (in press). The flowering of man: Naming of plants among the Tzotzil Maya of Zinacantán, Mexico. In W. Ahn, B. Goldstone, B. Love, A. Markman, & P. Wolff (Eds.), *Categorization inside and outside the lab: Festschrift in honor of Douglas L. Medin.* Washington, DC: American Psychological Association.

Ross, N., & Medin, D. (2000). *The development of folkbiological thought: A cross-cultural approach* (Unpublished manuscript). Seventh International Congress of Ethnobiology (Athens, Georgia).

Ross, N., & Medin, D. (2003). On the tip of the tongue: Cultural models, expertise, and the organization of knowledge. *Field Methods.*

Ross, N., Medin, D., Coley, J., & Atran, S. (2003). Cultural and experiential differences in the development of folkbiological induction. *Cognitive Development, 18,* 25-47.

Ross, N., & Sanchez, A. C. (n.d.). *Mexican migrants in Chicago.* Unpublished manuscript.

Röttger-Rössler, B. (1989). *Rang und Ansehen bei den Makassar von Gowa (Süd-Sulawesi/Indonesien).* Berlin: Reimer Verlag.

Said, E. (1979). *Orientalism.* New York: Vintage Books.

Schweizer, T. (1989). Margaret Mead und Samoa: Zur Qualität und Interpretation ethnologischer Feldforschungsdaten. In B. Illius & M. Laubscher (Eds.), *Circumpacifica, Festschrift für Thomas Bartels* (pp. 441-457). Frankfurt am Main: Peter Lang Verlag.

Schweizer, T. (1996a). *Muster sozialer Ordnung; Netzwerkanalyse als Fundament der Sozialethnologie.* Berlin: Reimer Verlag.

Schweizer, T. (1996b). Reconsidering social networks: Reciprocal gift exchange among the !Kung. *Journal of Quantitative Anthropology, 6,* 7-21.

Shankman, P. (2000, September). Mead Freeman déja vu. *Anthropology News,* p. 5.

Shore, B. (1996). *Culture in mind.* New York: Oxford University Press.

Shweder, R. (1991). *Thinking through cultures.* Cambridge, MA: Harvard University Press.

Sperber, D. (1985). Anthropology and psychology: Towards an epidemiology of representations. *Man, 20,* 73-89.

Sperber, D. (1996). *Explaining culture: A naturalistic approach.* Oxford, UK: Blackwell.

Spindler, G. (1955). *Sociocultural and psychological processes in menomini acculturation.* (University of California Publications in Culture and Society, vol. 5.) Berkeley, CA: University of California Press.

Stefflre, V., Reich, P., & McLaran-Stefflre, M. (1971). Some eliciting and computational procedures for descriptive semantics. In P. Kay (Ed.), *Explorations in mathematical anthropology* (pp. 79-116). Cambridge, MA: MIT Press.

Strauss, C. (1992). Models and motives. In R. D'Andrade & C. Strauss (Eds.), *Human motives and cultural models* (pp. 1-20). Cambridge, UK: Cambridge University Press.

Strauss, C., & Quinn, N. (1992). Preliminaries to a theory of culture acquisition. In H. Pick, P. van den Broek, & D. Knill (Eds.), *Cognition: Conceptual and methodological issues*. Washington, DC: American Psychological Association.

Strauss, C., & Quinn, N. (1997). *A cognitive theory of cultural meaning*. Cambridge, UK: Cambridge University Press.

Sturtevant, W. (1964). Studies in ethnoscience. In Transcultural studies in cognition [Special issue]. *American Anthropologist, 66(3)*, 99-131.

Trotter, R. (1981). Remedios caseros: Mexican-American home remedies and community health problems. *Social Science and Medicine, 15B*, 107-114.

Tylor, E. B. (1871). *Primitive culture: Researches into the development of mythology, philosophy, religion, art, and custom*. London: J. Murray.

Udvardi, M. (1989). Gender metaphors in maladies and medicine: The symbolism of protective charms among the Giriama of Kenya. In A. Jacobson-Widding & D. Westerlund (Eds.), *Culture, experience and pluralism* (pp. 45-57). Uppsala, Sweden: Almqvist & Wiksell.

Van de Vijver, F., & Leung, K. (1980). Methods and data analysis of comparative research. In J. Berry, Y. Poortinga, & J. Pandey (Eds.), *Handbook of cross-cultural psychology* (Vol. 1, pp. 257-300). Boston: Allyn & Bacon.

Viqueira, J. P. (1993). *María de la Candelaria, india natural de Cancuc*. Mexico: UNAM.

Vogt, E. Z. (1967). Tendencia de cambio en las tierras altas de Chiapas. *América Indígena, 27(2)*, 199-222.

Wagner, R. (1981). *The invention of culture*. Chicago: University of Chicago Press.

Wasserman, S., & Faust, K. (1994). *Social network analysis: Methods and applications*. Cambridge, UK: Cambridge University Press.

Wassmann, J. (1995). The final requiem for the omniscient informant? An interdisciplinary approach to everyday cognition. *Culture & Psychology, 1*, 167-201.

Wassmann, J., & Dasen, P. (Eds.). (1993). *Alltagswissen: Der kognitive Ansatz im interdisziplinären Dialog*. Fribourg: Mueller Verlag.

Weller, S. (1983). New data on intracultural variability: The hot/cold concept of medicine and illness. *Human Organization, 42*, 249-257.

Weller, S. (1984a). Consistency and consensus among informants: Disease concepts in a rural Mexican town. *American Anthropologist, 86*, 966-975.

Weller, S. (1984b). Cross-cultural concepts of illness: Variation and validation. *American Anthropologist, 86*, 341-351.

Weller, S. (1987). Shared knowledge, intracultural variation, and knowledge aggregation. *American Behavioral Scientist, 31*, 178-193.

Weller, S., & Romney, K. (1988). *Systematic data collection*. Newbury Park, CA: Sage.

Weller, S., & Romney, K. (1990). *Metric scaling: Correspondence analysis*. Newbury Park, CA: Sage.

Weller, S., Romney, K., & Orr, D. (1987). The myth of a sub-culture of corporal punishment. *Human Organization, 46*, 39-47.

Wellman, H., & Gelman, S. (1992). Cognitive development: Foundational theories of core domains. *Annual Review of Psychology, 62*, 1070-1090.

Wimmer, A. (1999). Comment to Brumann. *Current Anthropology, 40,* 19-21.

Wolff, P., Medin, D., & Pankratz, C. (1999). Evolution and devolution of folkbiological knowledge. *Cognition, 73,* 177-204.

Yager, T., & Rotheram-Borus, M. J. (2000). Social expectations among African American, Hispanic, and European American adolescents. *Cross-Cultural Research, 34*(2), 283-305.

Young, J., & Garro, L. (1982). Variation in the choice of treatment in two Mexican communities. *Social Science and Medicine, 16,* 1453-1465.

Zent, S. (2001). Acculturation and ethnobotanical knowledge loss among the Piaroa of Venezuela. In L. Maffi (Ed.), *On biocultural diversity* (pp. 190-211). Washington, DC: Smithsonian Press.

Author Index

Subject Index

About the Author

Norbert O. Ross is Assistant Professor in the Department of Anthropology, Vanderbilt University. Previously, he was Research Assistant Professor in the Department of Psychology, Northwestern University, where he co-founded the Program in *Culture, Language and Cognition*. His research deals with the broad issue of culture and cognition, targeting questions such as *effects of cultural change, the acquisition of cultural knowledge,* and *effect of culture on human thinking and behavior.* While most of his research is within the realm of folk biology, he also conducted research on issues of health and religion. He is principal investigator or co-principal investigator on several research grants from the National Science Foundation and the National Institute of Health.

Dr. Ross is fluent in two Maya languages and most of his research takes place among Maya people in Mexico and Guatemala. In addition, he also conducts research among Native Americans and Hispanic populations in the United States. He is the author of two books (published in Germany), several book chapters, and many journal articles. Originally from Germany, he earned a Ph.D. in Anthropology from the University of Freiburg.